ちちをかえせ ははをかえせ
としよりをかえせ
こどもをかえせ

わたしをかえせ わたしにつながる
にんげんをかえせ

にんげんの にんげんのよのあるかぎり
くずれぬへいわを
へいわをかえせ

The Day Man Lost

Hiroshima, 6 August 1945

by
The Pacific War
Research Society

KODANSHA INTERNATIONAL
Tokyo • New York • London

ACKNOWLEDGMENTS

The compilers and publishers are grateful to the following for permission to reproduce the photos in this book: Kyodo News Service; Kodansha Ltd.; Asahi Shimbun; Bungei Shunjū Ltd.; the Society for the Preservation of Material Associated with the Atomic Bombing of Hiroshima; and the U.S. Air Force.

Distributed in the United States by Kodansha America, Inc., 114 Fifth Avenue, New York, N.Y. 10011, and in the United Kingdom and continental Europe by Kodansha Europe Ltd., 95 Aldwych, London WC2B 4JF. Published by Kodansha International Ltd., 17-14 Otowa 1-chome, Bunkyo-ku, Tokyo 112, and Kodansha America, Inc.

LCC 76-174219
ISBN 0-87011-471-9
ISBN 4-7700-0959-3 (in Japan)

First edition, 1972
First paperback edition, 1981
95 96 97 98 99 10 9

CONTENTS

FOREWORD

None of mankind's conflicts has been so well covered or so voluminously documented as World War II. Hardly a segment of the worldwide theatre of operations has gone unexplored; hundreds of books have told us how the war started, how it was fought, how it was ended. We are given inside stories, definitive studies, untold stories, never-before-told stories, who-can-believe-it stories. We are treated to stories of heroism and cowardice in high and low places. We hear of the good emerging from war's horrors; of the evil arising from good intentions. We are told the war was meaningful, meaningless, avoidable, inevitable. No sooner has one massive volume filled with overwhelming "factual" detail proven a thesis than an even more massive volume appears completely refuting the first.

What is the confused reader to do? He has no legal recourse. There is no kindly God in a Machine who will point the way through the maze; nor a Super Critic to give advice. In fact the art of criticism has sunk to its nadir. It is the rare book that cannot boast from some pundit a "Superb!" or at the very least "Monumental!" This is the age of the polluted adjective and noun and a book that is merely "good" stands no chance at the booksellers. To pick one's way through the frightening (and often frightful) mass of overpraised war literature that has been dumped on us we must look for help from within. The solution is to set up our own rigid standards and then apply them ruthlessly to the growing mound of books beleaguering us.

I would like to suggest four simple requisites: 1) the book should be adequately written; that is, every page must be understandable, concise, interesting, and occasionally stimulating; 2) the author must supply us with new material of some importance, a realignment of old material giving new insight, or a fresh and valid overview that cuts through encrusted prejudices; 3) the book must be credible. It is not enough that the author makes his material come alive or seem plausible. It must have an unassailable base in evidence and documentation. It is not necessary or even desirable to document every fact. Obvious statements that are accepted by the body of reputable historians need no documentation. If, however, the author makes fresh disclosures—that the war in the Pacific, for example, began by mistake in Malaya some two hours earlier than the Pearl Harbor attack—then he must present proof. His unsubstantiated word is not enough.

Let us apply these first three dicta to a recent book which has attracted considerable attention, *Japan's Imperial Conspiracy,* by David Bergamini. That book claims that the emperor of Japan deliberately led his nation into war. It is adequately written and it presents new material. But is it credible? Its thesis, which runs completely in the face of Japanese tradition and culture and is contrary to the generally accepted belief held by historians, is so revolutionary that substantiated, detailed documentation should be presented. I had heard similar charges against the throne when I was in Japan researching *The Rising Sun,* but investigation merely dredged up baseless accusations, personal diatribes, and left-wing propaganda. Has Mr. Bergamini been more successful? His best witnesses are anonymous, his best testimony argumentative. His case would have been thrown out of any court of law. Therefore, despite the weight of thousands of pages of evidence expertly joined together, I must conclude that *Japan's Imperial Conspiracy* is not a history but an unfounded character assassination based on one man's fantasy.

The Day Man Lost makes no such sensational "disclosures", nor any appalling accusations. In fact, it is not even argumentative. Its purpose is simple—to tell the complete story of the atom bomb and Hiroshima. It does so without polemics or editorializing.

But why write another story about the bomb? Certainly this is one area which seems to have been completely covered in all its aspects. *The*

Day Man Lost is ably written and presents new information. Unlike Japan's Imperial Conspiracy, its new material is properly documented. Moreover, it fulfills my fourth rule of history: judicious selection of material and historical perspective. Any data collecting agency can interview hundreds of witnesses and collect thousands of documents. This is only the preliminary step; the resultant mountain of raw material must then be reduced to a controllable size by a rigid system of winnowing. Only that material which is significant and lies in the mainstream of history should remain. Then comes the final step— assembling the culled material into an artistic whole within the iron framework of history.

The compilers of The Day Man Lost have largely succeeded in doing this, and herein lies this work's lasting value. The awesome story of the atomic bomb is told effectively, step by step, from its developments in America, Germany, and Japan to its awful consummation on the morning of 6 August 1945.

Nowhere else can one find the details of Japan's nuclear experiments. The considerable efforts of Dr. Nishina and his assistants will probably come as a surprise even to the well informed. But the greatest contribution of this book is its comprehensive description of the bombing and its aftermath. Here research has been deep and original, and the result, while harrowing and revolting, always remains moving because the authors have not forgotten this is a human story that must be visualized in human terms.

As I read of the ghastly suffering in Hiroshima I could not help but wonder—what if Japan had succeeded in making the bomb before her enemies? What if the first two cities bombed had not been Hiroshima and Nagasaki but San Francisco and Los Angeles? If the Allies had still won, imagine, if you can, the moral rage at the Tokyo International Tribunal! The comparison to Hitler's crimes! The vengeance!

The world must therefore marvel at the "Christian" reaction of the Japanese. They alone endured nuclear attack; they alone experienced its horrors first-hand. Yet somehow they have as a nation transcended hate and can bring out a book conceived in objectivity and freed of petty indictment. To be sure, in conclusion, the authors pose a question painful to the West—"Why was the bomb dropped on Hiroshima?" But this is a question that all men of good will—west and east—will surely keep asking to the end of time.

JOHN TOLAND

PREFACE

As I write these words, Japan is commemorating the twenty-sixth anniversary of the end of the Pacific war—a war during which over three million of her people died. Every year, on this mid-August day, the nation mourns those dead and prays for the repose of their souls. It is a ceremony in which both the emperor and the prime minister take part, and their theme is a constant one. In the emperor's own words, when he spoke this year: "At the same time that I mourn the war dead, I pray for the peace of the world. . . ." Despite recent accusations from abroad that Japanese militarism is being revived, I am convinced that both the Japanese people and their government understand—as intensely as any other people and any other government in the world—the futility and waste of war. We would like to see war banished from the face of the earth, and it is with this unhappily remote but perhaps still attainable goal in mind that the members of the Pacific War Research Society have undertaken to write their second book.

Mr. Bergamini's attempt to resurrect the rejected hypothesis that the emperor himself was personally responsible for the war might have gained in plausibility had the author's citation been more precise and detailed. A man who advances a theory so wholly at variance with accepted history must, if he desires to be credited, be overgenerous in his use of notes and references; the author in question, having chosen the opposite course, does not, in our opinion, present a case that is sufficiently strong to justify the overthrow of the accepted interpretation of the events of World War II.

His wartime experiences were far from happy, and we understand his feelings. In fact, many survivors of the atomic bombing of Hiroshima share them. When suffering strikes on so grand a scale, we, the victims and potential victims, are hard pressed to ascribe it merely to the ignorance and shortsightedness, the mistakes, hesitations, and misunderstandings of the men who happen to be in positions of power at the time. Yet these all too human qualities, along with an impersonal and relentless logic once hostilities are under way, seem to supply the far from reassuring answer as to why these catastrophes occur. The Japanese emperor, it should be noted, despite his supremacy in the land, wielded no real power; and his final exercise of it, in order to bring the war to a long overdue close, was virtually unprecedented in his country's history.

The European war, with Russia and the United States as allies, ended on 8 May 1945. Elliott Roosevelt wrote ". . . before the [Yalta] Conference broke up, Stalin had once more given the assurance he had first volunteered in Teheran in 1943: that, within six months of VE day the Soviets would have declared war on Japan: then, pausing in thought, he had revised that estimate from six months to three months."[1] The Russians, therefore, were due to join the war against Japan on or before 8 August. The first A-bomb had been tested on 16 July. The second was dropped on Hiroshima on 6 August, the third on Nagasaki on 9 August. With facts like these, and with enough imagination, it would be easy for us Japanese to argue that the people of Hiroshima were the victims of a brilliant and imaginative anti-Communist conspiracy on the part of the Allies. We choose not to do so because, on the whole, the Allied leadership appears to have been as ordinary and shortsighted as the Japanese.

A few years ago we published an account of the twenty-four fateful hours that followed Japan's decision to surrender to the Allied powers in 1945. We thought of it not as a book of history but rather as an attempt to tell the story of "Japan's Longest Day" in human terms, from the point of view of the people who took part in reaching the decision and attempting to put it into effect as well as from the point of view of the average Japanese fighting man and the average Japanese man in the street. Although largely ignorant of what their civilian and military leaders were doing, they too were chief actors in the drama. Here, in our second book, we have tried to tell a similar story about another long day in Japanese history, not a day that ended a war but a day that irrevocably changed the nature of our planet. It is a story of the folly and inhumanity of war, of war's inexorably brutal logic—and for that reason it is a story that should never be forgotten so long as men are alive on earth.

In 1945, as the Pacific war entered its final stages, I was a third-year student in middle school and had been drafted to work in a munitions factory. I recall that my classmates and I were well aware that the tide of war had turned against our country: food was horribly scarce, enemy planes bombed our cities with virtual impunity, and there was obvious and widespread corruption among the rich and powerful, which was accompanied by an inevitable deterioration in public morale. Few people, in those closing days of the war, gave wholehearted credence to the optimistic communiqués issued by the army and the navy. I remember that our group laughed as it totaled up the number of enemy ships that imperial headquarters claimed had been lost or crippled: it was a figure that so far exceeded total Allied shipping as to be utterly ludicrous. Yet despite all this, I remained convinced that Japan would eventually emerge victorious.

My conviction did not falter even after the drastic fire-bombing of Tokyo on 10 March. During that raid, my family's house was burned to cinders, and I escaped only by jumping into a nearby river, where I stayed the whole night long. When dawn broke, I saw that the banks of the river were piled high with charred bodies, and many of those who had taken refuge in the water were dead as well. We were all victims of the logic of war—a logic that permits each belligerent to claim that he has "justice" and "right" on his side, but a logic that is, of course, dictated solely by selfish national and personal interests. That is intrinsic to the nature of war: war is waged by sovereign states; sovereign states are governed by men; men who govern sovereign states are, all too often, governed in turn by the lust for power; and the axiom that power corrupts is no longer open to question. How frequently have we seen the process in operation! Indeed, has there been a single day, since the Pacific war ended, when somewhere in the world men were not killing other men ostensibly in the name of "justice" and "right" but actually for other, infinitely less laudable reasons? Such thoughts are commonplace, yet they still have the power to arouse anger in our hearts. And against what is that anger directed? My own answer would be: "Against something that has no shape but that deprives us all of our human sentiments and thoughts."

The Japanese government succeeded in convincing itself that in initiating the Pacific war it was acting in the best interests of the country. The American government, in demanding unconditional surrender and in producing and ultimately using the atomic bomb, was also convinced that it was acting in its own best interests. Trapped between these conflicting beliefs were the draftees of two armies, the victims of conventional bombing, and the nearly half-million people who happened to be in Hiroshima on 6 August 1945 at 8:16 in the morning. When, in preparing this book, we interviewed the Hiroshima survivors, we found that they had no desire to speak of their experiences: those experiences, even after the lapse of twenty-six years, were still too terrible to talk about. Yet terrible as they were, we heard the victims express, time and again, the same thought: "Our agony that August day was nothing compared to the agony we have suffered in the long quarter of a century that has passed since then. If you tell our story, all we ask is that you tell the truth."

That is what we have tried to do, and it is all we have tried to do.

I would like to thank Yutaka Yukawa for his major role in the compilation of Part III.

> KAZUTOSHI HANDŌ
> Chairman,
> The Pacific War Research Society

Postscript: One of our members, reporter Yoshinori Takano, died in a traffic accident before this book was published. We offer this book to his memory.

PART I
1941-1944

CHAPTER 1   **1941**

In the fifth century B.C. a Greek philosopher named Democritus propounded the theory that matter, all matter, was composed of the same indivisible particles, particles that he called *atomos*, which means in Greek nothing more than "nondivisible."

For the next two thousand years little of significance occurred on the atomic front. Even the great Isaac Newton, toward the end of the seventeenth century, pronounced his agreement with Democritus that the atom could not be invaded. But then, in the early 1800's, came John Dalton and Michael Faraday, with their quite different theories on the nature of matter, and by the end of the century Western scientists agreed that these "indivisible" particles called atoms were divisible after all. The atom, however, proved a hard nut to crack.

In 1905 appeared Albert Einstein's special theory of relativity, and with that the story of the smashing of the atom gathered momentum. As the century wore on, the great names of modern physics made their varied contributions, and by the time the Second World War broke out it was apparent on both sides of the Atlantic, not only to scientists but even to statesmen, that the splitting of the atom, if it could ever be arranged and controlled, would result in a chain reaction that could produce an explosion incalculably greater than anything the world had ever known.

Despite this the problems involved in producing an "atomic bomb" seemed insuperable. How were adequate amounts of uranium 235 (by then considered essential) to be separated from uranium 238 so as to create the necessary critical mass? How was it to be stabilized, compressed, and shaped? How was it to be triggered so that there was no interference in a continuing chain reaction? Could all these problems be solved? And could they be solved quickly enough? Refugee scientists from Germany came to America with horrifying tales of the progress of Nazi research; Einstein wrote his famous cautionary letters to President Roosevelt; and in February 1940 the sum of $6,000 was allocated by the government of the United States for atomic research. Quite soon the sum was increased, geometrically, and research was correspondingly accelerated. Forty years after Einstein announced to the world that $E=mc^2$, the Little Boy fell on Hiroshima.

*

On both sides of the Atlantic, during those years, many scientists were aware of the enormity of the problems involved, perhaps of the impossibility of ever solving them; some politicians were aware of the need for haste, perhaps of the impossibility of ever achieving the necessary impetus. The same was true on both sides of the Pacific. Japan, recently so determinedly isolationist, was now, like some of the "advanced" countries of Europe, preparing for armed world conquest; and, though a late starter in the Western science sweepstakes, she was also keenly aware that the ability to make destructive use of atomic fission was a virtual guarantee of total victory in the fast approaching conflict.

The director of the Aviation Technology Research Institute of the Imperial Japanese Army was a highly educated man, who had majored in electrical engineering. His name was Takeo Yasuda, and his rank was that of lieutenant general, but unlike many who have attained that eminence Yasuda had not sunk into lethargy: he continued to study and to read articles and books pertaining to his chosen field. Among these were learned dissertations on the problems of nuclear fission. Yasuda came to the conclusion that this was a field where Japan, embarked on the path toward greater East Asian coprosperity, had better not be caught napping. Accordingly he initiated his own chain reaction, one familiar in all the armies of the world. In April 1940 he instructed

Lieutenant Colonel Tatsusaburō Suzuki, who was attached to Army
Aviation headquarters, to carry out a study of the question in relation
to Japan's potential.

Suzuki had studied at Tokyo University under the illustrious Professor Ryōkichi Sagane. He began researching the problem, reading
whatever foreign journals he could get hold of, and discussing the
question at length with Professor Sagane. Some six months after being
handed the problem, in October 1940 he turned in his report to Lieutenant General Yasuda. It was his conclusion that Japan possessed or had
access to sufficient deposits of uranium ore to produce an atomic bomb,
as it was already, although somewhat inaccurately, being called. Accepting the conclusion, Yasuda summoned Professor Masatoshi Ōkōchi,
director of Japan's Physical and Chemical Research Institute, and asked
him to investigate further the possibility of producing an explosive
device making use of nuclear fission.

Chain reactions are not confined to armies. Professor Ōkōchi soon
handed the problem child over to another professor, one Yoshio
Nishina, who headed a brilliant array of talented young physicists
within the same research institute. The choice was an obvious one.
Nishina, in his younger days, had studied in Copenhagen under Niels
Bohr, one of the century's most famous nuclear scientists; back in Japan, he had engaged in a number of joint research projects with promising young physicists; and by now he had working under him a
total of 110 researchers, including many of Japan's brightest young
scientists. Nishina's laboratory was, at that time, not only the nerve
center for Japanese physical research, it was a magnet that attracted
all the most brilliant minds in the field.

And it was also, so everyone agreed, an extraordinarily pleasant
place to work. Nishina himself, warmhearted and sympathetic, believed in letting his young men wander where their curiosity led them.
They were divided into four distinct research groups: the cyclotron
atomic nucleus group, the cosmic ray group, the theoretical group,
and a group devoted to investigating the effects of radiation on living
organisms. But the groups were not all that distinct. Where lines crossed, investigators followed; they were free to hold whatever debates

and discussions seemed desirable with whoever seemed most capable of supplying the right answers. To all his men Professor Nishina was known affectionately as *Oyabun* ("the Old Man"), and the atmosphere of his laboratory (considering the potentially lethal nature of the research that was being undertaken there) was relaxed and easygoing— positively convivial in fact.

When the young men on Nishina's staff heard they were to work on an atomic bomb, they were hardly surprised. They knew that research into the possibility of nuclear fission was being intensified in the West; they read whatever they could find on the subject in academic journals (German, American, and British, among others). Obviously they were aware of the enormous amount of energy that nuclear fission could produce, and they also realized, like nuclear scientists all over the world by that time, that that energy could be used destructively and decisively. It was in April 1941 that they were informed that the Imperial Japanese Army desired an atomic bomb, and in those days what the Imperial Japanese Army desired it was accustomed to getting.

In April 1941, at several locations, Germany's Kaiser-Wilhelm Institute of Physics was still trying to separate sufficient quantities of the uranium 235 isotope in order to create the necessary critical mass. By then the Germans had access to uranium deposits all over the European continent as well as to such installations as Norway's huge Vermork hydrogen electrolysis plant, to Belgium's enormous stockpiles of uranium compounds, and to Professor Frédéric Joliot's laboratory at the Collège de France. Professor Fritz Houtermans was even then in the process of writing a report in which he "for the first time made explicit calculations on fast-neutron chain reactions and the critical mass of uranium 235—i.e., that mass which, when assembled, would result in a spontaneous fast-neutron chain reaction and a violent explosion."[1] Despite all this, however, it was apparent that the Germans had not yet found the right road to the new weapon—and the new age.

On the other side of the Atlantic, the Americans, although they had nothing like the supplies of uranium that were available to the Germans, possessed one tremendous advantage of which the Germans had chosen to deprive themselves: they had many exiled and refugee scientists from the Axis countries (most of them Jewish). These scientists were not only brilliant physicists, but were also conscious of the progress of Nazi research into the destructive potentials of nuclear fission and had the keenest personal reasons in the world for desiring the enemies of the Nazis to reach the finish line first.

In April 1941 relations between Japan and the United States were growing increasingly strained, and would soon reach the breaking point. The day before that point came, a fateful meeting took place in Washington (on 6 December 1941 to be exact). The story of it is perhaps best told in the words of Arthur Holly Compton, who (in that same April of 1941) was made chairman of a committee of the National Academy of Sciences to study the possible military use of atomic energy. Compton writes:

"In September 1941, Ernest Lawrence of the University of California met President James Conant of Harvard and me in our home in Chicago. He told us of calculations indicating that an atomic bomb of great effectiveness could be made using much smaller amounts of uranium 235 than had previously been thought necessary. The British scientists responsible for these calculations were so convinced of their significance that they were eager to get going on a full-scale effort to produce the required U-235 and to make the bomb. Lawrence told us further of the discovery, just made in his laboratory, that the new element plutonium that Seaborg, Kennedy, and Wahl had made with the California cyclotron has the same fission characteristics as does U-235. But this new element might be produced in a nuclear reactor and be separated chemically from its parent uranium. Here was an alternate approach to making the material for an atomic bomb that would not require the very difficult process of isotope separation.

"We all became convinced that these possibilities called for quick and thorough examination. Conant turned to Lawrence. 'Ernest,' he said, 'does this seem important enough to you to devote to it the remaining years of the war?' Lawrence paused, and swallowed hard: 'If you tell me that's my job, I'll accept it.'

"Conant then turned to me. 'Arthur,' he said, 'it's up to you to get

together the people who can judge the merits of this atomic bomb proposal, study it with all the available data, and give us a report on its
importance and feasibility. And don't lose any time. If the possibilities
are what they seem to be, with the head start the Germans have, it may
well be a race for the key to victory. We have no time to lose.'

"That was September. Enrico Fermi, then at Columbia University
in New York, gave his quick calculations about the bomb. Harold
Urey and John Dunning supplied the latest reports on isotope separation. Engineers from Westinghouse and General Electric gave practical counsel. In November we turned in our report. The bomb would
probably be made. It might well be of decisive effect in the war. Three
or four years of all-out effort would be needed, at a cost of roughly a
billion dollars. If the Germans got there first, they might yet snatch
victory out of the hands of defeat.

"Vannevar Bush went to the President. Our report paralleled closely
one from the British. On 6 December 1941 several of us were called
to Washington and were given instructions from the President to put
all possible effort into experiments that would show how U-235 could
be separated and how an atomic bomb might be made.

"After the meeting I lunched with Conant and Bush. I explained
that there was just a chance that producing plutonium by means of a
nuclear chain reaction might be a cheaper and quicker way of getting
the material for the bomb than by separating the uranium isotopes. We
discussed the enormous difficulties involved—setting up a controlled
nuclear chain reaction, which was as yet only an idea on paper, learning
the chemistry of plutonium, and developing a method for separating
it from other substances in the presence of lethal rays of tremendous
intensity. Difficult, but not impossible, we agreed. Thus, as an after-
thought, I was commissioned to bring together the physicists who
would endeavor to set up the chain reaction and the chemists who
would look for a method of extracting the plutonium after it was
produced."[2]

The following day, with that ghastly irony that seems so to delight
the muse of history, a total of 350 Japanese aeroplanes attacked Pearl
Harbor. The United States replied with a declaration of war. The other

two Axis powers, in turn, declared war on the United States. Now the whole world was a tremendous volcano erupting its fire everywhere. The United States, ever 'more fearful that the Nazis would win the atomic sweepstakes, went into highest gear. The muse, with her gentle smile, decreed that the Japanese, who had brought the United States into the war, were destined to be the ones to suffer from the swift and prodigious achievements of American technology.

CHAPTER 2 **1942**

The Imperial Japanese Army was confident of its invincibility, and millions of the Japanese people accepted that myth wholeheartedly. Thus, despite the relatively small size of the country and its extremely limited resources, they were ready to take on the colossus across the ocean; as for the rest of the world they believed that Germany could handle that easily enough.

Japanese-German domination appeared inevitable; and, for a time, that belief seemed well founded. Immediately after the outbreak of hostilities between Japan and the Allied powers, Japan's armed forces were victorious wherever they went. After the smashing success of the attack on Pearl Harbor came the triumphant battle for the Malayan Sea, then a series of conquests in the South Sea islands. In the homeland the people rejoiced, carrying brightly lighted lanterns in their hands as they marched in victory parades.

As he watched the parades, Professor Nishina remarked to one of his staff, "What an insane war Japan has launched! Any fool knows the power and the might of the United States. The consequences to Japan can only be disastrous." Those were dangerous sentiments and danger-ous statements, for the army at that time controlled the country; no one had any choice but to follow its dictates. Yet, "We are all aboard a sinking ship," the Old Man added recklessly, "a ship called Japan. We must do what we can to save it."

Although born in the Meiji era, imbued with its enthusiasm and patriotism, filled with pride at the way in which Japan, in only half a century, had raised itself from a remote, isolated country of little consequence to a first-rate world power, Nishina was also a man of great common sense and great compassion. He loved his country and his emperor; he did not want to see them embarked on an adventure that he was convinced could only end in disaster. Yet he was the man entrusted with the development of the atomic bomb, the sole weapon that might have ensured Japan's final victory.

Meanwhile, the war, from the point of view of the Imperial Army, had been progressing extremely satisfactorily. In the first five months after the attack on Pearl Harbor, the Japanese had taken Singapore (15 February), terminated (except for Corregidor) the war in the Philippines (9 April), and occupied the whole of the Dutch East Indies (9 March). Such overwhelming successes were even greater than the arrogant, self-assured army had anticipated in its arrogant, self-assured calculations. General headquarters was by now convinced that the end of the war was in sight; Japan, they believed, was already in a position to insist on highly advantageous peace terms.

The German high command was in much the same ebullient frame of mind as the Imperial Army; they were, and with apparent good reason, even more optimistic than the Japanese. They saw no great urgency about pursuing the production of the atomic bomb, and they chose to ignore the dissatisfaction of German scientists at the way in which the nuclear program was being superseded by other, seemingly more practical, less chimerical programs. The high command was convinced that the war would be successfully ended long before an atomic bomb could be made operational.

Albert Speer, Hitler's minister of armaments, was, however, less sanguine. General Friedrich Fromm had persuaded him that, despite Germany's victories on the continent, she was in danger of ultimately losing the war unless she came up with a new weapon of enormous destructive power. Accordingly, on 4 June 1942, Reichsminister Speer called a conference of many of Germany's chief scientists as well as members of the Munitions Ministry and the general staff. This may well have been the first time that the scientists had an opportunity to come into direct personal contact with high government officials.

It was at this conference that Professor Werner Heisenberg, a Nobel Prize winner and one of the world's most illustrious theoretical physicists, reported on the progress being made in the field of nuclear fission, and on how it could be used to produce an atomic bomb. This was the first time that many of those present at the conference had heard those two fateful words. Heisenberg said he feared that the Americans were devoting enormous sums of money as well as their finest talents to the production of such a bomb, and, if his fears were justified, they might well be in possession of a uranium bomb within two years. Germany, on the other hand, was lagging far behind in nuclear studies. Her talents and resources were being devoted to the development of other weapons that cost far less and that were of far more immediate practical application. Heisenberg's report produced both amazement and apprehension.

It did not, however, produce the atomic bomb. When Speer, after the meeting ended, asked Heisenberg how long it would take Germany to make such a bomb operational, the professor replied that "theoretically" it ought to be possible within those same two years he had anticipated it would take the Americans—provided, he added, that the project enjoyed the government's "full financial support." It was an unsatisfactory reply. Two years, by Speer's calculations, were too long. Further, Speer knew that Hitler was interested in immediate results, not in some "theoretical" long-range atomic project. On 23 June, the reichsminister, in his own words, "Reported briefly to the führer on the meeting concerning atomic fission, and on the assistance we have rendered."[3] This, so far as is known, is the only occasion on which Speer and Hitler discussed the atomic bomb out of a total of 2,200 conferences that took place between the two men!

On the other side of the world the problem was being considered more seriously, and this time it was the Imperial Japanese Navy that stepped in to invigorate the flagging project. When, as early as 1938, the United States embargoed the overseas shipment of uranium ore, the navy suspected that something was afoot; but at that time the navy's Technological Research Institute was preoccupied with the problem of developing a warning system resembling what later came to be known as radar, and consequently had no time or talent to spare to attempt to determine precisely what that "something" might be.

Then came Pearl Harbor and the consequent declaration of war between Japan and the United States. As time went on, Japanese losses, both on the sea and in the air, mounted staggeringly, and now the navy found itself forced to consider the feasibility of producing a new and powerful weapon. That weapon was the atomic bomb. Accordingly, Lieutenant Commander Kiyoyasu Sasaki of the Electrical Research Division of the Naval Technological Research Institute went for advice to Professor Ryōkichi Sagane and Professor Juichi Hino, both of Tokyo Imperial University, the former in the Department of Physics, the latter in the Medical School. As a result of these consultations, the navy determined, in the spring of 1942, to undertake studies on the utilization of atomic energy—studies to be directed by the Technological Research Institute.

The project was given the name of Research on the Application of Nuclear Physics and was known as B-research for short. At the time the project was initiated, it was described in the following terms: "The study of nuclear physics is a national project. Research in this field is continuing on a broad scale in the United States, which has recently obtained the services of a number of Jewish scientists, and considerable progress has been made. The objective is the creation of tremendous amounts of energy through nuclear fission. Should this research prove successful, it would provide a stupendous and dependable source of power which could be used to activate ships and other large pieces of machinery. Although it is not expected that nuclear energy will be realized in the near future, the possibility of it must not be ignored. The Imperial Navy, accordingly, hereby affirms its determination to foster and assist studies in this field."

The energy was to be used, according to the navy, for such peaceful purposes as the turning of engines, the creation of artificial radium, the production of luminous paint, and the study of mineral alloys. Nowhere was the phrase "atomic bomb" employed, but that was not because the navy did not have the atomic bomb in mind; the sole purpose of B-research was, in fact, the production of the bomb, no matter how assiduously, for purposes of counterespionage, the navy attempted to camouflage its intentions. Of interest also is the fact that the navy, although well aware that results were uncertain and could in any case only be long-term, considered B-research to be a "national project." Quite obviously, the navy had come to the conclusion that, despite time and chance, it had no choice but to initiate the project.

In an effort to accelerate preliminary studies, the Naval Technological Research Institute created a committee for the study of the application of nuclear research, to which it named many of Japan's leading scientists. These included Yoshio Nishina, Hantarō Nagaoka, Masaharu Nishikawa, Ryōkichi Sagane, Juichi Hino, Sanichirō Mizushima, Tsunesaburō Asada, Masashi Kikuchi, Satoshi Watanabe, Tamotsu Nishina, and Masamichi Tanaka, representing the country's chief universities and private industry. Professor Nishina was elected chairman of the committee.

It held its first meeting on 8 July 1942 just a little over a month after Speer made his brief, noncommittal report to Hitler on the subject. The venue of the meeting was the Suikosha, a naval officers' club, at Shiba Park in Tokyo. Virtually all the navy's chief technical officers were present at the meeting.

"The American embargo on exports of uranium, thorium, and radium," Professor Kikuchi informed them, "seems proof enough that the United States is undertaking intensive research into the production of the atomic bomb." Professor Sagane added: "Our chief problem, then, is twofold: can Japan produce the bomb and, if so, how soon?"

These were, of course, the two questions that the navy wanted definitive answers to, answers that the scientists were quite unable to supply. Once again they explained the extreme difficulty of isolating sufficient quantities of U-235, and to the navy's insistence on knowing whether the process was possible, the scientists could only reply: "We cannot say that it is impossible, only that it is so difficult as to be uncertain. That is as far as we can go at this time."

Thus the first meeting of the committee ended on this inconclusive note, the members having resolved that research on the project was to continue as intensively as possible, and that the committee was to convene once a month until the researchers were able to supply a positive answer, one way or the other. Professor Nishina himself, it is interesting to note, had little to say at this first meeting. He may have felt that the atmosphere was not a congenial one in which to speak frankly; having been requested first by the army to conduct nuclear research for military purposes, he may have been aware of the rivalry between the two services and decided it was the better part of valor to maintain a discreet silence. To get its B-research under way, the navy appropriated the munificent sum of ¥2,000, which at that time had the value of some $4,700.

The United States, on the other hand, was ready to take the plunge. The special "S-1" committee appointed by the president had reported back; their conclusion was that an all-out program would cost at least a hundred million dollars and might result in a usable bomb by July 1944. The committee's conclusion was accepted: the United States was embarked on "the greatest scientific gamble in history," a gamble that was eventually to cost considerably more than that paltry hundred million dollars first envisaged by the committee.

On 13 August a top secret project was organized within the Army Engineer Corps, and shortly thereafter Brigadier General Leslie R. Groves was named to head it. The ultimate aim of the project was the production of a bomb utilizing the chain reaction of nuclear fission; it had to be a bomb small enough, and stable enough, to be transported by plane and, above all, it had to be completed before the enemy could get their own version of the bomb into production. As one journalist described it: "In September 1942, when Brigadier General Leslie Groves took over the newly designated 'Manhattan Project,' he was certain that never in history had so many embarked on so fateful an undertaking with so little certainty about how to proceed. The only solution seemed to be to charge ahead on a number of fronts and, by elimination, arrive at the production process that held the most promise."[4]

And that is precisely what happened: cyclotrons at Berkeley, nuclear reactors at Chicago and Columbia, theoretical research at Harvard and Princeton, separation plants at Oak Ridge, Tennessee, plutonium reactors at Hanford, Washington. Eventually some one hundred fifty thousand people were to be engaged in one form or another of atomic research and production, and, as President Truman would point out after Hiroshima, the bomb was to cost two billion dollars.

So much, and such diverse, activity could not be kept altogether quiet. At one point the problem of atomic energy was actually discussed on the floor of the Senate! Groves did all he could to keep the project as secret as possible, but inevitably, especially in the beginning, there were leaks. Rumors reached the Japanese that the United States was engaged in an all-out effort to produce an atomic bomb.

"So it can be done after all!" cried navy captain Yōji Itō at the second meeting of the special committee for the study of the application of nuclear research. This meeting also was held at the Suikosha, on a hot, muggy summer day, the kind of day that is not conducive to the clearest thinking or the most even of tempers. "So it *can* be done!" Captain Itō repeated excitedly, and the other officers looked at each other in open consternation, hardly able to credit the unconfirmed rumors that so stupendous an undertaking was in progress on the other side of the Pacific.

Then Professor Sagane took the rostrum. He revealed the results of the calculations that he had been making over the past month. If, he said, the experimental reactor was increased so-and-so many times and if the volume of raw material was expanded by so-and-so many kilos, then so-and-so many grams of U-235 might be produced each second. Then, he went on, if several new reactors were constructed and operated around the clock, the grams of U-235 might be measured in terms of kilos. He concluded that the process would clearly require a number of years. It was not an encouraging report, and it was followed by a few moments' silence.

Captain Itō then spoke again. "You college professors," he said, "are apt to be too conservative. You tell us that the problem is so difficult that success within a reasonable time is impossible to hope for. But listen to me. People who make warships have a different way of approaching problems. Even though they may feel that it is impossible to have the ship finished in time, they do their best, and in most cases, let me tell you, that ship is off the production line ahead of schedule. I ask you, then, not to tell us that you are unable to produce the bomb within the necessary time but rather to exert every effort to do so. I want you to continue your research." The navy had only recently completed construction of two giant battleships, the *Yamato* and the *Musashi*; Captain Itō felt that his optimism was justified.

The physicists, however, with their cooler heads (despite the August heat) and their accurately adjusted calculations, remained convinced that it would take the Japanese at least a decade to produce an atomic bomb even if all the matériel, all the funds, and all the manpower available in the country were to be mobilized for the project. Nonetheless, the scientists did not feel obliged, at this second meeting, to express opinions of so negative a nature to their fellow members of the committee, officers of the Imperial Navy, so they agreed to follow Captain Itō's recommendation that they continue their research. On that note the conference ended.

Virtually no one who had been present at the meeting, neither the men of science nor the men of war, could have foreseen how fast time was running out for the Japanese. After those six glorious months of victory that followed the outbreak of hostilities, both the army and the navy had been halted in their progress through the Pacific. The shocking defeat at Midway indicated the turn of the current; the Japanese, whether they knew it or not, were now on the defensive. Then came the retreat from the Solomons and the fall of Guadalcanal; yet still the military persisted in fostering the myth of its invincibility, and still the people of Japan seemed willing to accept that myth.

One man at least did not. A year and eight months had passed since Professor Nishina had first been asked by the army to research the possibility of developing an atomic bomb. What his true reaction to that request may have been is not known. Then came the navy's B-research conferences, and once again Nishina, for the most part, kept his own counsel. But he was not only a man of great compassion and an illustrious scientist, he was also a staunch patriot. Now, with the tide of war turning against Japan, he apparently decided that his country stood in dire need of a new and powerful weapon and that that weapon could only be the atomic bomb.

Accordingly, at the year-end, he summoned Tadashi Takeuchi, a member of the cosmic ray group of the army's Aviation Technology Research Institute, and remarked, somewhat nonchalantly, that he was about to start research on the production of an atomic bomb, and he asked Takeuchi to assist him. The latter was, at first, taken aback; the request was unexpected. Then he recalled how Nishina had solemnly stated, during the celebrations marking the first anniversary of Pearl Harbor, "We must all do everything we can for our country if a time of crisis arises." Takeuchi was a much younger man, just turned thirty-three, and he was not imbued with the lofty patriotic ideals of the Meiji men, like Nishina. He felt himself to be a scientist first, a patriot second: it was the problem of smashing the atom that attracted him, not what use the military might make of it. Thus, although his motives were not the same as those of Nishina, he enthusiastically joined forces with him in an attempt to solve the overwhelming problems of nuclear fission. Japan, however belatedly, was at last a serious contender in the atomic sweepstakes.

Had the decision come too late? Perhaps it had, for it came at a time when a group of American scientists, gathered around the world's first atomic reactor in an old, musty squash court at the University of Chicago, were engaged in a final, crucial experiment. The story has been told by one of the eminent men who were present on this now historic occasion, Dr. Arthur Holly Compton.

"On the morning of December 2, a reviewing committee of eminent engineers came to my office. They had been charged with recommending to the War Department whether actual construction of atomic bombs should be undertaken, having in mind the half-million man-years of effort that the task would require. Their visit to the Chicago laboratory was to see whether they could recommend proceeding with the project with the full resources of the nation.

"The reviewing committee met me in the conference room. 'Where is Fermi?' they asked. Enrico Fermi was the great Italian physicist who eight years before, working in his laboratory in Rome with the help of a single assistant, had shown how to handle the neutrons that play the vital role in the nuclear reaction. He was now directing the construction of our experimental atomic reactor. 'I'm sorry,' I replied, 'Fermi is engaged in his laboratory and has asked to be excused. Perhaps I can answer your questions.' After an hour of discussion the telephone rang. It was word from the research team. 'We are ready to try the critical experiment.' I took with me the youngest member of the reviewing committee, Crawford Greenewalt of the Du Pont Company, and walked over to the laboratory.

"We entered the balcony at one end of the room. On the balcony some twenty scientists were watching the instruments and handling the controls. Across the room was the large cubical pile of graphite and uranium blocks in which we hoped the atomic chain reaction would develop. Inserted into openings in this pile of blocks were the control and safety rods. When inside the pile these rods absorbed so many neutrons that the chain could not start. Just beyond, standing on a platform overlooking the pile, was the 'suicide squad.' These men were armed with equipment to destroy the pile and thus quench the chain reaction if all went wrong. A hundred feet away, behind two concrete walls, was a third group of men who followed the experiments with remote control instruments, and who could set off the electrical mechanism for throwing in the safety rods in case the reaction became too violent.

"After a few preliminary tests, Fermi gave the order to withdraw the control rod another foot. We all knew this was the real test. The Geiger counters registering the neutrons from the reactor began to click faster and faster, until their sound became a rattle. Now the galvanometer pointer, indicating the current in the ionization chambers, began to move, at first slowly, then faster and still faster. The reaction grew until there might be danger from the rays coming from the pile. 'Throw in the safety rods,' came Fermi's order. Immediately the pointer moved back toward zero. The rattle of the counters fell to a slow series of clicks. For the first time atomic power had been released, and it had been controlled and stopped."[5]

It was 3:20 P.M., 2 December 1942, less than a year after Pearl Harbor, that matter released its energy to mankind. The men who were present at the experiment were well aware of the awesome nature of that energy and deep in their hearts most of them hoped that it would never have to be used destructively. But the world was at war. No one was sure how advanced the Germans were; no one was sure what the Japanese were up to. Clearly the United States was committed to producing the bomb if it could. The Chicago experiment was a green light.

After it was over, Compton telephoned James Conant, President of Harvard. Using the wartime code name for Fermi, he said, "The Italian navigator has just landed in the new world."

"Were the natives friendly?" asked Conant.

Compton's reply was, perhaps, more cryptic than prophetic. "Everyone landed safe and happy," he said.

CHAPTER 3   **1943**

As the new year dawned, the staff of Nishina's laboratory held their first conference on the subject of separating the U-235 isotope. The date was 15 January 1943 and the aim of the conference was to examine the various methods available and to determine which of them, under the circumstances, was likely to prove the most practical. Taking into consideration the material, technology, and funds at their disposal, as well as that all-important factor, time, the Nishina staff came to the conclusion that their best, and quickest, chance of success was what was called the "dialytic method of elimination." They realized that other methods might well prove more effective, but they also realized that, because of the limited budget and time available to them, those other methods were beyond their scope.

After that first meeting, work intensified and further conferences were of frequent occurrence. Tadashi Takeuchi, on 28 February, presented a report summarizing various complex calculations that he had made. Japan still did not possess an atomic reactor, but plans for the reactor were by now at least on paper. Yet everyone realized, uneasily, that in this all-important field of nuclear fission, Japan was still proceeding at a snail's pace.

On the very same day that Takeuchi made his report, German nuclear progress sustained a severe blow. A small task force of Norwegian
saboteurs, ten men in all, undertook the incredibly difficult and dangerous mission of dynamiting the huge hydrogen electrolysis plant at
Vermork (Norsk-Hydro). "It was," to quote David Irving, "a perfect
piece of sabotage. The bottom had been knocked off every cell and the
priceless fluid had flooded down the drains; to compound the damage,
the flying shrapnel had punctured the tubes of the plant's cooling
system, and the room was full of spraying jets of water. This *ordinary*
water had effectively swirled the remains of the heavy water away.

"All eighteen cells had been completely drained of their contents,
almost half a ton of heavy water; even after the torn and blasted instal-
lation had been replaced it would still take weeks of full-power working before each cell's contents had been put through nine stages of concentration; months would pass before any heavy water could be tapped
from the rebuilt plant. In short, a delay of many months had been
inflicted on the German uranium research program—a delay which it
could not afford."[6]

This bold, daring, and eminently successful act of sabotage had the
further effect of dampening the führer's enthusiasm for nuclear research. Already he had contemptuously termed this research "Jewish
physics," and so, inevitably, "decadent." As Irving puts it, a little later
on in the same book on the German atomic bomb; "Repeated meetings
were called in various parts of the Reich to try to find ways of using
Albert Einstein's theories while denying his authorship of them. How
could the German physicists hope to exploit atomic energy if the Party
disapproved of Einstein's special theory of relativity?"

Reichsminister Speer, ever sensitive to Hitler's moods and none too
confident himself about the possibility of Germany's developing the
atomic bomb in time for it to be of use, now publicly declared that
other projects had higher priority. Hitler wanted, as he always wanted,
instant weapons, but the atomic bomb still lay uncertainly in the dim
future. German nuclear research continued, to be sure, but under the
double disadvantage of being both "Jewish" and problematic.

In Japan, the navy's nuclear research program, while it suffered from no strong religious or "racial" scruples, also came under the pressure of immediacy and priority. With American naval might in the Pacific growing ever more threatening, the Japanese navy came to the conclusion that what it chiefly needed was a new weapon today, not on some distant tomorrow. It needed more and better aircraft, and it needed radar. Accordingly, on 6 March, it convened a meeting of the committee for the study of the application of nuclear research (which had already held more than a dozen conferences) and asked for some definitive conclusions on the question of the atomic bomb.

The members of the committee seemed agreed that an atomic bomb could unquestionably be produced, but they doubted that any of the belligerents could produce it in time for it to be of strategic value in the war. Japan labored under the added disadvantage of requiring imported uranium ore. There were uranium deposits in Korea, but Korea was still undeveloped; Burma, which was then occupied by Japanese troops, was more promising, but was it promising enough? The committee thought not. It further thought that neither Germany nor the United States could reach the finish line in time.

Captain Itō, who was present at the 6 March meeting on behalf of the navy, says of the decision: "The best minds of Japan, studying the subject from the point of view of their respective fields of endeavor as well as from that of national defense, came to a conclusion that can only be regarded as correct. The more they considered and discussed the problem, the more pessimistic became the atmosphere of the meeting." The navy's committee for the study of the application of nuclear research was dissolved. Its scientists were asked to undertake other, more pressing tasks. Japan failed in its effort to recapture Guadalcanal; Admiral Isoroku Yamamoto, commander in chief of the Japanese Combined Fleet, flew to the Rabaul front; the war in the Pacific had doubled, then redoubled, in fury. Obviously, the Imperial Japanese Navy was convinced it had quite enough to do without undertaking so doubtful, so chimerical a project as the production of a bomb making use of the energy released by nuclear fission.

Still, the country had not altogether abandoned hope of achieving that bomb: the Nishina laboratory, under the auspices of the Imperial

Army, continued its search for a practical method of isolating the essential isotope. On 19 March, two weeks after the dissolution of the navy's B-research project, the Nishina laboratory came to a definitive conclusion. It discarded the electromagnetic method because that would entail the construction of a massive magnet beyond Japan's resources and technology; it discarded centrifugation because at least two to three years would be required to produce a separator revolving at super-high speed; it discarded separation by gaseous diffusion on much the same grounds: lack of technology, time, and money. What remained, then, was the heat dispersion method, and this is where the Nishina laboratory decided to concentrate its efforts.

On 5 May it presented a report to the army announcing, first of all, that in the opinion of the staff the production of an atomic bomb was technically possible. The report then proceeded to give details of how the heat dispersion method might be most successfully employed. It is doubtful whether most of the officers were any better equipped than the man in the street to understand those complex technical details, but one fact emerged clear and triumphant: the nation's most eminent physicists believed that it was possible for Japan to produce an atomic bomb. Accordingly, the army's aviation headquarters inaugurated a top-secret, high-level project called N-research, the "N" being derived, not from "nuclear," but from "Nishina."

It was soon apparent that the members of the Japanese Diet were no better equipped than the average army officer to comprehend either the complexities or the overweening importance of the nuclear bomb. In a speech that he made before the House of Peers, in a plenary session of the Diet, Professor Aikitsu Tanakadate, an aerodynamics engineer, attempted to enlist the support of the legislators for an all-out effort. In the course of his speech, he said, "You gentlemen who are gathered here today are probably unaware of the fact that the progress of nuclear physics has made it possible to utilize atomic energy. It is now possible to produce a bomb the size of a matchbox which has the explosive power to sink a battleship!"

The legislators yawned. The idea was obviously absurd. Further-more, Professor Tanakadate was widely considered to be pretty much of a crank. At a time of intense nationalism' he persisted in advocating the replacement of the age-old Japanese system of writing, making use of Chinese characters and *kana*, with the Roman alphabet. The professor's matchbox seemed about as sensible as introducing a wholly new system of writing into a country at war.

However, now that it had been made public on the floor of the Diet, it was far too good a story for the newspapers to ignore. Headlines told of "a matchbox that could sink a battleship," and the Japanese people seized eagerly on this "new weapon." For it was apparent that a new weapon was desperately needed because hostilities, for the moment, seemed to be at a deadlock, a deadlock that the matchbox could put an end to in a moment's blazing flash of light and power. The people assumed that secret researches on the matchbox were being pursued.

And they assumed more or less correctly. N-research was going on in a building belonging to the Aviation Technology Research Institute—a building with a total floor space of only 330 square meters! Here were gathered all the scientists chosen by Professor Nishina to solve the problems and conduct the experiments necessary for the production of the new weapon. To the army's credit, it must be noted that the young men Professor Nishina asked for were demobilized at once and placed under his charge. One such was twenty-six-year-old Kunihiko Kigoshi, who had already researched methods for producing uranium in a gaseous state (sexa-uranium fluoride). He now continued with that research in the Nishina laboratory. Another member of the staff was Hidehiko Tamaki, who was charged with the task of determining the volume of U-235 required in order to release its energy. To Tadashi Takeuchi, of the cosmic rays group, was delegated the all-important problem of developing a separation device.

N-research, then, had the men it wanted; but where was it going to find the material it required? Where, in other words, could it find the absolute minimum of two tons of high grade uranium ore that were essential for its experiments? This problem was handed over to Professor Satoyasu Iimori. At first, much hope was placed in the so-called Monazu ores of Fukushima Prefecture, but, after a great deal of time and effort were expended in digging, the ore was determined to be not only of poor quality but also of hopelessly insufficient quantity. The only alternative, then, was to find the ore outside Japan, in areas under Japanese occupation. The army issued orders to its field commanders in Manchuria, China, the South Sea Islands, and elsewhere to make an intensive search for the needed ores. It even, forlornly, requested the cooperation of the Germans.

Thus, although Japan had highly competent and enthusiastic physicists to direct the various departments of its N-research program, it still lacked the essential material. This fact did not, however, dampen the enthusiasm of the researchers; they worked at the problems assigned to them with almost demonic fury, but, because of the scarcity of available ore, their progress was inevitably slow.

What about the situation on the other side of the ocean? The story of Los Alamos is too familiar to be retold again in any great detail, but it is interesting to note that it was coming into being just about the time the staff of the Nishina laboratory was preparing its report for the Imperial Army. At first the process of getting under way was a chaotic one, but gradually "Y" site, as it was known in code, took shape; gradually the scientists under Professor Robert Oppenheimer, men who had come to Los Alamos secretly from all over the country, found a tenuous modus operandi with the army engineers under General Leslie Groves.

"Only the urgency of the task ahead," writes Lansing Lamont, "submerged the troubles that threatened to abort the new laboratory before its birth.

"The very remoteness of Los Alamos—selected for its secrecy and distance from possible enemy air attack—was paramount to the scientists' purpose: to contemplate, without harassment, the nature of the new weapon, and to design its assembly and determine how to produce it—all in advance of receiving the vital nuclear components which would comprise its very soul. It was a horrendous undertaking, a bit like trying to manufacture a new automobile with no opportunity to test the engine beforehand."[7]

However, it worked. The eminence of the scientists and the intense, unprecedented security precautions that were being taken caused Los Alamos to be known as "a concentration camp for Nobel Prize winners." It was this intense security that the scientists (the longhairs) found most irksome; it was even more irksome than the discomforts of the hurriedly built site. Yet they persevered, and in the end their efforts were rewarded, however unhappy some of them may have felt about the nature of those rewards.

Still, it was slow work, and Groves was impatient. Roosevelt feared that the Nazis were ahead of the Americans in the nuclear race, but Groves himself was more cheerful. A man of great energy and singleness of purpose, he believed that the Americans would win the race in time, he hoped, to drop one of those bombs over the Nazi fatherland.

Rumors of a Japanese bomb he discounted. For one thing, the United States had a first-rate intelligence network in Japan and knew pretty well what was going on within the country. Groves was sure that Japan did not have the needed ore, and he doubted very much that her technology was sufficiently advanced. Only once, so the story goes, did Groves question an American physicist about their capabilities. "I don't believe they can do it," the American is said to have replied. "There simply aren't enough first-rate Japanese scientists."

Groves, accordingly, dismissed Japanese efforts in the field, but rumors about German progress grew more persistent and more alarming. The German government, in the autumn of 1943, went so far as to declare publicly that it was in possession of a new and secret weapon of unimaginable power. Consequently various American agencies, including both army and navy intelligence, combined to create a group of men who were to prepare to follow the Allied invasion of Europe the following year and attempt to determine the precise state of German nuclear research. The Alsos mission, as it was called (after the Greek word meaning "grove"), was to be commanded by Lieutenant Colonel Boris T. Pash, of the United States Military Intelligence Service. Their insignia was to be a badge with a white α pierced by a bolt of lightning, a rather conspicuous means of identification; but it is said that the men who wore the badge were proud of it, for they felt the bolt of lightning symbolized the dawn of the new atomic age.

At the end of the year the Alsos mission went to Italy, where they were able to determine that the Italians had done nothing in the way of nuclear research; but their investigations in regard to German research remained inconclusive. The United States was still in the dark, still fearful, but still hopeful.

Around the time that the Alsos mission was being secretly organized in the United States, Takeuchi in Japan was on the point of completing the highly complex and extremely ingenious separator he had been working on, and Kunihiko Kigoshi, on the floor above, was engaged in the production of sexa-uranium fluoride, the gas that was to be used in the separator. These two young men, then, constituted Japan's sole hope of ever winning the war, or even holding her own against an increasingly powerful enemy. There was no question, by now, that the tide of war had turned; the daily necessities of life were fast disappearing from the nation's markets; and the daily necessities of the scientists were growing increasingly hard to obtain. The two young physicists found, for example, that they had to make thirty-two copies of an application for needed steel from the Arms and Munitions Ministry. The fact that the N-research project was top secret did not make their task any easier. Further, in addition to Takeuchi and Kigoshi there was only one other scientist, Takehiko Ishiwatari, directly engaged in the project, along with two women assistants.

By the end of November Takeuchi's separator was ready to be tested. He was making use of two cylinders, one inside the other, with the space between filled with gas. When the temperature of the two cylinders was changed, it was expected that the gas would move, the lighter gas going to the top, the heavier gas settling underneath. This, much simplified, was the principle behind the heat-dispersion method; it had been shown to work with plain argon, but would it also work with the uranium isotopes? There was nothing in the institute's vast library that would answer that all-important question.

Nor was much known about the nature of the sexa-uranium fluoride that was to be used in the separator. One thing that was known about it was that it was so powerful it would corrode even glass; steel, therefore, was out of the question. What was needed was either gold or platinum, both highly resistant to fluoride, but these were unavailable in sufficient quantities. Takeuchi decided to gamble on copper. Kigoshi, meanwhile, had evolved a process for obtaining the coveted sexa-uranium fluoride. Uranyl nitrate was burnt in order to produce uranium dioxide. By mixing this with carbon powder and heating the mixture in an electric furnace to a temperature of $1,500°$ C., a carbonized uranium could be obtained. Reacting this with fluoride should result in sexa-uranium fluoride.

This was all very well in theory, but would it work in practice? Could sufficient U-235 be obtained? Reluctantly, the researchers came to the same conclusion as those who had been engaged in the navy's B-research, which had been shelved: the atomic bomb could be produced but Japan could not produce it in time to change the tide of the war. To think otherwise was to cherish a forlorn hope.

Sensing this mood of growing pessimism in his laboratory, Professor Nishina, as the year drew to a close, called one of the men into his office. "What attitude," he asked, "motivates your work? Do you truly believe we are capable of producing the bomb?"

The young man was silent for a moment. Then, "No," he said, "I don't believe we are."

At this Nishina's usually benign expression swiftly changed, and behind his spectacles his eyes flashed angrily for a moment. Then he called in the other researchers, and to each, individually, he put the same question. From each he received the same answer.

His rage mounted. "If that's your attitude," he cried, "then . . ."

Suddenly he paused.

In the silence that followed, everyone mentally completed the sentence: ". . . then stop your work!"

After a moment, Nishina completed the sentence himself, aloud, in a quiet voice: "Go on with your work," he said, "at any rate." Then he shook his head, and as his staff filed out, they sensed that his own answer was the same as theirs.

CHAPTER 4   **1944**

The first of January marked the opening of the third year of the war. Typical of the feeling in the country was the entry in the journal of Yoshishige Kozai, the well-known Japanese philosopher: "Another new year has dawned in the midst of a world war. The Japanese flag flutters at every gate, but the footsteps of the people are not to be heard in the streets. The city is silent. In this coming year, 1944, no doubt a tremendous upheaval will be felt throughout the world, nor will Japan be an exception. She will be confronted by extremely grave problems, both internally and externally. I cannot imagine what will happen to me and my family."

The armed forces were suffering defeat after defeat, on virtually every front. Production lagged far behind what was needed to replenish the losses in matériel that were being sustained day after day. Ships were being sunk in increasing numbers while steel production diminished. News from everywhere was discouraging. Yet the military, determined to pursue the war to the very end, continued to express its optimism, although there was no longer any doubt that the high command knew secretly it had no further cause for the optimistic view it kept insisting on. All hope of victory was fast vanishing.

At home, although the flags continued to flutter patriotically, the Japanese people welcomed the new year with deep anxiety and apprehension. They tightened their belts and patched their old clothing as the necessities of life continued to disappear from the markets and the shops. On 1 February 1942 a rationing system for clothing had been established. People who lived in cities were given a hundred points a year; those in rural areas, eighty. It was hardly enough, because a man's suit required fifty points, a shirt twelve, a pair of trousers four, stockings two, and a suit of work clothes twenty-four. By 1944 the allocation had been considerably reduced: fifty points for people under thirty, forty for those thirty years old or older. But even Japanese who had enough points found that the points were useless to them: the shops were empty. They lived increasingly frugal lives, repeating, as the military desired, the patriotic but empty slogan, "All we want is

to win the war!" As Kozai suggested in his diary, everyone was beginning to feel a deepening sense of anxiety about the future; every man,
deep in his heart, was wondering what that future held in store for him
and his family.

But was there, at last, a ray of hope that the Japanese people knew
nothing about? The answer was still uncertain, but shortly after the new
year dawned Kigoshi, working through the night, succeeded in producing crystals of sexa-uranium fluoride. In a quartz tube he placed the
uranium carbide he had obtained from uranyl nitrate along with fluoride; then he heated the tube, and as the carbide began to burn, it
emitted sexa-uranium fluoride gas. After the gas cooled, it formed into
a crystal. The process was, after all, relatively simple, but it had taken a
long time to evolve, and it had exacted much hard work on Kigoshi's
part.

The crystal was only as large as a grain of rice, but it was a tremendous breakthrough. Kigoshi and Ishiwatari, who had worked with
him, danced for joy. It was a bitterly cold, midwinter night, but neither man felt the chill. Nor did they feel sleepy: they were too excited,
too eager to report their success to Nishina, who was expected, as
usual, to appear for work early in the morning.

Japan's N-research project had labored and produced a rice-sized
crystal of sexa-uranium fluoride. But what was happening on the other
side of the ocean? There too scientists were laboring mightily, including the refugees and scientists in exile as well as Britain's top physicists
and vast numbers of Americans. Excitement mounted as the projects
seemed to be drawing to the desired conclusion, but there was no slack-
ening, for although fears that the Germans might produce the bomb
first had diminished, there remained the constant awareness that the
bomb could shorten immeasurably both the war in Europe and the
Pacific war.

Oak Ridge, where the Clinton plant was engaged in separating
U-235, had grown into a town of nearly eighty thousand people. The
plant itself was so enormous workers used bicycles to get from one part
of it to another. At Hanford, Washington, some sixty thousand people
were engaged in the production of plutonium; the temperature of the

nearby Columbia River, whose waters were used for cooling purposes, rose when the plant started operating. The entire Manhattan Project required a total of more than 539,000 man-years of effort. It was indeed, as Henry Stimson, the secretary of war called it, the greatest scientific project in the history of the world.

The same could hardly be said of Japan's N-research project, although in March its personnel was increased considerably; that is considerably more than the three or four people who had hitherto been engaged on it directly. The additions were some ten young men, mainly of lieutenant rank, who had only recently left university, where they had majored in physics, and been drafted into the army. They had been assigned to the project by army aviation headquarters. Casting aside their uniforms with alacrity, they went happily to work in the Nishina laboratory.

Four of them were immediately assigned to the mass production of sexa-uranium fluoride under Kigoshi's direction, while Kigoshi himself now had more time to determine its precise chemical properties, knowledge which was essential for carrying out further experiments. Of particular importance was the viscosity coefficient of the gas. If they knew that, the scientists could work out exactly how the separation process would occur once the gas was in the separator.

On 12 March the Takeuchi type separator had been redesigned in order to eliminate unstable heat distribution. But there were still a number of major problems to be solved, for although it was now possible, theoretically, to separate U-235, the separation process had never actually been carried out. Perfecting the separator had been a long, arduous task, and the mere fact that it was already in existence seemed almost to transcend the technological knowledge in Japan's possession at the time. It marked a major advance by Japanese science.

But far greater quantities of U-235 were essential, and this in itself posed a seemingly insurmountable problem, for the production of only one kilogram of U-235 necessitated the use of literally thousands of separators. One kilo was the minimal amount needed for the completion of one bomb. Thus, N-research required not only vast quantities of material but astronomical sums of money as well in order to construct the separators. Could all this be made available? Assuming that it could, the researchers next had to tackle the problem of the volume of electric current needed for the nichrome coils within the separators. This, according to the calculations made by the so-called military scientists in the Nishina laboratory, would amount to about one-tenth of the total amount of electricity in use in the entire country. The figure was a dismaying one for Takeuchi, since it was quite impossible for the laboratory, at that time, to obtain such an enormous amount of electrical power. However, despite the mounting, and apparently insurmountable, problems that faced them, the N-researchers continued their work. If, as seemed all too likely, they could never succeed in producing an atomic bomb in time for it to be of strategic value during the war, they worked on with the thought that their research might still be of tremendous importance in a postwar future.

Meanwhile, work on the Manhattan Project was proceeding at an ever accelerating tempo. In the words of W. L. Laurence, science reporter of the New York Times:

"If a Rip Van Winkle had gone to sleep at the turn of the century and awakened to behold modern airplanes, radio, television, and radar, he could not have been more surprised than I was when I first visited the mammoth plants in which U.235 is being pried loose from U.238, or the great atomic piles in which U.238 is being transmuted into plutonium. . . .

"The surprises that meet the visitor to the various plants are not confined to the plants as a whole, their enormous dimensions, their novelty in design, their Olympian grandeur, their unique processes, and their awesome products. Individual surprises relating to the multifarious components and apparatus in each of the plants await the visitor at every turn. He no sooner recovers from one than he is confronted by another equally if not more startling. And when he thinks he has reached the saturation point, he soon discovers that he has barely scratched the surface.

"For example, he enters one of the great buildings in which U.235 is being concentrated by the electromagnetic method. He no sooner passes through the door than he finds himself confronted by a monumental structure that practically fills the entire space of the building. Merely the appearance of this inner structure is impressive enough, but suddenly he learns the incredible fact that practically the entire monumental mass, occupying many tens of thousands of cubic feet, constitutes one gigantic electromagnet. Nothing approaching a magnet of this size was even considered possible before the war.

"As though that were not enough, the visitor soon learns that this is only one of many such magnets, scattered in various other similar buildings of this one plant, sprawling over an area covering five hundred acres."[8]

It was a kind of twentieth-century shotgun wedding between science and industry, where the justice of the peace, oddly enough, was the American military establishment, while the shotgun was the possibility that Nazi Germany might still produce an atomic bomb. Spinoza has said that there can be no hope without fear, and the Manhattan Project is a classic example of his dictum. They hoped against hope, and smothered as best they could the inevitable frictions. Science, industry, and the army combined their efforts to produce the bomb before Germany could, and, in doing so, they ushered in a new era in the history of mankind.

Fear of German scientific prowess was particularly sharp on the part of refugee scientists from Europe, who had had ample opportunity to observe German skill, German organizational power, and German ruthlessness. Strangely enough, the Germans, aware of those qualities and convinced that Allied skills could never equal their own, had little fear of an enemy atomic bomb. They were convinced that no such bomb could come into being within the near future. They constructed their atomic reactors not to produce an atomic bomb but in order to obtain a new and powerful source of energy. Less than a hundred scientists and workers were engaged in their nuclear project, and by the time the war ended they had spent less than ten million dollars on it.

They continued to concentrate their efforts on other, more immediate projects, such as jet fighters, bombs that could be dropped by remote control, rocket aircraft, rocket bombs that could strike enemy planes by means of heat rays, and torpedoes that could home in on a zigzagging ship by tracing its sound. They had, in fact, so many such projects that many of them were far from completion when the war ended. If it seems strange that a powerful authoritarian dictatorship was unable to concentrate its efforts as a free democracy did, in the Manhattan Project, then at least part of the explanation must lie in Hitler's own peculiar disinterest in nuclear research. He reached that private decision early and, luckily for the Allies, he abided by it. There is the further consideration that, with so many diverse projects in the developmental stage, competition for priorities was inevitable. Thus, each project was the rival of every other; Nazi nuclear scientists' most powerful enemies may not have been the Allies at all but rather their own scientist colleagues.

The Allied forces landed in Normandy on 6 June 1944; the Germans were driven back; the authority of the Third Reich then crumbled throughout occupied Europe; and soon much of Europe was no longer occupied at all. The liberation process was advancing rapidly and Germany had all but lost the war. What then was to be done with the atomic bomb if Germany was defeated before the bomb could become operational? The Manhattan Project had been aimed at Germany. If Germany fell, would the gun base swivel in another direction?

Defeat was dogging the footsteps of the Japanese as well. The imperial forces had declared the Mariana Islands to be their last defense line—but the Marianas fell. Some of the army's most indefatigable diehards began to experience a feeling of pessimism, a premonition of irreversible defeat. Then, on 9 July, came the fall of Saipan. The army had repeatedly assured the Japanese people that Saipan was unassailable, much as the American navy had assured the people of the United States that Pearl Harbor was "an impregnable fortress." But there was an all-important difference. Nearly three years of war and attrition had intervened. Pearl Harbor set the American war machine in motion; Saipan was the beginning of the end for the Japanese. The people themselves were shocked, and their rulers realized that the time had come for peace feelers to be put out in earnest. Or was the time past? Was it already too late?

On 18 July the Tōjō cabinet, which had been conducting the war for two and a half years, resigned en masse. Of this event Misao Ōki, chief secretary of the House of Representatives, wrote in his journal: "I arrived at the Diet at ten o'clock. Soon after came Mr. Tadahiko Okada, chairman of the House, who said: 'I was right. I have just heard at the headquarters of the Taisei Yokusan Kai[9] that the cabinet has resigned. The senior statesmen met last night at Hiranuma's house. What I said must have been effective. I will now prepare a statement on the resignation of the cabinet.' "

On the very same day that General Tōjō presented his resignation to the emperor a new and hopefully final, or near-final, experiment on U-235 separation was inaugurated at the Nishina laboratory: a flask of sexa-uranium fluoride (which by that time was being produced in greater quantities) was to be attached to the under section of the separator. For this first experiment only 170 grams were used; the flask was small enough to be held in a pair of hands. By a complex process making use of different degrees of heat, U-235 was to rise to the top of the separator, while the heavier U-238 was to fall to the bottom.

But so many factors were still unknown, such as the precise degree of heat necessary to create a convective current, the correct space between the inner and outer tubes, and the very nature of the gas itself. But time was now, if ever, of the essence: despite the crucial unknown factors, the Nishina men had no choice but to make the test. Scientists working in unknown fields have sometimes experienced the strange phenomenon of a sudden and mysterious power that unexpectedly solves all problems. It was this that Japan's nuclear physicists now hoped for—that, indeed, they depended on.

By watching the flask attached to the under section of the separator and seeing to what extent the flouride diminished, they could tell whether the gas was entering the separator. At last one member of the "military group" cried: "It is becoming noticeably less! Without doubt it is changing into gas!" Takeuchi nodded silently and then ordered the flask to be replenished with more of the material.

As the days passed, the young scientists took turns at their vigil, meanwhile collecting all available data from the various instruments connected to the separator. The lay visitor would have seen only a group of young white-clad men, with tired, bloodshot eyes, tinkering endlessly with mysterious gauges and meters, and then hastily writing down the results. It would have been a boring sight, but the young men were far from bored! Each moment they expected the unexpected, the sudden mysterious solution to unsolved problems.

Then the unexpected came. But it solved no problems; it only presented more. Two specially made gauges had been attached to the top and bottom of the separator; by checking the difference in pressure between the two gauges, the men of the N-group believed they would be able to determine whether U-235 was actually being separated. But although the volume of gas continued to diminish, there was no perceptible difference in pressure. In fact, it tended to fall. Takeuchi instituted certain slight changes in method and added more sexa-uranium gas. But the pressure continued to diminish. There seemed to be various possible explanations, but none of them was particularly satisfactory.

Takeuchi took the problem to Nishina. After pondering for some time, Nishina said, "Well, don't worry. Just keep on with it, just keep giving it more gas." This confirmed Takeuchi's own conviction that he had no choice but to go on trying: to continue with the experiment, to take as accurate data as possible, and to use whatever new methods seemed most likely to prove effective. Day after day he and his colleagues worked around the clock. It was not only sleep of which they were deprived, because food had become scarcer than ever. Their stomachs rumbled emptily as, like young doctors with a cranky premature baby, they tended the precious separator, which continued to refuse to behave as it should. They were, in a sense, Japan's only hope, for the day of reckoning was about to dawn.

In Europe that day had already dawned, and the clock was racing onward as the Allied armies dashed across the continent. In France, American tank units advanced forty miles a day. On 2 August, in an address to the House of Commons, Winston Churchill said there was no longer any doubt of an Allied victory in Europe in the very near future.

A week later the second Alsos mission, still under the command of Colonel Pash, was in France interviewing French atomic scientists, including of course Professor Frédéric Joliot. In the course of their investigations they learned that some of Germany's most eminent nuclear researchers were at the Reich University of Strasbourg. But Strasbourg was still under German control. Brussels meanwhile was liberated, and the files of the Union Minière there revealed the enormous quantities of both crude and refined uranium that had been shipped to Germany. It was a disquieting moment. Germany was losing the war, but she might still pull that trump card out from under her ravelled sleeve.

It was, to be sure, only a remote possibility. Equally remote was the likelihood that the Americans would have an atomic bomb operational before the European war ended. This did not, however, have a deterrent effect on the Manhattan Project, which proceeded at top speed. What had begun as "the greatest scientific gamble in history" was fast becoming a near certainty, and if it was not to be used against the Nazis, then clearly there was but one other target.

On 18 September Roosevelt and Churchill concluded an aide-mémoire on the subject of the bomb in which they agreed that all possible precautions should be taken to prevent nuclear information from reaching the Russians. The same memorandum included another historic statement: "When a bomb is finally available, it might perhaps, after mature consideration, be used against the Japanese, who should be warned that this bombardment will be repeated until they surrender."

On this point Lamont writes, "The scientists at Los Alamos, their waking hours consumed by work on the device, had for the most part given little thought to the prospect of the bomb being used against Japan. Some of their colleagues at Chicago, with more time on their hands to ruminate over the moral implications of the bomb, had given it deep thought however. The Chicago scientists found it difficult to adjust to the idea that the bomb was no longer simply an anti-Nazi weapon. They also genuinely feared for the future peace of the world if the United States undertook to release atomic power in a destructive act of war.

"The Los Alamos scientists seemed detached from all this. Absorbed in their labors, swept up in the invigorating atmosphere of the mesa, they lived remote from the problems of Washington and the world."[10]

The commander of the Manhattan Project, General Groves, had no nagging doubts. His attitude toward dropping the bomb on Japan is certainly best given in his own words:

"There has been much discussion since the war about the decision to use the atomic bomb against Japan. Decisions of this nature must always be made by only one man, and, in this case, the burden fell upon President Truman. Under the terms of the Quebec Agreement, the concurrence of Prime Minister Churchill was necessary; nevertheless, the initial decision and the primary responsibility were Mr. Truman's. As far as I was concerned, his decision was one of noninterference—basically, a decision not to upset the existing plans.

"When we first began to develop atomic energy, the United States was in no way committed to employ atomic weapons against any other power. With the activation of the Manhattan Project, however, the situation began to change. Our work was extremely costly, both in money and in its interference with the rest of the war effort. As time went on, and as we poured more and more money and effort into the project, the government became increasingly committed to the ultimate use of the bomb, and while it has often been said that we undertook development of this terrible weapon so that Hitler would not get it first, the fact remains that the original decision to make the project an all-out effort was based upon using it to end the war. As Mr. Stimson succinctly put it, the Manhattan Project existed 'to bring the war to a successful end more quickly than otherwise would be the case and thus to save American lives.'

"Certainly, there was no question in my mind, or, as far as I was ever aware, in the mind of either President Roosevelt or President Truman or any other responsible person, but that we were developing a weapon to be employed against the enemies of the United States. The first serious mention of the possibility that the atomic bomb might not be used came after V-E Day, when Under Secretary of War Patterson asked me whether the surrender in Europe might not alter our plans for dropping the bomb on Japan.

"I said that I could see no reason why the decision taken by President Roosevelt when he approved the tremendous effort involved in the Manhattan Project should be changed for that reason, since the surrender of Germany had in no way lessened Japan's activities against the United States."[11]

Another man intimately associated with the development of the bomb, this time a scientist, Dr. Arthur Holly Compton, has also noted (in his book, *Atomic Quest*) that after the Battle of the Bulge in December, it became clear that the capitulation of Germany was not far off, in which case the bomb would inevitably be used against the Japanese rather than the Germans.

So it was that Japan had in a sense already become the target of the bomb. But no Japanese, of course, was aware of the fact; hardly anyone even considered the possibility. What chiefly concerned the Japanese at this moment in their history was what would happen to them if, or rather when, Germany was defeated. On 20 July, at the time the Tōjō cabinet resigned, an attempt was made on Hitler's life; although the attempt failed, it cast its shadow ahead. The supreme command of the Imperial Army came to the reluctant conclusion that their chief ally was doomed.

In an attempt to cope with this eventuality, the Koiso cabinet, which had succeeded that of Tōjō, drafted a statement of "new national policy" on 21 September (three days after the date of the Roosevelt-Churchill aide-mémoire on the use of the bomb). The "new" policy declared that Japan, in the event Germany surrendered, would have to be prepared for intensified Allied attacks. The government, however, would have to make the people realize a German surrender need not greatly affect Japan's own position, pointing out that:

(1) inevitably there would be increased friction among the Allied powers in Europe as a result of the German surrender, and it would therefore be impossible for the three belligerents to deploy all their forces in the Far East;

(2) a termination of the war in Europe would lead to diminution of the Allied will to fight, whereas Japan was more than ever determined to pursue the war to a victorious conclusion, a fact that would have an

additional deteriorating influence on the enemy's fighting spirit; and

(3) it would not be possible for the enemy to conduct massive air raids on the Japanese islands on a scale comparable to those it conducted in Europe.

Did the new government truly believe the points it was trying to make? If so, it was either unduly optimistic or extremely badly informed, since as far back as 30 June, soon after the Americans had captured Saipan, they had begun the construction of a huge air base there. Saipan was only a little over fifteen hundred miles from Tokyo. Further, in their raids over Japan, the Americans proposed to make use of bombers far larger than those that had been used in Europe; these were the B-29s, the so-called superfortresses. In view of these facts, the policy statement of the new Koiso cabinet can only be seen as the result of some elaborate wishful thinking. It is also, of course, further evidence of the extreme reluctance of the Japanese military establishment to admit that, in provoking America into war, it had bitten off a great deal more than it could chew.

By the end of that same month, September 1944, over fifteen hundred men had converged on a desolate air base in the Utah desert. They were members of the newly formed 509th Composite Group, commanded by Colonel Paul Tibbets. The name of the remote and dusty air base was Wendover Field, but that was a name known only to very few; in code it was called Kingman, or just plain K. When Wendover telephoned Los Alamos, for of course there was a connection between the two, it was K calling Y. It was all very well to manufacture an atomic bomb if you could, but there was little point to it unless you could also drop it safely on a selected target. This was to be the task of the 509th Composite Group, a task that bore the code name of Operation Silver Plate.

The delivery of the atomic weapon itself was assigned to a section of the 509th called the 393rd Bombardment Squadron. After the personnel of the squadron, all highly trained and experienced men many of whom were old friends and flying companions of Colonel Tibbets, had been assembled, they underwent intensive training in a type of bombing that was wholly unfamiliar to them. They had fourteen new

B-29s at their disposal, planes that had simply seemed to vanish from the air force rolls, and these, once they reached Wendover, were lightened by removal of most of their armament, for although the bomb itself was still in the production stage, its makers knew that it was going to be extremely heavy, and they also knew that the plane that delivered it was going to have to fly at an altitude of 30,000 feet for reasons of safety.

The crews under Tibbets's command took the planes, each carrying one large bomb, up to an altitude higher than the necessary 30,000 feet, released the bomb over a white circle painted on the desert surface, made a sharp turn within thirty seconds of dropping the dummy bomb, and swerved in a 155-degree arc. The scientists had calculated that when the actual bomb was dropped, it would fall about six miles before exploding some two thousand feet above ground. The plane that had dropped the bomb, if it followed the maneuvers for which it was training in the Utah desert, would be eight and a half miles away at the moment of explosion, at which point it would take longer than one minute for any shock waves to reach the bomber itself. The purpose of the sharp turn and consequent swerve was to permit the bomber to escape the worst shock, but this was not, of course, known to the men who were undergoing the training. Security precautions at Wendover were as strict as those at Los Alamos itself.

The Japanese caught their first glimpse of the new and ominous B-29 on 1 November: it was a lone plane that had taken off from the Saipan air base. Shōgo Nakamura, a reporter for the *Asahi* newspaper, has described that day in his journal:

"The members of the cabinet were just about to begin their lunch in the Diet restaurant when shrill air raid warnings were sounded all over Tokyo. Simultaneously came the roar of antiaircraft guns, and the bursting shells left trails of white smoke that looked like tufts of fluffy cotton against the blue background of the sky. Through the cottony smoke could be seen a single glistening plane, flying high over the official residence of the Prime Minister and headed in a south-westerly direction. It could only have been a B-29.

"The members of the cabinet took refuge in the bomb shelter at the prime minister's official residence. As they huddled there in that cramped bomb shelter, packed as tightly as sardines in a can, the telephone went dead. The information that trickled through turned out to be mostly inaccurate. I began to wonder what would happen should Tokyo be visited by a massive air raid if this was the condition of things at the prime minister's official residence."

There was no longer any doubt that the target of American air raids was to be the Japanese homeland. Could Japan defend herself? No one who had any accurate information felt very optimistic on that point. The Combined Fleet had suffered great losses at Leyte, and by this time there were no more than about twenty-five hundred fighter planes scattered over the entire country. Fuel was in extremely short supply, and casualties had been so heavy that the men who were now flying the planes were doing so without adequate training. To make the situation even more hopeless, Japanese antiaircraft guns were not powerful enough to reach the new planes capable of flying at very high altitudes. The prospects for Japan, her people, and her emperor, seemed dismal indeed.

As that month of November was drawing to a close, the city of Strasbourg fell into Allied hands, and on the heels of the frontline troops came Colonel Pash with an advance group of the Alsos mission. They hoped to capture some of Germany's top nuclear physicists, who had been working there; in particular, they wanted Professor Carl-Friedrich von Weizsäcker, a key figure in Germany's attempt to produce an atomic bomb; but Pash's first impression was that all the scientists, including von Weizsäcker, had already fled the city. Then came word that a "nuclear physics laboratory had been found in a wing of a Strasbourg hospital, and staff who had at first been thought to be doctors had turned out to be physicists."[12]

Dr. Samuel A. Goudsmit, the famous Dutch physicist who was now a member of the Alsos team, set out at once for Strasbourg, accompanied by another member of the mission, Fred Wardenburg. There, in von Weizsäcker's office at the university, they found a great treasure trove of documents, including letters exchanged between the various physicists reporting on their progress along with the addresses of the various institutes throughout Germany that had been working on the nuclear project. This latter discovery was, of course, of extreme importance. When they made it, so the perhaps apocryphal story goes, Goudsmit and Wardenburg cried out with excitement.

"What happened?" asked one of the guards. "Draw a winning number in the lottery?"

"I think so," Goudsmit replied, for it appeared from the documents that there was no longer any possibility Germany might suddenly produce an atomic bomb. "We've won the war!"

"Sure we have," said the guard. "You can't beat GIs."

In any case, in Goudsmit's words, the documents "gave an authentic picture of the uranium research program as of the summer of 1944." Hitler, convinced of German invincibility and blindly disinterested in long-range projects, had been informed as far back as 1942 that an atomic bomb was within the realm of possibility, but he had persisted in giving the project low priority. As a result, two years later, when the Strasbourg papers fell into Allied hands, it became clear that the Germans, although they continued to work on nuclear research, had, as Goudsmit said, "given up altogether the idea of making a bomb."

Under these circumstances, should the Manhattan Project be abandoned? Had the United States any justification for continuing its all-out effort to produce, and presumably use, the new catastrophic weapon? This was the beginning of top-level debate in the United States to go on for several months before a decision was finally made; it was the beginning of a controversy that can still produce heated argument.

A squadron of B-29s raided Tokyo for the first time on 24 November. The designated target had originally been the Musashi plant of the Nakajima Aircraft Manufacturing Company but was changed, because the sky had clouded over, to Tokyo itself. The raid, which began at 1:00 P.M., came in three waves. The people of Tokyo counted eight B-29s in the first, twelve in the second, and twenty-three in the third. To these people the long glistening craft, flying high over the city, looked like handsome new toys, but after the bombs began to fall (a total of 2,700 tons of them, chiefly aimed at munitions plants) the toys took on a deadly air that, as time went on, was to grow disastrously familiar.

As the planes invaded the sky over Tokyo, antiaircraft guns spread a heavy blanket of shells, and fighter planes flew up in an attempt to engage the enemy. One fighter crashed into the tail of an invading B-29, and the B-29 fell into the sea. Government officials who had taken refuge in shelters heard the bombs dropping overhead, while at the same time they listened to a broadcast from Los Angeles describing the raid. The broadcast announced that a hundred planes had taken off from a base in the Mariana Islands and were even then bombing the Japanese capital. The government had no choice but to believe the substance of the American broadcast, and for three hours, while the raid went on, the administration of the country ground to a halt.

It almost seemed as though the life of the whole country was grinding to a halt. How can people wage a war, how can they resist a powerful enemy, when their stomachs are crying for food? The Japanese have always, in their history, been a notably frugal people, but the frugality that was now imposed upon them, by an ever harsher rationing system, was almost more than even long-suffering Japanese flesh and blood could bear. The newspapers printed daily lists of allowable amounts of food, and it could not have been very enticing for a housewife to read that for herself and her family of four she was to be permitted that day to purchase two sardines. To make matters worse, even the skimpiest rations were not always available and were often of the poorest quality; the autumn rice harvest had been unusually small, while imports of foodstuffs from Manchuria were growing increasingly meager. Children under fifteen and people over sixty-five were allowed candy once a month. To help allay the gnawing pangs of hunger, indeed to help stay alive, those who had a bit of land or a small garden took to growing pumpkins and squash, but those are not foods that stick to the ribs. In November the cigarette allowance was reduced to six a day for each adult.

The government fostered such inspiring slogans as "We ask for nothing but to win the war," "The enemy must be defeated," and "A hundred million people will advance like a ball of fire." Daily the newspapers and the radio carried stories about suicide pilots who had intrepidly crashed their planes into enemy aircraft and ships; both the army and the navy spotlighted their suicide corps. In December the age of conscription was lowered to eighteen, but even younger recruits, inspired by the ubiquitous banners of the rising sun, applied daily for enlistment at military barracks. Middle school pupils were mobilized to work in munitions plants.

Apparently the Japanese people were united in their determination to fight to the end, no matter how bitter it might be. But the fact is that incessant enemy air raids, combined with the drastic food shortage, were grossly undermining that determination, and the government had little to offer to bolster morale save to call upon the "spiritual strength" of the people. On 11 December, accordingly, the prime minister asked the whole people to offer a silent prayer to the Ise Grand Shrines at exactly 1:22 P.M. During the thirteenth century, a "divine wind" (*kamikaze*) had suddenly sprung up and driven the invading Mongol fleet from Japanese shores. Could the combined prayers of the whole people muster sufficient spiritual strength to induce another divine wind to spring up and scatter the enemy warships and the fleets of B-29s?

The army did its best to allay the apprehensions of the people by pointing out that only a very small percentage of the thousands of bombs being dropped by the enemy could make direct hits: one out of fifty at most, perhaps only one out of a hundred. Four thousand incendiary bombs, the army insisted, would claim the lives of at most a hundred people. The war must go on, cried the army, and to that end no sacrifice could be considered too great. Would such repeated declarations dissipate the country's growing sense of defeat, which the army feared as greatly as it feared the growing military might of the enemy? Could the people be persuaded to fight to the end, even though the end might mean annihilation?

OP-16-W said "No!" This was the code name for a secret research and planning section of the United States Navy that had been established as far back as August 1942 to aid in psychological warfare against the Germans. Now, with the German defeat, they turned their attentions to Japan. One of the questions to be answered was whether the Japanese people were indeed so emotionally channeled that they could be induced to continue fighting until the whole country had committed suicide (taking with it, in the process, millions of enemy troops).

The chief of the section, Dr. Ladislas Farago, made an intensive study of Japanese history in an attempt to answer that question. He found that while the Japanese had fought few foreign wars, they had frequently fought amongst themselves, and that these internecine conflicts had generally ended not in mass suicide of the defeated but in their surrender. Surrender was not, then, intrinsically repugnant to the Japanese spirit, not even to the spirit of *bushido*, the ancient "way of the warrior." Despite popular tradition, Japanese history produced few instances of samurai who had chosen suicide in preference to surrender·

Japan would probably, as she had during the Russo-Japanese war of 1905 when the tide turned against her, ask some third power to act as mediator in bringing about a cease-fire. In the Russo-Japanese war, the Japanese army, after suffering its first defeat at Shaho, south of Mukden, had requested President Theodore Roosevelt to arrange an end to hostilities. A similar situation, Dr. Farago's section concluded, could now be brought about in the present conflict: the Japanese could be persuaded to lay down their arms rather than fight, as the Imperial Army kept insisting they must, to "the last man."

It was through the Turkish embassy in Tokyo that Dr. Farago's group came to learn that standing in the way of an early end to hostilities there was, on the Japanese side, but one unnegotiable condition: the status of the emperor. The Turkish embassy, under the code name Shark, had proven a valuable source of information in the past to the United States, but never before had they passed on so hopeful a message. Like a most welcome Christmas present, it reached the group on 23 December.

The news it contained was startling as well as auspicious. The present Koiso cabinet, according to the message, would shortly resign en masse, and a new cabinet would be formed by Baron Kantarō Suzuki, retired admiral and former grand chamberlain to the emperor. At the same time, the peace faction within the government was growing increasingly influential and was now apparently prepared to act, using the emperor as its spearhead, provided only that the Allied powers were willing to guarantee that his present status would remain unchanged after the war. Should they indicate their readiness to do so, the Suzuki cabinet would then resign and a member of the imperial family, probably the emperor's cousin, Prince Naruhiko Higashikuni, would form a new cabinet to effect the terms of surrender. With the emperor himself commanding capitulation, the Japanese armed forces would obey; the war would be over.

Further encouraging news reached Dr. Farago's group around the same time. The hitherto invincible Kwantung Army was now being deployed on southern fronts, where it was being inexorably annihilated. There were virtually no Japanese troops at all remaining in Manchuria. With Japan's lifelines ruptured in both north and south, the country was left gasping for breath. It was clearly ready for surrender.

Unfortunately, the conclusions reached by Dr. Farago and his group carried little weight in Washington, which appeared unwilling to commit itself on the question of the emperor and which, furthermore, did not credit the Japanese with the willingness to surrender. Indeed, an intensification of kamikaze attacks hardly appeared to reinforce Farago's position, while the ferocity of the battle for the Philippines all too clearly indicated the opposite. Neither the State Department nor the Joint Chiefs of Staff expressed interest in acting on the information gleaned by OP-16-W; neither appeared willing to believe that Japan was in reality prepared to surrender.

Whatever the Allied powers may have chosen to believe, there is no question that numerous groups within Japan were secretly working to end the war; secretly because they were subject to close surveillance by both civil and military police which naturally hampered their effectiveness. Freedom of speech was, of course, an unknown luxury in Japan at the time, and, with the truly remarkable obtuseness that often characterizes such people, the military police (the dreaded Kempei-tai) attempted to control freedom of thought as well. Using hired civilian informers, they arrested and interrogated during 1944 over six thousand people suspected of harboring antiwar sentiments or of disseminating rumors derogatory to the Imperial Army or Navy. If the military police came to the conclusion that there was substance to the accusation not only the suspected person himself was liable to punishment but members of his family as well. Under such circumstances, it is hardly surprising that peace groups had to work both secretly and deviously, and on the whole ineffectively.

One of the most powerful of these groups was headed by Shigeru Yoshida, a former vice-minister of foreign affairs who was later to become Japan's most highly esteemed postwar prime minister; Binshirō Obata, a retired lieutenant general and former superintendent of the Japanese War College; and Tatsuo Iwabuchi, who had once been a columnist for the *Mainichi* newspaper. Aiding and abetting them was Prince Fumimaro Konoye, an ex-premier of Japan.

As far back as 1942 these men had begun making their joint effort to put an end to the war, seeking ways and means of achieving their goal in a country strictly dominated by a military establishment supported to the full by big industry. It was a formidable combine to work against, yet they continued trying. Their first hopes centered on Kazushige Ugaki, a retired general who still wielded considerable influence within the army but who, they believed, would be amenable to putting out tentative peace feelers. Ugaki, however, refused to commit himself. They then turned to a retired admiral, Seizō Kobayashi, in the expectation that he would be willing to form a cabinet looking toward peace, but Kobayashi adamantly refused to have anything to do with the plan.

Undaunted by these two rebuffs, they next turned to another retired admiral, Baron Kantarō Suzuki. Yoshida and Konoye conferred with him at Yoshida's house in October of 1944. (This was, it will be noted, at a time when the 509th Composite Group was learning how to drop a single unwieldy bomb on a target in the Utah desert from a height of over thirty thousand feet.) Suzuki was an old man and rather hard of hearing, but he had no difficulty understanding what the two men were asking of him and no hesitation at all in expressing his opposition to their plan. Suzuki had been captain of the crew of a torpedo boat way back in 1905 during the Russo-Japanese war, when he had engaged the enemy in a courageous action in the Japan Sea, and despite the forty years that had intervened he appeared to be as full of beans as ever.

"The final outcome of a war," he told his two visitors, "can never be known unless the war is fought to the very end. Therefore, while the war is still going on, we must not even think of either compromise or surrender. If we are exhausted by the war, we should bear in mind that the enemy too must be tired and worn out. He who perseveres hardest will emerge victorious. We have before our eyes a good example in Chinese history, when the Southern Sung dynasty yielded to the Yüan dynasty because one of its statesmen made premature concessions. Japan must not become a second Sung."

Konoye now gave up hope of persuading Suzuki to form a cabinet, but Yoshida refused to be discouraged. He remained convinced that Suzuki, who was one of the men closest to the emperor, was the only one capable of forming a cabinet that could bring the war to a close, and so he continued meeting Suzuki in the hope of eventually persuading him to change his mind. In addition to his other objections, however, the octogenarian retired admiral pointed out that he considered himself far too old to undertake so arduous a task. To make matters worse, Yoshida's self-appointed mission was now rendered infinitely more difficult by the fact that the Kempei-tai had got wind of his meetings with Suzuki and had begun keeping close watch on the two men. The Turkish embassy in Tokyo, incidentally, was also supposed to have been aware of Yoshida's efforts and to have been keeping OP-16-W informed.

Yoshida was not, by any means, the only man in the country secretly working toward the war's end. There was in the navy Captain Sokichi Takagi, who was attached to the ministry; in the army, Colonel Makoto Matsutani, chief of the 20th section of Army Staff headquarters; and in the Foreign Ministry, Toshikazu Kase. There were also peace groups outside the military or the government, many of whom acted not out of hatred of war but out of fear that Japan was doomed to annihilation if the war was allowed to continue. This fear became intensified when it was apparent that a disastrous defeat at Leyte was imminent.

None of the peace groups apparently was in communication with any other; their only known liaison was in Kempei-tai's files, which were exhaustively thorough. Little, probably nothing, of a "subversive" nature escaped their everwatchful eyes. And the peace groups themselves were hardly more sanguine about the Japanese temper than the American State Department or the Joint Chiefs of Staff. Pessimistically they feared, as did Washington, that Japan would refuse to surrender until its last soldier lay dead. Nonetheless, despite their discouragement, they continued to do what they could, hoping against hope, wondering if the moment would ever come when they would be in a position to take positive and constructive action. Meanwhile, as ordered, they bowed low when they passed before the Imperial Palace to express publicly their unswerving loyalty.

On 30 December, General Groves submitted to General George Marshall, army chief of staff, a memorandum that was in turn passed on to Henry Stimson, the secretary of war, and then finally to President Roosevelt himself. In this new memorandum Groves predicted that the world's first bomb making use of nuclear fission would be ready for delivery by 1 August 1945 and that adequate amounts of plutonium for the first implosion bomb would be available by the latter half of July. He noted also the progress of the 509th Composite Group. Groves proposed, therefore, that the time had come to inform top-level commanders in the Pacific of what had hitherto been the world's closest-guarded secret.

Groves had never been in doubt that if the European war ended before the bomb could be used and if the Pacific war was still continuing, then the bomb must be directed against Japan. "It was always difficult for me," he was to write later, "to understand how anyone could ignore the importance of the effect on the Japanese people and their government of the overwhelming surprise of the bomb. To achieve surprise was one of the reasons we had tried so hard to maintain our secrecy."[13]

As the year ended, Japan was in a sorry state. She was unquestionably losing the war abroad, while at home the situation had gone from bad to worse. Her armed forces had suffered a resounding defeat at Leyte, and Allied troops were about to land on Luzon. Loss of the Philippines would be a major catastrophe. At the same time swarms of B-29s were reducing Japan's major cities to rubble; people were left homeless and very nearly foodless. Military production, despite the recruitment of ever younger workers, was almost at a standstill. How could a nation fallen into such disarray continue a war to the bitter end against the mightiest military power in the world?

Yet continue it to the end, even to the very bitterest end of all, was what the military-dominated government kept insisting upon. Now was the time, they said, for Japan's hundred million to unite in an indivisible bond, to make whatever sacrifices were necessary, to fight to the last man. Or woman. Or child.

The army continued to turn defeat into victory in its reports to the people, but the people no longer believed the reports. They knew now, deep in their hearts, that the war must end in their defeat, but they did not know how to bring about that end or how disastrous it might be. Perhaps fighting on was the lesser of the two evils. How could they tell? Bellies empty, eyes red from tears and lack of sleep, bodies insufficiently clad against the December cold, they walked the ruined streets of their cities and cowered in whatever blackened shelter they could find against the incessant bombing of the enemy. They were cornered animals, animals that could do nothing but await in dumb fear whatever dreadful fate destiny had in store for them.

PART II
1 JANUARY–5 AUGUST 1945

PART II
1 JANUARY-5 AUGUST 1945

CHAPTER 1 **JANUARY 1945**

On 1 January 1945 the people of Hiroshima witnessed a most unusual phenomenon: snow began to fall before dawn, and the fall grew heavier as the day wore on. This was unexpected because Hiroshima, spreading out like a fan on the delta of a river entering the Inland Sea, generally enjoys a rather warm winter. Older citizens racked their brains, trying to recall the last time they had seen a white New Year's Day and wondering what so strange an occurrence might portend. Some insisted it was an auspicious omen; others, more pessimistic, believed that it boded ill for the city, that some dreadful catastrophe would befall Hiroshima before the year was out.

But the latter did not give voice to their fears, for every quarter of the city, as elsewhere in Japan, was closely watched by a group whose duty it was to ensure that no one said or did anything that might undermine public morale. These *tonarigumi* ("neighborhood associations"), as they were called, publicly denounced such traitors and threatened to haul repeated offenders before a military tribunal. Thus, those among Hiroshima's citizens who saw something ill-omened in the New Year's Day snowfall kept their mouths shut tight as they wandered through the unaccustomed white streets of the city, as they paused on one or another of the city's many bridges that spanned its seven rivers, or as they looked down onto the clear, still unpolluted waters flowing toward the Inland Sea.

Compared with many of the other cities of Japan, Hiroshima had been extremely fortunate; a man could walk its streets, as he could not, for example, those of Tokyo or Osaka, without fearing the imminent wail of a siren and then a rain of bombs. So far the people of Hiroshima had not even so much as glimpsed a B-29 invading their skies. Where Tokyo was already something of a shambles, Hiroshima still enjoyed what was almost a peacetime existence. There were, certainly, the usual shortages of food and clothing, but those shortages were not so acute as elsewhere, and those people who had been born in Hiroshima and had gone to the larger cities to seek their fortunes were now fleeing back in ever increasing numbers. The first question they asked the friends and relatives who had come to meet them at the railroad station was: "Is there anything to eat here?"

There was. There was no surplus, to be sure; there were no gourmet dinners to be had; but neither was there the near starvation diet that was imposed on the people of the larger or more strategic centers. Here in Hiroshima the bombed out newcomers were overjoyed to discover that they could undress and sleep through the night without being awakened by the shrill, menacing howl of the sirens, and without huddling in a shelter for hours on end, listening and waiting. Hiroshima was not alone in this: throughout the country there were still many towns and villages whose inhabitants led what amounted to a comparatively normal daily life.

While the soft, unaccustomed snowfall awakened some of the citizens of Hiroshima and left them sleepless for a time, the people of Tokyo were aroused by a harsher sound. At 12:05 A.M. on that first January day the sirens began their shrill wail. No one could sleep through that caterwaul, but nevertheless most people continued to lie in bed for a while longer. Then, when the sirens grew more insistent, they wearily rose to seek doubtful shelter, for by this time they were so familiar with the death and destruction that rained down upon them from the skies that they accepted both with resignation, almost with equanimity.

Musei Tokugawa, a writer and radio personality, noted in his journal: "The screeching of the alarm bell and the rattle of antiaircraft fire woke me at three in the morning. I found that the enemy planes had already passed over our house and were dropping incendiary bombs in the far distance. What a horrible way to begin the new year! Immediately after the all clear came, my daughters went to the Hachiman Shrine to pray for victory. Today the temple bells that signal the end of the old year did not sound."

The first of January in Tokyo, unlike that in Hiroshima, dawned clear. Iwabuchi and Obata (who, along with Yoshida, had been trying to persuade Suzuki to form a new cabinet looking toward peace) conferred outdoors under the blue skies, where they could speak together without fear of being overheard. They agreed that immediate action was essential and that, since Suzuki remained adamant, their best hope now was to persuade Prince Konoye to appeal privately to the emperor. Not only was he a former prime minister, he also retained His Majesty's confidence. Accordingly, on the following day, the two called on Yoshida at his villa at Ōiso, in Kanagawa Prefecture. The chief defect in the plan was the difficulty of access to the emperor: the closer Japan came to defeat, the more impassable grew the gates of the Imperial Palace. They remained shut to high-ranking government officials, to senior statesmen, and even to members of the imperial family. Would Konoye be able to make his way through those barred gates, across the moat, and into the imperial presence?

The three men came to the conclusion that they had no choice but to ask him to try. On 6 January they went to Hakone, where Konoye was resting, with the draft of an appeal to the emperor. Their objective was the formation of a Konoye cabinet, and the first step in achieving that objective was, they considered, a direct appeal to His Majesty—an appeal that they now asked Konoye to present personally. Konoye replied that while he was in general agreement with the plan, he feared the consequences if the plan miscarried. He lacked, he said quite frankly, both the courage and the perseverance to embark upon it.

Would he have given a different reply if he had known that the emperor was cautiously moving in the same direction? That very day His Majesty had summoned Marquess Kido, lord keeper of the privy seal, who was always in attendance, and said that he might shortly find it necessary to hold an audience with the *jūshin*, the senior statesmen, and ask their opinion about the course that Japan ought to follow if the war continued in her disfavor. The *jūshin* were former prime ministers who, although they had no constitutional authority, wielded considerable influence. Despite the fact that the army continued to insist it was still winning victory after victory, there would seem to be little doubt that the emperor, however remote he was kept from affairs of state, was aware that these claims were, if not an outright lie, at least a distortion of the truth. Had he, by this time, reached his own private conclusion that he might soon be called upon to take decisive action himself?

And what about the citizens of his capital? Did they still believe the army's optimistic communiqués? The mere struggle to stay alive had by now grown so severe that probably very few of them had the energy left to examine the claims, to sift what little evidence was given them, to believe, or to disbelieve. They had turned into automata, zombies, spurred to action by their rulers and numbed to inaction by the increasing ferocity of enemy raids over the city.

Large areas of the capital were mere heaps of rubble. The only things to be seen were the burnt-out shells of buildings and a few objects that had refused to burn, such as refrigerators, metal files, and steel safes. Placards announcing where former residents had moved to grew more numerous and so did professional safe openers. Safes in homes and offices that had burnt down had to be left for a couple of days to cool before they could be safely handled, and even then it was no easy job to open a safe that had been baked by fire. This gave rise to a new profession, that of safe opening. After a raid, groups of men would roam bombed out districts shouting, "We open safes! Twenty yen each! Just ten minutes!" A man whose only possessions left in the world lay in that safe had no choice but to cough up the fee of nearly $50.

In fact, the people of Tokyo had little choice about any aspect of their lives those unhappy January days. Whether or not there was an alert, they were required to turn their lights out at ten o'clock and, with no street lamps burning, Tokyo by night became a ghost city. Despite the fact that it was a cold winter, there was little or no fuel. People who used more than their allotted amount of gas were immediately deprived of it altogether. Neither charcoal nor coal was any longer being rationed because there was none of either available for nonproductive use. In order to keep warm people burned whatever they owned that would burn. In offices, books and files went first, then empty bookshelves, and then desks and chairs that had been used by men who were now in the armed forces. Employees wore overcoats and gloves at work.

Complaints grew sharper and more frequent. Newspapers went so far as to publish in their columns letters like the following: "It is bitterly cold, but we have no charcoal or wood to burn. They promised us they would bring wood from faraway Hokkaido, but should the people of Tokyo wait patiently until that wood arrives? No! Right within our city there are plenty of trees, in parks and gardens, alongside streets, and in front of large houses. We have a source of fuel right before our eyes. I suggest that we cut down all trees in Tokyo except those that are essential for one reason or another, and use the lumber as fuel. The land where the trees grew can be converted into vegetable gardens. Labor for the job can be obtained by making use of students mobilized to work in munitions plants who are idle because there is no raw material for them to work with. The trees of our city are only waiting for the opportunity to be of service to the country!"

Meanwhile, people tried to keep warm and clean (everyone seemed to be infested with lice these days) by using the public baths. There they sat around in silence, for they no longer had anything to talk about. In earlier days there were the glorious victories of the Imperial Army to discuss, then there was rationing, then factory work, then the black market, then the first air raids. By January 1945 there was nothing. Nor were there any able-bodied men to be seen: in the words of the flippant American wartime song, everyone was "either too young or too old."

And everyone was undernourished. The last harvest of rice, the staple food of the Japanese people, had been shockingly small. Now the government was growing large amounts of both sweet potatoes and Irish potatoes using army-owned land and military personnel, but almost all the potatoes were being allotted to the production of isooctane as fuel for aircraft.

Even the emperor, the chief of state, lived an extremely frugal life. Although he frequently worked from dawn to long past dusk, his diet was little better than that of the rest of his people: rice mixed with barley once a day, a bowl of soup, a bit of fish, and an egg or two. The empress herself picked wild grass in the palace grounds, a food that the emperor found highly palatable. The imperial pair lived in only a few rooms in the newly reinforced Obunko, the palace library area.

Everything was so topsy-turvy that the abnormal seemed normal. Even the great Army Day parade on 8 January was a skimpy affair, inspiring little in the beholder but an awareness of the obvious desire of everyone concerned to get it over with as quickly as possible, lest the enemy use the occasion as a fine excuse for a really bang-up air raid. Only one division paraded briefly on the Imperial Palace Plaza in front of the emperor; gone were all the splendor and grandeur of the imperial reviews of former years. When it was over, everyone sighed with relief that there had been no raid.

That came on the following day. Perhaps the Americans had planned it that way. In any case, it was a massive raid, and it came in broad daylight; there was no wind, and the sky was a brilliant blue. The citizens of Tokyo had an excellent view of the spectacle. Breathlessly they watched as a Japanese fighter plane rammed into a B-29, burst into flame, and began its long descent to earth, leaving a trail of white smoke as it fell. The B-29, inexplicably, remained aloft, although gradually it began to lag behind its formation. A heavy cloud of smoke erupted from an engine, then seemed, to the watchers on the ground, to be slowly winding a white ribbon around one of the wings. But, even more inexplicably, the wounded B-29 continued flying, and soon it disappeared into the eastern skies. The spectacle was a horrifying one, and it brought home to the people of Tokyo, as perhaps nothing else had so far done, the terrible might of the enemy and the terrible weakness of Japan.

Yet still the radios blared the army's defiance. "If the Philippines are lost," cried the announcers, "then we'll fight on the Chinese mainland. And if China is lost, then we'll continue the battle in the homeland to the last man. Fight on, people of Japan! The first to compromise is the first to lose! Look at Italy, Romania, Bulgaria, Finland. . . ." Were the people still listening? Or did they hear rather the cries of a flock of crows that also vanished into the clear blue sky, cawing derisively?

It was on 13 January that the emperor once again spoke with Marquess Kido about the advisability of consulting the senior statesmen. Clearly His Majesty was by now extremely apprehensive about the outcome of the war and was ready to seek means of terminating hostilities. But here Kido's own position was highly ambiguous. As privy seal he was expected to attend the emperor at all times, to keep him informed, to answer his questions, and even to offer him advice; at the same time, he was constrained from meddling in politics or from seeming to favor one faction over another. The duties of his office were not easily reconciled with its prohibitions, and this may account for his apparent equivocation, since there seems to be little question that Kido himself had long been convinced that Japan should seek the most favorable peace terms she could secure, and accept them. He may also have feared the effect that a meeting between the emperor and the senior statesmen might have on the army at that stage. In any case, whatever his motives, his journal for that day merely records baldly: "His Majesty expressed his desire to meet with the senior statesmen, but I replied that the matter ought first to be studied more deeply."

Japan's military establishment, meanwhile, was using every means in its power to intensify the martial ardor of the people. Everywhere, on the ruined streets of the capital, appeared placards bearing such slogans as: "Give cotton! It can be made into the gunpowder that will sink enemy ships!" or "Turn in your silver—the army needs it!" or "No more travel till the war is won! Make every effort to increase production and help defend the homeland!" The newspapers, spurred on no doubt by the army, now began to advocate general mobilization of the entire country.

At the same time, on the radio, interspersed with bouts of martial music, came communiqués describing Japanese victories. On 7 January it was announced that Japan's fighting pilots had sunk thirty-two enemy warships at Lingayen Gulf and at Mindanao on the previous day. The communiqué of 10 January claimed that out of sixty B-29s which had raided Japan twenty-nine had been shot down; two days later, it was reported that nine enemy ships, including several aircraft carriers, had been sunk in Lingayen Gulf; three days after that, reporting a raid over

Nagoya, the radio announced that forty-three out of sixty B-29s had
been downed, adding that twenty-seven enemy ships were sunk during
the landing of American forces at Damortis. The supreme command
knew, of course, that such reports were false, but it believed that in
the perilous state in which Japan now found herself such distortion was
justified. The military justified these outright lies and, as so often happens, ended up believing their own lies. Even the evidence of their
senses, that more and more enemy planes were invading the Japanese
skies and that more and more enemy ships were taking part in the
battles of the Pacific, failed to convince them otherwise.

And if the enemy dared to invade Japan proper, why, they were
ready for that too. In fact, they anticipated that an enemy invasion
might take place around the middle of the year, and they were ready
to sacrifice every last Japanese in repelling the attack. On 11 January, the
war guidance department of the supreme command began making
contingency plans for such an invasion, and on 20 January the roles to
be played by both the army and the navy were tentatively decided
upon.

Meanwhile, in an all-out effort to forestall that invasion, kamikaze
attacks were to be intensified. Young men in increasing numbers were
taught to crash their flimsy but nonetheless sometimes lethal planes
into enemy targets to cause the maximum amount of damage, and they
were also taught to throw away the dearest thing they owned as though
it were a careless trifle. The training was a harsh one, as indeed it had to
be. At Tsuchiura Naval Air Base (in Ibaraki Prefecture), instructors used
thick hickory staffs, baseball bats, and rope bound rubber hoses as
educational aids. "Spiritual training," one officer is quoted as having
said, "is based on unswerving loyalty to the emperor. The baseball bat
is a short cut to help the pilots resign themselves to certain death."

Horrified by the callousness of the supreme command in so casually
tossing away the lives of Japan's youth and by the intensified devastation of the country itself, Yoshida, along with Iwabuchi and Obata,
once again approached Prince Konoye on 19 January. Marquess Kido
was still adhering, apparently, to his policy of noninterference, of
steadfastly keeping the emperor above and beyond factional strife; but

the three men persisted in their belief that somehow they must, and would, get through to him with a personal appeal to take action that only he, in his godlike eminence, was capable of.

With enemy air raids increasing, with the food shortage growing continually more acute, and with the cities flooded with bombed out families, even the overcautious Konoye agreed that it was time for him to listen more sympathetically to the pleas of the would-be peace-makers. As prime minister when the Sino-Japanese incident erupted and when negotiations between Japan and the United States broke down, Konoye was as familiar as anyone with the immediate causes of the war. "One must reap the harvest," says a Japanese proverb, "of the seeds one has sown." It is a proverb that is familiar the world over, but there, and then, it seemed to have a peculiar and terrible applicability. Konoye finally agreed to join forces with the three "conspirators" for peace and even promised that he would himself write the letter of appeal to the emperor.

There still remained the problem of somehow getting through the barriers that isolated the descendant of the Goddess of the Sun behind the wide moats of the Imperial Palace. Here Baron Suzuki still seemed the best bet, and Yoshida approached him once again with a plea for cooperation. Suzuki now said he agreed that Japan must somehow find a means of achieving peace (recent events had apparently changed his mind about the inevitability of pursuing the war to the end), but he continued to insist that he was himself too old a man to play a leading role in the peace effort. He was willing, however, to do what he could behind the scenes. Accordingly, at Yoshida's request, he asked Hisanori Fujita, the grand chamberlain, to entreat the emperor to summon the senior statesmen to an immediate conference.

Fujita now had a quiet talk with Kido on this point. There is no question that Kido was well aware that imminent disaster faced Japan (although he could not, obviously, have been aware of the full extent of it), and there seems to be little question also that he had come to the conclusion that he could no longer follow the long tradition that kept him apart from political differences, and that kept the emperor himself high on a cloud above the earth, wholly isolated from problems unworthy of troubling so august a mind. At last the moment had come for the emperor to enter the arena: there was clearly no other way to stop the bloodshed that could only end in the final annihilation of the country.

But in Japan action does not follow hard upon consensus (a process that replaces the need for individual decision). It never has, and perhaps it never will; in any case, it did not that cold, disastrous January. The American tempo is, or at least was then, quite a different matter: it wanted things done yesterday instead of tomorrow. And one of the things that was being done, while the princes, the barons, the marquesses, and the grand chamberlains groped toward agreement, was to accelerate bombing raids over Japan, in particular Tokyo. Another thing that was being done, of which the Japanese were of course unaware, was to continue building the atomic bomb, for which, by now, there could be only one possible target.

Typical of conditions in the capital was the incendiary bombing of 27 January, which occured in daylight and in which sixty American bombers, in six formations, took part. Equally typical was the fact that the air raid siren, because of some mechanical defect, sounded the all clear prematurely. People who had taken refuge in a shelter near Yūrakuchō railway station left the shelter and began to line up to buy tickets. The bomb that made a direct hit upon this queue killed seventy people outright. The havoc was so absolute that identification was almost impossible; the bodies were transported to nearby Hibiya Park, where they had to be left for several days until grieving relatives could come to make what identification they could. One of the officers from Marunouchi police station who rushed to the scene of the tragedy said afterwards, "All we could do was scoop up the bits and pieces of human flesh, as though it was so much rubbish, and put it in trucks to be carried to the park."

This was not an isolated incident, neither in the capital itself, nor in the country at large. Yet there was nothing the beleaguered people could do save grumble at the ineptitude of their municipal governments, which procrastinated about repairing dwellings, roads, and broken water mains, about clearing away dangerous debris, and about looking after the injured and the dead. Yet they could not grumble at the government itself. They were cold and hungry and exhausted, and subjected to incessant raids; but the military police redoubled their surveillance, while the military establishment continued to insist that death was the only acceptable alternative to victory. Defeat, said the military, was no longer in the Japanese vocabulary.

But was victory still possible? There seemed no likelihood of it as this month of January drew to a close. Of the 2,260 aircraft that were scheduled for delivery that month, only 800 left the assembly line. There was virtually no steel left. Then how were Japan's millions to be armed so as to fight their last-ditch battle for the homeland? The government itself seemed to be in a kind of trance; on 29 January, according to a reporter for the *Asahi* newspaper, the Diet and the cabinet were unable to agree on "problems of national organization," so they spent the entire day "in idle chatter." Both the army and the navy were determined to go on playing their little game, though the dice were obviously loaded against them—and the stakes were a hundred million of their fellow countrymen.

Japan's only hope of survival rested with that tiny group of men who were working so tenaciously yet so terribly, terribly slowly for peace. To this end they still hoped to make use of the senior statesmen and the members of the imperial family. Yet the military police were well aware of these aspirations and kept everyone whom they knew to be in any way connected with the peace movement under the closest possible surveillance. The mass of the people were still willing to go on fighting, for no alternative had been offered them; but were they to realize that there was another way out of this apparent impasse, would they still be ready to fight and die? The military police grew ever more vigilant.

On 30 January Prince Konoye once again held a talk with Marquess Kido. The prince felt that if the emperor were made fully aware of the situation as it then stood, he would be ready, willing, and perhaps even anxious to take action. But how was the emperor to be reached? If the moment was not right for a meeting with the senior statesmen, then perhaps an imperial audience with the chiefs of staff of the army and navy would be helpful. What did Kido think? Apparently there was still no consensus.

The night of 30 January was clear and bitterly cold. The moon shone bright, stars twinkled overhead, and the wind was still. Jun Takami, the author, described a conversation with his novelist-friend Nitta in his diary: "The moon sheds a brilliant light over the deserted streets of Tokyo. I turned to Nitta and said I wondered why there was no one to be seen. [The time was then only about ten o'clock.] He replied, 'Probably everybody went to bed early so they could get as much sleep as possible.' It seemed to me that the empty streets were an omen—an omen of something evil and disastrous."

CHAPTER 2   **FEBRUARY 1945**

While the people of Tokyo shivered, heatless, in the bitter February cold, Hiroshima was enjoying a mild, almost balmy early spring. Lying at the head of Hiroshima Bay, on the Inland Sea, it was protected on three sides by mountains that helped to screen it from chill northerly and westerly winds. Its mountains also gave it an air of grandeur that made it the envy of much of the rest of Japan, where an appreciation of natural beauty is, or was, an intrinsic part of the life of the people. When the sun set in the west, it dyed the mountaintops red, while the many rivers that traversed the city reflected the crimson glow. Now and then a cormorant could be seen diving into the placid waters and coming up, when it was lucky, with a fish in its bill. But the people of Hiroshima had little opportunity, this month of February 1945, to enjoy the scenic evening beauty of their city, for it was becoming an increasingly important military center, and blackouts were strictly enforced.

It had not always been known as Hiroshima. The first settlement on the site was called Ashihara, for the delta was thick with reeds, and Ashihara means simply "reed field." Then, in 1594, a feudal lord named Motonari Mōri erected a castle there which he called Hiro-shima-jō ("Broad-island-castle"), and soon that became the name of the entire settlement. In the following century, the Mōri family removed itself to

Hagi, on the north shore of the Inland Sea, and the castle on the broad island in the reed field passed into the possession of Masanori Fukushima, in whose hands it remained but briefly, for the Asano family were soon named lords of the district. This distinction they retained for thirteen generations; their sovereignty came to an end only with the restoration of imperial rule at the time Emperor Meiji ascended the throne in 1867.

Hiroshima became a municipality in 1889, when its port was completed. During the Sino-Japanese War (1894–5), that port grew to be of enormous strategic importance, for imperial headquarters were established in the castle, which was also the scene, on one occasion, of an emergency session of the Diet. From that time on, Hiroshima became an increasingly important military center, with an economy that was largely dependent on army and navy expenditures. Nearby was the port of Ujina from which soldiers and supplies were shipped to the fronts in continental China and further south. By the time the Pacific war erupted, the city housed the Hiroshima Eleventh Regiment, an army transport headquarters, a quarantine station, munitions and supplies depots, as well as a number of other important military installations. With a population of some four hundred thousand, it was the seventh largest city in the country.

Under the circumstances, one might have thought that it would have been an early target for Allied raids, but so far Hiroshima had had a charmed life. Its citizens listened with numbed shock as homeless refugees from Tokyo and Osaka described the horrors of incendiary bombs falling from heights that Japanese antiaircraft guns were powerless to reach. As they listened, the people of Hiroshima silently resigned themselves to the sad inevitability of their lovely city being fire-bombed before the war ended. They did not know (indeed, no one in the world then knew) that the fateful morning when nine-tenths of the city would vanish in the blinking of an eye lay only half a year ahead.

On 1 February word reached the nation that the Soviet army was only sixty miles or so from Berlin. Italy had already fallen, and the surrender of Germany was both certain and imminent: Japan could look for no aid from her wartime allies. Alone, the nation was facing

a final showdown with the victorious powers of the West, and meanwhile her cities were the targets of incessant raids. Much of Tokyo was
already destroyed; its citizens were by now so familiar with death and
devastation, with hunger and homelessness, that no one gave much
thought to whether he would live to see more than one more day. He
knew that if his future lay in the laps of the gods, it also lay in the hands
of the American strategists whose forces were leapfrogging across the
Pacific, from island to island, headed inexorably in but one direction.

It may have been the news of the imminent fall of Berlin that enabled
Marquess Kido to arrive at a decision. It may have been the fact that the
senior statesmen were making their displeasure increasingly apparent at
being shut away from the emperor by Kido's "chrysanthemum cur-
tain." In any case, Kido apparently reached the conclusion that unless
the emperor took immediate action, His Majesty's role in history would
be a shadowy, negative, perhaps even an ignominious one. Yet still
Kido did not move directly. He consulted first with the minister of the
imperial household, Yasumasa Matsudaira; only then did he undertake
to arrange private audiences in which the senior statesmen might convey their opinions to the emperor about the future conduct of the war
and express any ideas they might have about how to terminate it. The
audiences were to be private and individual, and ostensibly, so as to
avoid antagonizing the army, each man was to come only to pay his
respects to the emperor and inquire after his health. The first meeting,
with Baron Hiranuma, was arranged for several days later.

Meanwhile, the army continued to make preparations to counter
an Allied invasion of Japan proper should one occur. The supreme
command divided Japan into six military districts: Northern, North-
eastern, Eastern, East seaboard, Central, and Western, each with a commander and chief of staff. When the division was announced in the
newspapers, it elicited little reaction from the mass of the people.
Accepting the fact that there was nothing, literally nothing, they could
do to alter the course of the war, and precious little they could do to
alter the course of their own lives, they seemed to have fallen into a
kind of apathy, acceding to whatever their leaders told them, doing
whatever their leaders commanded them to do.

In the words of the writer Musei Tokugawa, "War progresses by a logic of its own." The entry in his diary for the day on which the supreme command made its announcement continued: "No anxiety we may feel about the future changes the fact that war is bestial and nonhuman. What is the point, then, in provoking ourselves into a state of nervous tension about the course of the war? All we can do, whatever happens, is persevere and never say die."

War was certainly progressing by a logic of its own on Ichigaya Hill, in Tokyo, which for seventy years had been the mecca of the Imperial Japanese Army. There the general staff, in the belief that only by repelling an invasion of the homeland could Japan hope to win final victory, was making preparations for a last-ditch stand by the more than six million soldiers garrisoned in Japan and at the same time attempting to foment a do-or-die spirit in the country at large.

In this they had, of course, the invaluable assistance of the controlled news media, which sang whatever tune the army played for them. "The battle for the Philippines," they had cried earlier, "is a crucial one. Japan must never give up Luzon!" But after Japan was forced out of Luzon, the newspapers blandly announced that "The Philippines are of little importance. What the nation seeks is to inflict the greatest possible losses on the forces of the enemy." With the fall of Guadalcanal and Saipan much the same thing occurred: it was a card the military establishment had played time and again, yet it always, at least with the mass of the people, seemed to take the trick.

On 6 February, at Ichigaya, chiefs of departments met in the office of the general staff of the Imperial Army. There they heard the chief of the military operations department, Lieutenant General Shūichi Miyazaki, sketch out a rough draft of the steps to be taken to repel an invasion. After pointing out that it was no longer possible for Japan to retake the Philippines, Miyazaki continued: "We shall turn the tide of war by meeting the enemy on the homeland, for which we are now preparing sixteen new divisions. By pouring twenty divisions into the battle within two weeks of the enemy's landing, we will annihilate him entirely and ensure a Japanese victory." The staff officers at the meeting nodded their agreement with this nonsensical wishful thinking.

Then General Michirō Umezu, army chief of staff, took the rostrum. "If the enemy should invade Japan proper," he declaimed, "martial law will be declared throughout the country. The army will of course be the ultimate authority and will take final responsibility, but the execution of the law will rest in the hands of local legislative bodies."

Once again the officers nodded their approval. The only points on which they were not agreed was when, where, and in what numbers the Allied forces would make their initial landing. The fact that Japan's most experienced troops were not in Japan at all but were fighting on the Chinese mainland and on Pacific islands appeared not to dismay the officers, nor did the fact that the army was grossly deficient in both weapons and ammunition. They would call upon reserve troops, however inexperienced, however unready; they would hurl them in their millions—if necessary, unarmed—against the well-armed and well-trained invaders. Victory was inevitable, they all agreed, for the Japanese possessed a mystical strength that metamorphosed unarmed men into "human bullets" that would pierce the steel armor of the enemy and drive him back into the sea.

On the following day General Miyazaki, meeting with the commanders of the six newly established military districts, went into the army's defense plans in greater detail. After pointing out that the enemy might approach from either the Chinese mainland or upward from Okinawa, he said that he considered the most probable date for the projected invasion to be either August or September. Preparations, in that case, must be completed by summer, and since railways are always among the first targets of enemy bombs, troops must be moved by night in trucks. Miyazaki then listed the number of divisions that would be deployed in each of the six districts. "It is essential," he said, "to concentrate at each front three times the firepower of the enemy."

The six commanders rose to signify their agreement. Then they set about solving the strategical and logistic problems that the deployment of this vast army of men would present. The whole project was, of course, classified as top secret; the people were hardly aware of the tremendous bustle and activity within the long corridors and the conference rooms of the Ministry of War at Ichigaya.

Not far away, on the very same day, within the compounds of the Imperial Palace, Baron Hiranuma, who had been prime minister in 1939, was in audience with the emperor. When asked to give his opinions on the course of the war, Hiranuma, an ultranationalist, refrained from referring in any way to either surrender or peace. The chief problems facing the nation, he said, were maintenance of adequate defense, increased production of arms, and the ensurance of sufficient supplies of food: these were the problems that must be given priority over all others. The emperor listened in silence and, after Hiranuma had finished, made no comment.

His own private opinions at that time are not known. Most people are of the opinion he had come to the conclusion that Japan's defeat was inevitable and that immediate measures must be taken if the country was to be saved from annihilation. These presumably were his reasons for assuming the initiative in conferring with the senior statesmen. A far more unlikely hypothesis, held by few, is that it was the emperor himself who had ordered the supreme command to make a final stand on Japanese soil.

Whatever the truth of the matter, the fact remains that the peace movement was gathering momentum and that it was taking as its spearhead the sacred person of the emperor, with all the mystical power, the aura that he then possessed. But so also were those who advocated fighting to the end gathering momentum, to whom the word "surrender" was tantamount to treason.

And it was the latter who were still effectively in control of the country; the former had no choice but to work by stealth. The secrecy they sought, however, was denied them. On the very day that the emperor conferred with Baron Hiranuma, a commander of the military police reported to the army chief of staff: "The chief pacifists in the country are Shigeru Yoshida, Aisuke Kabayama, and Kumao Harada, among others. These men are in liaison with Fumimaro Konoye and Keisuke Okada and are making use of both the Vatican and neutrals now in China. Discontented about the course of the war, they must be kept under close surveillance."

Presumably, then, the military police were quite well aware of the fact that, two days after he granted an audience to Baron Hiranuma, the emperor conferred with Kōki Hirota, the doyen of Japanese diplomats who had been prime minister in 1936. Hirota's chief preoccupation was the Soviet Union: he considered it absolutely essential to Japan's welfare that the latter should remain neutral and that every possible precaution should be taken not to provoke her into a declaration of war. Hirota pointed out that if Japan was confronted by an enemy on both sides of her, she would be no better off than Germany. When asked by the emperor if he had any concrete suggestions to offer, Hirota seemed to feel that a necessary first step was the replacement of Naotake Satō as Japanese ambassador to Moscow.

That does not, at this distance, seem like a very conclusive or positive act, but it must be borne in mind that Satō himself, who knew the Russians well, was not very sanguine about the possibility of maintaining Soviet neutrality. Hirota may have thought that an ambassador with a more optimistic attitude might prove more effective. That the Soviet posture was a crucial one was a fact of life recognized by everyone in the government as well as by the military. To the dismay of both, anti-Japanese overtones had begun to appear in Russian newspaper articles and editorials after the Allied landing on Leyte in October 1944. Even more ominous was the fact that on 6 November, the eve of the anniversary of the Soviet revolution, Stalin openly criticized Japan for the first time. Now that the war in Europe was approaching an end, how was Japan to ensure Soviet neutrality? It had begun to seem a matter of life and death.

On the same day on which the emperor saw Hirota, he conferred with General Umezu, the army chief of staff, who also spoke to him about the Russian question. After reporting on the war situation in general, Umezu said that in the opinion of imperial headquarters the United States was determined to lay waste the country as well as destroy the national polity (that is to say, the emperor system) whereas the Soviet Union appeared to have adopted a friendlier attitude. Therefore, in the opinion of the army, Japan should seek Soviet assistance in order to pursue the war against the United States to a final conclusion, even though that might well mean the devastation of the country.

War does indeed progress with a logic of its own! The invincible Imperial Army, which had proposed to divide the world with Nazi Germany, now proposed, Germany having been defeated, to form an alliance with Germany's ex-enemy and the ally of Japan's chief enemy. It is hard to imagine now what tortured thinking led to this conclusion; one can only suppose that the supreme command's hatred for the United States, against which it had expected to gain an easy victory, was so great that the army preferred to see the country devastated rather than admit defeat at the hands of the enemy whom it had provoked into war. Were the military so deluded as to suppose that their own "logic," or rather lack of it, could be imposed on the emperor and his people? Was Japan expected to follow the Soviet apparition to her own destruction?

But of course the army was blissfully unaware that on 11 February a secret agreement was signed at Yalta, on the southern tip of the Crimean peninsula, by Stalin, Roosevelt, and Churchill. The three men agreed that "in two or three months after Germany has surrendered and the war in Europe has terminated the Soviet Union shall enter into the war against Japan on the side of the Allies on condition that: (1) The status quo in Outer-Mongolia (The Mongolian People's Republic) shall be preserved; (2) The former rights of Russia violated by the treacherous attack of Japan in 1904 shall be restored. . . ." The "rights to be restored" included the handing over of the Kuril islands and the southern part of Sakhalin to the Soviet Union, the internationalization of the commercial port of Dairen, the re-leasing of Port Arthur as a U.S.S.R. naval base, and certain other provisions in regard to Chinese and Manchurian railroads.

Apparently Roosevelt was deluded both by reports of Japan's military might and by his own conception of Russia's postwar intentions. There seems to be no question that, having been misinformed about Japan's potential, he quite honestly believed that Soviet entry into the war would help shorten it and save American lives; nor, presumably, did he foresee the imperialistic objectives of the Soviet government.

If only he had known how truly desperate Japan was by then! Alas, the "logic of war" does not permit such ifs. One may only surmise, sadly but uselessly, how different the course of history might have been; one may even speculate whether the bomb would have been dropped on Hiroshima, despite the frivolity of such speculations when confronted by the inexorable logic of war and the sometimes disastrous inadequacies of the men who wage it.

However extensive its information apparatus, the American command seems to have had no idea how exhausted Japan was, militarily, physically, and morally. A joke of sorts that was going around Japan at the time is suggestive:

"QUESTION: 'What things have multiplied since the war broke out?'"

"ANSWER: 'Laws, paper money, music without songs, and lice.'"

"QUESTION: 'What things have diminished?'"

"ANSWER: 'Commodities, food, and kindness.'"

"QUESTION: 'What things have grown doubtful?'"

"ANSWER: '*Yamatodamashii* ["the Japanese spirit"] and the will to win.'"

The diary of Fūtaro Yamada, the novelist, who was then a medical student of twenty-three, lists the high prices of various staple goods. "Of these items," Yamada's diary continues, "sugar, eggs, and saké are classed as luxuries. Thus, the people who buy them are to blame for permitting black marketeers to reap such enormous profits. At today's session of the Diet, one member asked the government whether it was aware of the tremendous role the black market played in the daily lives of the people. The relevant minister replied that he had not made a study of the problem!

"This is the kind of government official who will eventually destroy the country. When one considers the indifference behind that reply! The feigned ignorance! The outright deceit! Does the minister really not know that most of the food the people eat is purchased on the black market? Has he not heard, day after day, their bitter complaints against black market practices? The chief problem to be solved now, if Japan is to be saved, is how to put enough food in the mouths of the people for them to go on living."

True, if a man ate only rationed foods, he could live on a few yen a month, but he would be almost too weak to climb the stairs of his own house! On the black market, that same amount of food would fetch twenty times the price, and obviously few people could afford to patronize the black market to any great extent. In these circumstances, the mass of the people, those who went to bed hungry night after night, could not avoid envying and censuring their leaders—high echelon military officers, top bureaucrats, munitions makers—who by making use of the black market continued to live lives of luxury. In the locked storerooms of their houses lay mountains of food and gallons of rice wine. At night, while the rest of the people huddled hungry in bombed out dwellings, those in power entertained one another at luxurious dinner parties, parties that often turned into nightlong orgies. It is hardly surprising that *yamatodamashii* was on the wane.

This increasing demoralization of the people was what chiefly preoccupied Prince Konoye, who feared that if, or when, Japan lost the war, the masses would turn to communism as a panacea. He was firmly convinced that if Japan was to survive defeat and rebuild the nation, she could do so only under the old imperial system; and the only way to retain that system, he now believed, was to terminate the war as swiftly and painlessly as possible. In his mind, it was the fanatical army officers who, by their insistence upon pursuing the war to the end, were paving the way for a Communist revolution in Japan. It was chiefly this fear that induced him to throw his still powerful influence onto the side of the would-be peacemakers.

He was scheduled to be the third of the senior statesmen to present his views to the emperor. On 13 February, the day before his audience, he conferred with Yoshida at the latter's house, at which time he showed Yoshida a draft of the written appeal, the so-called memorial to the throne, that he had addressed to the emperor. After Yoshida had suggested certain changes, Konoye returned home, where he spent a large part of the night completing the final version of the memorial.

On the following day, with the memorial in his waistcoat pocket, he was driven to the Imperial Palace in Yoshida's car. It was his first audience with the emperor since he had relinquished the premiership to General Tōjō just before the outbreak of the Pacific war. The meeting was, no doubt, highly charged with emotion on both sides, for

Konoye, staunch in his devotion to the imperial house, was the emperor's favorite among all the senior statesmen.

After an exchange of greetings, Konoye began to read his memorial, which opened with the unequivocal statement: "Sad though it is, I believe that Japan has already lost the war."[1] Konoye continued, "Although defeat will be a great strain upon our polity, it need not necessarily occasion undue concern especially since public opinion in America and Britain, on the whole, has not yet gone so far as to demand a fundamental change in our national structure. . . . From the standpoint of maintaining Japan's imperial system, that which we have most to fear is not defeat itself but, rather, the threat inherent in the possibility that a Communist revolution may accompany defeat. . . .

"The situation within Japan is such that every possible factor favorable to the accomplishment of a Communist revolution is on hand. There is poverty in the life of the people, a rise in the voice of labor, and an expansion of pro-Soviet feeling growing out of an increase in enmity towards America and Britain. In addition, there are the actions of the national renovationists—a movement championed by a certain faction within the military, the activities of the so-called new bureaucrats—the 'fellow travelers' of this movement, and the secret machinations of the leftists who are pulling the strings from behind. . . .

"The more critical the war situation becomes, the louder we hear the cry, 'One hundred million die together!' Although the so-called right-wingers are the ones who shout the loudest, it is the Communists, in my opinion, who are the instigators of it all, for they hope to achieve their revolutionary aim by taking advantage of the confusion that will arise out of defeat. . . .

"The question would be different if there were even some slight hope of the fighting taking a turn for the better, but with defeat staring us in the face we shall simply be playing into the hands of the Communists if we elect to continue a war wherein there is no prospect of victory. From the standpoint of preserving the national polity, therefore, I am firmly convinced that we should seek to end the war as speedily as possible.

"The greatest obstacle to a termination of the conflict is the existence of that group within the military which ever since the Manchurian Incident has driven the country to its present plight. Although the military men have already lost confidence in their ability to prosecute the war to a successful conclusion, they are likely to continue fighting to the very end merely to save face.

"Should we endeavor to stop the war abruptly without first rooting out the extremists, I fear that they—supported by sympathizers within both the right- and left-wings—might perpetrate internal disorder thus making it difficult for us to achieve our desired goal. The prerequisite to a termination of the war is therefore the elimination of this extremist element within the military. . . ."[2]

After Konoye had finished reading his memorial, the emperor asked him to be seated and then put a number of questions to him. His Majesty noted, for example, that the army kept insisting that the Americans would institute drastic changes in the national polity, and asked whether Konoye agreed.

"The army exaggerates," Konoye replied, "in an attempt to persuade the people to continue fighting." He noted that Joseph C. Grew, when he left his post as American ambassador to Tokyo, expressed the highest regard for the imperial family. "However," Konoye went on, "since the government of the United States is necessarily influenced by public opinion, it is impossible to predict that no changes will be made. That must depend on the future course of the war. It is why I consider an immediate termination of hostilities to be essential."

The emperor then asked why Konoye thought it so important to eliminate extremists from the army, and Konoye repeated his belief that it was the extremists who were playing into the hands of the Communists and that bolshevism was a real and present threat to the country. In that case, said the emperor, it is a question of finding the right people; he asked whom Konoye would suggest. Konoye replied that he would prefer to leave that question in the hands of the emperor, but the emperor persisted, noting that it would be extremely difficult for him to take any action if Konoye himself refrained from naming names.

Konoye then suggested certain of the retired generals who were free of the extremist taint, such as Kazushige Ugaki, Kiyoshi Kōzuki, Jinzaburō Masaki, Binshirō Obata, and Kanji Ishihara. He then went on to say that if it was thought these men would be likely to cause friction within army ranks, then possibly officers on the active list such as Korechika Anami or Tomoyuki Yamashita might take over the task of purging the army of its most dangerous elements. At that time Anami was inspector general of the army air corps; Yamashita was commander in chief of the Japanese forces fighting the battle of the Philippines.

The emperor made no comment on any of the men Konoye had suggested. Perhaps he was remembering the so-called incident of 26 February 1936 when a group of fiery young ultranationalist officers attempted a coup in the course of which they succeeded in assassinating statesmen close to the emperor whose influence upon him they held to be "treasonous." Among the would-be usurpers were both Masaki and Obata.

Changing the subject, the emperor now asked Konoye to comment on the army's conviction that more favorable peace terms might be secured if Japan were first to achieve victory in one important battle. The chiefs of staff of both the army and the navy, the emperor said, had informed him that, if the enemy could be induced to invade Taiwan, a major enemy defeat would be inevitable, thus paving the way for a more favorable peace.

"But is time on our side?" asked Konoye. "A victory on Taiwan would indeed be advantageous to Japan—but only if it were to come within the very near future. If we have to wait another six months or a year for that victory, it would be of no use to us."

Konoye's audience ended on an inconclusive note, and he was more than a little dispirited when he reported to Yoshida the substance of his conversation with the emperor. Summing up, Konoye told Yoshida that His Majesty did not seem to be as well informed as he might be on the actual course of the war; further, since his informants were the chiefs of staff of the army and the navy, the emperor did not appear unduly pessimistic about the immediate future. "That," said Konoye, "is what I fear most of all."

Konoye's reasoning that the Japanese communists were gaining strength and planning to create a revolution in their homeland may or may not have been justified, but it was a fact that the army and navy were seriously thinking of gaining at least one big victory over the enemy before making peace with him. Certainly some of Konoye's fears were justified, as a large part of the country was to discover on 16 February, when a number of the enemy's carrier-based bombers swooped down on Japan in four raids so intense that they were thought to be a prelude to a general invasion. According to Tokyo air defense headquarters, alerts were sounded at 7:09 and 10:47 in the morning and at 12:33 and 2:55 in the afternoon. Each raid lasted over an hour.

Kenji Nagai, then a high school student of sixteen who had been drafted to work at the Nakajima Aircraft Manufacturing Company in the city of Ōta (Gumma Prefecture), described the last of the raids in his diary:

"It was after two in the afternoon when the fourth warning was sounded. I started running toward the bomb shelter, and as I did, I could see single-engined fighters streaking over Ōta from west to east with a high metallic whine. To drop their bombs on us, they descended to heights as low as a mere 150 feet, and when the bombs started falling we thought at first that they were the planes themselves and we all shouted, 'Banzai!' Then from the planes we heard the rattle of machine guns aimed at us as we were running toward the shelter; the planes were flying so low we could see the faces of the crew. At that I jumped into the shelter, where I clasped my hands in front of my face in prayer. The roar of the bombs and the guns was so constant and so near I felt I was already dead. When at last the roar ended, we left the shelter. I could see the bright silvery planes disappearing over the horizon. A fellow worker shouted *Bakayarō!* ("stupid bastards!") at them. Out of the plant where we had been working billowed clouds of thick black smoke." At that one factory, that one day, eighty-six planes which had already been assembled and were ready to be fitted out were extensively damaged, fifty-six planes were damaged in part, and twenty-six planes were damaged only slightly. The enemy had had it all his own way; what else could a man do but cry, *Bakayarō!*

Indeed, despite the military's continually optimistic communiqués, it began to look as though the enemy was going to have it all his own way from then on. The military ranted, but the people saw with their own eyes; and the rift between the two (which was later to be known as a credibility gap) kept growing wider. The air corps said its fighters possessed mysterious, godlike powers; but the people saw no evidence of it. The navy said its ships were invincible; but where were the ships? At the bottom of the sea? The army announced that it had developed a new type of bomb which was to be carried to the American mainland by balloons; but so far the revolutionary new "balloon bombs" were only just becoming operational.

In fact, the army was still pinning its hopes on winning the final battle, the "battle of Japan," and to win this it had to have the whole-hearted, unstinting collaboration of the entire people. The hundred million had to be ready to suffer any hardship in order to drive the invader back into the sea. In an act unprecedented in the Imperial Army's seventy invincible years, one of its top-ranking officers, the chief of operations, went so far as to address a civilian gathering. In the course of his speech on 19 February, General Miyazaki said, "The course of the war will force us at last to meet the enemy on our own soil. After the retreat from Guadalcanal, the army has had little opportunity to engage the enemy in land battles, but when we meet on Japan proper, our army will demonstrate its invincible superiority."

The army reasoned that in fighting the island battles for Guadal-canal, Saipan, Guam, Tinian, and the Philippines, it had been dependent upon the navy for its supplies, and because the navy had been de-feated in these battles, defeat inevitably followed for the army. But in fighting the battle of Japan, it would have no need of the navy; it could freely deploy its tens of divisions on a vast battlefield. To a con-temporary strategist, it would seem that the Imperial Army was still fighting the First World War; it was ignoring altogether the revolu-tionary changes that made the second war so different from the first.

As though in answer to Miyazaki, the Americans landed on Iwō Jima on the very day that he condescended to explain the Imperial Army's strategy to mere civilians. Within four days the Stars and

Stripes was raised (in the presence of a photographer) atop Mount Suribachi, although it was not until the middle of the following month that the island was officially considered secure. The Imperial Army could hardly have been unaware of the fact that Iwō Jima was but a three-hour flight from Tokyo.

On 22 February all the Japanese people could read in their newspapers that twelve Allied powers had reached an agreement on the fate of Japan once the war ended. Among the ten articles that had been agreed to the previous month were those that called for a change in the country's national polity, the punishment of the men responsible for the war, and the reorientation of the Japanese people. All this, cried the newspapers indignantly, amounts to the enslavement of the population; Japan now has no choice but to fight the war to the end!

While the fierce battle for Iwō Jima was being fought, the physicists who were working on Japan's N-research project reached the conclusion that they had overcome the major obstacles that had arisen since sexa-uranium fluoride had first been placed in the separator over six months before, and they were ready now to try an even more critical experiment. If it succeeded, potentially Japan would have in her possession a new weapon, one capable of tremendous devastation. The men had been instructed to devote all their time and effort to this research; they had been told that their country's fate was in their hands as it was in the hands of other men, hardly younger than themselves, who were piloting their planes in suicide attacks on enemy aircraft and shipping. The researchers had done their best, and now they hoped that before the day was out they would see their strenuous efforts crowned with success.

Briefly, without undertaking to go into complex scientific detail, the experiment may be described as an attempt to bombard uranium oxide and sexa-uranium fluoride with a beryllium neutron. For this purpose the men were making use of a cyclotron to produce what they hoped would turn out to be nuclear fission and a Lauritsen electroscope to measure the amount of radioactivity. The experiment was put in the hands of a man not directly connected with N-research who, for that reason, would be less likely to be swayed by preconceptions. The ex-

periment ended in failure, for it demonstrated conclusively that virtually no U-235 had been extracted from the sexa-uranium fluoride that
had been placed in the separator. Nishina shrugged, when informed of
the failure; Takeuchi, who had worked so hard on the separator, went
back to work on it some more. That was his job; he considered he had
no choice.

In higher places there seemed to be a choice, but whether the men
who were going to make that choice were going to make the right one
appeared uncertain. On the day that an army communiqué announced
the landing of enemy forces on Iwō Jima, the emperor conferred with
two men: Baron Reijirō Wakatsuki, who had twice been prime
minister of Japan, and Count Shinken Makino, a former lord keeper
of the privy seal. Makino's daughter, incidentally, was married to
Shigeru Yoshida.

Wakatsuki said that in his opinion Japan should seek to make peace
only on the premise that there could be no final victory or defeat for
either side. When asked if he had any concrete suggestions as to how
this could be accomplished, Wakatsuki replied that he could see no
alternative but for Japan to continue prosecuting the war until the
enemy realized its futility. Only then could an acceptable peace treaty
be arrived at.

Makino, whose audience with the emperor was interrupted for a
time by an enemy raid, was also of the opinion that this was not a
propitious moment for Japan to sue for peace. He agreed with the
military that Japan must first gain a major victory because she would
then be in a position to propose favorable peace terms. The same point
was made a few days later (on 23 February) by Admiral Keisuke Okada,
who had been prime minister at the time of the 26 February incident.
Japan, Okada repeated, must wait until the war had taken a more
auspicious turn.

The emperor had by now conferred with six senior statesmen, but
none had offered any concrete proposals for negotiating an acceptable
peace treaty with the enemy. All had counseled waiting at a time when
it should have been obvious to them that waiting could only lead to
greater and still greater disaster. Was it merely a lack of information on

their part? A failure of vision? Or was it the fact that Japan, in her long history, had never been defeated by a foreign power, and these retired leaders of the nation were still unable to envisage the possibility?

The enemy, meanwhile, was increasing the tempo of its air raids over the country, and the Imperial Army was elaborating plans for what it foresaw as the coming "battle of Japan." On 26 February army leaders met for three days to discuss details. There were widely divergent opinions, but the majority favored mobilizing a million and a half men who were on the retired list as well as new recruits to add to the thirty or forty divisions of trained troops that would be available within a month or two. The army's rather simplistic idea was to turn its men into human waves that would inexorably push the enemy back into the sea; that casualties in this operation would occur on an undreamed of scale appeared to be of little interest to the organizers of the plan. It was like asking all Japanese girls of twelve to thirteen years to bear children.

Nor did they make any secret of their intentions. The information bureau of the army convened a joint press conference with managing editors as well as political and economic editors of the various newspapers at which Lieutenant General Jōichirō Sanada, chief of the bureau of military affairs, made an impassioned speech about the coming "battle of Japan." His words were duly listened to and reported; the the people of Japan learned what a glorious opportunity was soon to be theirs—a gift of the invincible Imperial Army.

Also on 26 February the emperor gave audience to the last senior statesman he was destined to see that month, Hideki Tōjō, prime minister at the time of Pearl Harbor. Bellicose as ever, General Tōjō pointed out that the United States had boasted it would conquer Japan within four weeks, yet four years later it had only got as far as Iwō Jima. Further, he said, air raids over Japan were on a considerably smaller scale than those which had devastated Germany, nor did he believe that the United States could increase them to any appreciable extent. He considered that there was a very good chance that the Soviet Union would not enter the war and, even if it did, would not be able to deploy enough troops on the Asian front to make much difference.

No, Japan's chief enemy, he informed the emperor unequivocally, was a sense of defeatism on the part of her people: it was that which must be combatted by every means in the power of her leaders. If leaders and people were united, Tōjō concluded, they could still win!

It was on this boastful, wishful note that the last February of the war came to an end.

CHAPTER 3   **MARCH 1945**

One of the sights of Hiroshima was the great Industry Promotion Hall, built in 1915 by the Czech architect, Jan Letzel. With its soaring dome and its brilliant and (at the time it was built) unique lighting system, it had for thirty years been a landmark of the city. When, in good weather, the people of Hiroshima strolled along the banks of the Motoyasu River, beside which the hall stood, they would pause for a moment to admire its impressive bulk before, perhaps, continuing on their way to one or another of the riverside restaurants that stood near the hall.

Only the year before, those restaurants would have been crowded with people attending farewell parties for young soldiers going off to fight. Because of the blackout, the passer-by would have seen no lights inside the restaurants, but he would have heard the stirring, martial sound of war songs being sung by the assembled guests. He would have straightened his back a bit before he continued, proud of his victorious country and its invincible army.

This spring, although the weather was clement, the banks of the Motoyasu River were very quiet. There were no farewell parties, nor did any groups join happily in martial harmony as they nibbled tidbits and downed cups of saké. Indeed, there were no tidbits to nibble, no rice wine to drink, nor were there any longer joyous groups of soldiers going off to fight the good fight in distant lands. Victory Hall, where they had customarily received their final instructions, stood silent and empty. Ujina, Hiroshima's port, some three and a half miles from the center of the city, a port from which many thousands of troops had in earlier days sailed to Pacific battle fronts, now seemed like a ghost town.

Demolition work had begun for the creation of three fire prevention areas running though the city from east to west. Although Hiroshima's seven rivers were natural fire barriers, the municipal government hoped to ensure that if incendiary bombs struck the city, so many of whose houses were wooden, the fires could be contained. In the three selected areas buildings were being torn down, and, as the fire prevention belts were cleared, the people found they could now see the great dome of the Industry Promotion Hall from afar, as well as the feudal castle that for so many centuries had played a role in Japanese history.

It was the creation of these three fire zones that brought home to the people of Hiroshima, as nothing else so far had done, the fact that they might not be altogether immune to enemy attack, although they still did not realize quite how devastating those attacks could be. The newspapers and the radio duly noted that Tokyo, Osaka, and Nagoya had been bombed but went into little detail about the effects of the raids, preferring to concentrate instead on Japanese victories in the field despite the fact that this was becoming increasingly hard to do. Refugees from the bombed out cities had horrendous tales to tell, but somehow the tales lacked immediacy. Hiroshima, after all, although it was the seventh city of Japan, had no great manufacturing plants for munitions or aircraft (which seemed to be the chief targets for heavy bombing), and its once bustling port was now deserted. Mitsubishi, it is true, had a factory for the manufacture of aeroplane engines, but it was so small it was unlikely to attract raiders. Most of the city's industry was devoted to the production of alcoholic drinks and tinned beef, and surely, thought the people of Hiroshima, American bombers would not bother about little things like that. But now those three vacated fire prevention belts made the citizens of Hiroshima uneasy. Would the enemy come anyway, they wondered, despite the fact that Hiroshima was such a harmless city?

Orders from Washington to the Twenty-first Bomber Command, in the Mariana Islands, were to give first priority to Japanese aircraft production, second to urban industrial areas, and third to shipbuilding. Although air force photographers flew almost daily over Japan in an effort to pinpoint targets for the bombers, and although the hordes of B-29s that invaded Japan's skies were indeed a frightening experience for her people, the fact is that in the four months since the B-29s started bombing the home islands, they had not, from the American point of view, proved very satisfactory.

General Tōjō, in offering his calculations to the emperor at the end of February, had had every reason to disparage their efforts. Although they were in all ways a superior weapon, a weapon the Japanese could not hope to rival, they had failed to live up to American expectations. Because of the distance between base and target and because of the extreme heights (to avoid interception) at which the planes flew, they could carry only a relatively small bombload. Even then, if they encountered trouble, they frequently ran short of fuel and drifted down into the sea; frequently also, because of the strain on the engine of flying so great a distance at so high an altitude with so heavy a load, the planes malfunctioned, and then the mission had to be aborted. The weather between the Marianas and Japan was particularly disagreeable and particularly hostile to long-range flights. Further, the heights at which the planes flew, as well as the weather over Japan, made visual sighting a virtual impossibility; radar was still undependable; and finding the target was a highly doubtful business. Probably there were yet other considerations: the fact remains that throughout four months of intensive bombing, the B-29s had not yet put even one of Japan's eleven priority targets out of action.

But General Tōjō, in his optimism, had reckoned without one of America's most gifted veteran bomber pilots, General Curtis LeMay. LeMay had first joined the Army Air Forces in 1928; by January 1945, when he took command of the Twenty-first bombers in the Marianas, he had had long years of experience, including numerous encounters with the Luftwaffe. In June 1944 he was recalled from Europe to the United States, where he was given command of the B-29s based in the vicinity of Chengtu in China. He found that attempting to bomb enemy positions from Chengtu presented insuperable obstacles, and, since Washington also was dissatisfied with the Chengtu operation, LeMay was transferred, in January 1945, to Guam.

After two months there, he decided he had figured out how to improve dramatically the effectiveness of the B-29s in accomplishing their mission of destroying Japanese war production (and, incidentally, of reducing the home islands and the people who lived there to a state of chaos, despair, and submission); and he was prepared to stake his career on his decision.

The planes, he determined, were henceforward to fly at low altitudes and at night; they were to carry little or no armor; they were to drop only incendiary bombs; and they were to fly singly, dispensing with the need for a rendezvous. Low altitudes meant less fuel, lack of armor meant less weight; together, the two meant a far greater bombload. The low altitude also meant less strain on the plane itself. Since much Japanese war production was now taking place within private dwellings, incendiary bombs dropped on a thickly populated area could have a catastrophic effect on production, as well as on the people who were doing the producing. It was a bold, indeed a revolutionary, plan; and LeMay determined to test it on the night of 9 March. He further determined to do so on his own initiative, without consulting General Hap Arnold, who was chief of staff of the United States Air Corps. The B-29s had been designed expressly to fly heavy bombloads at a high altitude; now LeMay was deliberately sacrificing that advantage. If the mission he had planned for 9 March had turned out to be a disastrous failure, it is possible he would have been relieved of his command. He was counting heavily on two factors: the undependability of Japanese radar and the unfamiliarity of Japanese pilots with night fighting.

Japan, however, was not wholly unprepared. On 6 March the morning newspapers reported that the number of enemy planes taking off and landing by night was increasing and that Japan might therefore, before very long, expect a massive night raid. Radar stations on four islands (Chichijima, Hahajima, Hachijōjima, and Ōshima) had picked up a number of night radar signals, while the army's Central Communications Research Department was listening around the clock to radio waves emanating from the great new American air base at Saipan. On a frequency of 12,500 kilocycles, they often used the code

NPN5PPP. Lieutenant Masataka Hakata, of the army communications department, checked with the navy, and together they came to the conclusion that NPN5 referred to the air base command, while PPP meant an air raid alarm.

"I used to pick up Saipan very clearly," Lieutenant Hakata recalled later. "I noted a tremendous increase in such code numbers as 15V425 and 16V425. It seemed obvious that the figures referred to B-29s, and that 15V425, for example, meant the fifteenth plane of the 425th squadron. We read the figures as '15th Victor of 425.'" The number of these references seemed to increase day by day; indeed, by the time the month of March rolled around, there were more than three hundred B-29s based on the Marianas.

Other observations Hakata made, listening to the radio waves emanating from Saipan, were that planes reported the results of an air raid in code as well as whether they had had to use radar or had been able to sight-bomb. If a B-29 had suffered severe damage, it reported the extent of the damage in plain English, without using code. "We are at such and such a place," the radio would report; "send us—" and then there came a word that sounded to the Japanese like *bambo*. In time Hakata learned that *bambo* referred to a remodelled B-24 that was used as a rescue hydroplane. The army learned also that a B-29 which had emitted a signal of that nature never again reappeared over the skies of Japan.

And there were many such. Up to the time that LeMay inaugurated his own bombing plan, the Seventy-third Bomber Wing on Saipan had flown the fifteen hundred miles of the route they called "Hirohito Avenue" and had bombed the Nakajima Aircraft Manufacturing Company plant at Musashino, on the outskirts of Tokyo, a total of eleven times without inflicting any great damage; although in the process they had lost a total of fifty-eight planes.

Now LeMay was planning to send his men in at low altitudes by night to bomb the best-defended city in the country. American intelligence on Guam had made fairly accurate estimates of the capital's defensive capacity and had found it to be a formidable one. Yet LeMay was prepared to risk his men and his planes as well as his own career on the basis of a highly experienced conjecture that that defensive barrage would be inadequate against low-flying planes dropping incendiary bombs by night.

His conjecture was more than vindicated by the event: Tokyo had never before undergone such hell, never before been subjected to such an inferno of destruction. The sky was clear that night, although there was a northerly wind blowing at some thirty miles an hour. It was because of this wind that Japan's air raid detection apparatus was not functioning normally, and as a result the Tenth Air Division, which was charged with the defense of Tokyo, was unaware of the approach of a large number of B-29s. These included three wings, the 73rd, the 313th, and the 314th, and their target was a highly concentrated urban area between the Imperial Palace and Nakagawa. Its code name was Meetinghouse. The area consisted largely of flimsy wooden houses which would, obviously, be particularly susceptible to incendiary bombing.

An air raid warning sounded over the Kanto district at 10:30 P.M., but the raid was not actually scheduled to begin until after midnight. The three wings consisted of over three hundred B-29s. The first twelve of each wing were to act as trail blazers, marking the target with an enormous fiery cross by dropping highly inflammable canisters of magnesium and phosphorus. After crossing the Bōsō Peninsula, southeast of Tokyo, they dropped and, making use of radar, glided toward their target. The Bay of Tokyo gleamed bright in the moonlight, and so did the waters of the Sumida River, which traversed Meetinghouse.

The first canisters fell at 12:08 A.M. Seven minutes later the air raid alarm was sounded. Tokyo might as well have saved its breath: there was nothing that anyone could do. Within half an hour the fires were completely out of control. Flames shot hundreds of meters into the air, and the smoke and heat rose so high that late-coming pilots had difficulty keeping their aircraft under control. Some crews had to use oxygen masks.

On the ground there was indescribable chaos; there were no oxygen masks, nor was there any air to breathe—there was only fire. Those who did not perish in the flames choked to death or were trampled under the feet of mobs seeking escape from the inferno of Meeting-house. The only exits seemed to be the bridges that crossed the Sumida River, and panic-stricken thousands made for them. Some were pushed into the river and drowned, others were crushed to death.

Koyo Ishikawa, a cameraman attached to the Tokyo Metropolitan Police Department, who photographed the raid, described it in the following terms: "Huge pillars of orange-red flame spurted high into the sky, while the fires leapt unchecked from house to house. The very streets were rivers of fire. Everywhere one could see flaming pieces of furniture exploding in the heat, while the people themselves blazed like match sticks."

Another witness was Masao Nomura, a reporter for the *Asahi* news-paper, who visited the scene after the worst was over: "Corpses without number," he wrote, "lay everywhere in the streets: naked bloated bodies, bodies of policemen still in uniform, bodies of women lying beside their children. Here and there smoke still smoldered from ruined streetcars. Long lines of ragged, ash-covered people straggled along, dazed and silent, like columns of ants. They had no idea where they were going; all they knew was that they were still alive. I wanted to interview some of them, but I lacked the courage. My only interview was with this vast desolation."

Sixteen square miles of eastern Tokyo were completely destroyed, leaving 88,793 people dead and 130,000 injured. A total of 268,000 dwellings were burnt down; a million inhabitants were left homeless. The raid lasted two hours. Looked at by the light of the logic of war, it was a brilliant success. General LeMay was satisfied, and so were his superiors in Washington.   His strategy had succeeded beyond expecta-tion, and accordingly the decision was made to repeat it. Some thirty-six hours after the B-29s returned to their base, they took off again; this time the target was Nagoya, in central Japan. On 13 March it was Osaka's turn, and four nights later Kobe was visited. In eight days, eleven thousand tons of incendiary bombs were dropped on those four cities. Washington, delighted by LeMay's new strategy, designated thirty-three more cities as future targets, and LeMay promised that in the month to come he would hit them relentlessly with three thousand planes.

Meanwhile, in Europe, Allied armies were crossing the Rhine and racing into the heart of Germany; Soviet forces, attacking with great ferocity, were aiming for Berlin in an attempt to take the German capital before their Western allies could reach it. In both hemispheres great cities were being destroyed and their citizens massacred while opposing armed forces clashed in fierce battles. If a terrible new weapon were now to emerge, would the politico-military leaders on either side hesitate to use it? Would moral scruples deter them? What use would they make of it? The questions answer themselves: no matter how greatly firepower and mobility increase, military men are notoriously reluctant to alter established strategy or tactics. Presumably they would then, if given an atomic bomb, plan to use it in the context of such familiar strategy and tactics.

After some two months of training in Cuba, the 509th Composite Group of the United States Air Corps was ready to occupy an airfield in the northwest corner of the island of Tinian, in the Marianas. Tinian had been selected as a base for the 509th by Commander Fred Ashworth of the navy, who the month before had conferred with Admiral Chester Nimitz on Guam. Hidden on his person Ashworth carried a secret letter addressed to Nimitz and signed by Admiral Ernest King, chief of naval operations. Nimitz, who commanded the Pacific fleet, had been curious about the new group that was to join his forces; the letter that Ashworth brought him explained who they were and why they were coming. Nimitz's curiosity was satisfied.

Tinian was chosen, apparently, for several reasons, chief among which was the fact that it was some hundred miles closer to Japan than Guam, a fact that might turn out to be of paramount importance considering the anticipated weight of the revolutionary bomb that was being produced back in the United States. Another consideration was the fact that Tinian's harbors were superior to those of Guam; while, at the same time, being much smaller, it offered greater security. Its shape was so similar to that of the island of Manhattan that the men who were stationed there took to calling its roads Fifth Avenue,

Madison Avenue, and the like. The Manhattan Project, on the way to fulfilling its final destiny, was to make use of a tiny, Manhattan shaped island in the South Pacific. It is one of history's minor ironies.

An irony of somewhat more major dimensions rose out of the choice of the target. The decision was now reached that, *if* it was found desirable to use the atomic bomb in the war against Japan, the target should be one that possessed military and strategic importance and (perhaps even more important) one that would be likely to destroy finally the crumbling Japanese morale. Further, it should be a target that had not been previously bombed, where the effects of the bombing could be clearly observed and confirmed, and preferably the target should have a radius of approximately one mile with a dense population. A number of small and medium-sized Japanese cities fulfilled all these requirements; Hiroshima was only one of them.

But there still remained the fateful question to be answered: *was* the bomb to be dropped on Japan? General Groves was untroubled by doubt, but some of the other men who had worked on the bomb were more uncertain about the desirability of using it, now that the European war was virtually ended. Professor Leo Szilard, the eminent physicist who had contributed so greatly to the development of the bomb, was particularly beset by anxiety. He was later to describe his state of mind at the time in the following words:

"During the war, while we worked on the bomb, we scientists thought for a while that we were in a neck and neck race with the Germans and that getting the bomb first might make the difference between winning or losing the war. But, when Germany was defeated, many of us became uneasy about the proposed use of the bomb in the war with Japan. Many of us were uneasy about how the existence of the bomb would affect the position of the United States after the war."[3]

Dr. Arthur Compton reported to Henry Stimson, the secretary of war, that there was wide divergence of opinion among the scientists, a fact that Stimson passed on to President Roosevelt when he saw him for the last time, on 15 March. Roosevelt was ill and extremely tired; he had just returned from Yalta, where he had found the going anything but easy; and he was then on the eve of his departure for Warm

Springs, Georgia, where he was to have a period of rest and recuperation.

He seemed depressed by the number of decisions that he believed he was going to be called upon to make in regard to the bomb. In fact, he was to be spared them by his death less than a month later; his successor would inherit them; but meanwhile, on that mid-March day, Roosevelt listened quietly to Stimson, who was, it appears from his own report of the interview, more interested in the postwar implications of the bomb than in its wartime use. After reassuring the president, who still remained somewhat doubtful, that the bomb would almost certainly not be a failure, Stimson writes:

"Then I outlined to him the future of it and when it was likely to come off and told him how important it was to get ready. I went over with him the two schools of thought that exist in respect to the future control after the war of this project, in case it is successful, one of them being the secret close-in attempted control of the project by those who control it now, and the other being the international control based upon freedom both of science and of access. I told him that those things must be settled before the first projectile is used and that he must be ready with a statement to come out to the people on it just as soon as that is done. He agreed to that. . . ."[4]

Professor Szilard and his colleagues were not the only men in the United States who hoped that the war might now be brought to an end without further prolonged fighting, without making use of some new and terrible weapon, and without continued suffering and loss of life. Captain Ellis Zacharias and Dr. Ladislas Farago believed that intense psychological warfare aimed at Japan's leadership could produce an atmosphere conducive to surrender. A campaign of this nature they considered to be of special urgency when it was learned, upon President Roosevelt's return from Yalta, that the United States and the Soviet Union had entered upon a secret military agreement. This, they reasoned, could mean only one thing: that the Soviet Union had undertaken to enter the war against Japan; and this, they reasoned further, was at all costs to be avoided, for it would only broaden and lengthen the conflict and wreak further destruction on an already vanquished country. The problem was to persuade that country to admit it was vanquished, as quickly and as painlessly as possible.

Captain Zacharias had had long and extensive experience with the Japanese over a period of two decades, and it is quite probable that he understood their ways of thinking and acting better than any other man in the United States armed forces. He believed that the Japanese process of reaching a decision by consensus was a "weakness which must be exploited to the fullest" in exerting the necessary psychological pressure on Japan's leaders. They must be persuaded that continuing the war was now an exercise in futility, convinced that making peace immediately was their country's only guarantee against devastation and possible annihilation, and shown that the "unconditional surrender" called for in the Cairo Declaration was not an insuperable obstacle to peace; that segment of the leadership which still remained opposed to surrender must be confounded and silenced so that the desired consensus favoring surrender might be reached.

For more than a week, meeting in the suburbs of Washington, in an old building that had once been a garage, a group of men under the direction of Captain Zacharias and Dr. Farago made plans based on these essential conditions. Implementation of the plans, they determined, would require a budget of something under one hundred thousand dollars. Could it be done? A hundred thousand dollars as against two billion! An end to killing instead of the use of the most terrible weapon the world had ever known! If psychology, rather than nuclear fission, could now win the war, the world would be the gainer; no one (save a handful of fanatic Japanese militarists) would be the loser.

It would not, however, be easy, for the basic problem remained: how to induce Japan's leadership to reach a consensus without any single person feeling he had taken the responsibility for the decision, particularly a decision of such consequence. Inside Japan too, but outside the mainstream of the war, there was a group prepared to work toward the same end. In Japan, however, this group had to operate with a desperate secrecy that was then unfamiliar to Americans, even in wartime, for if the Japanese military police got wind of their activities, those activities would be abruptly eliminated. And so might the men themselves.

The head of this group was Professor Shigeru Nambara, who, on 9 March, was appointed dean of the College of Jurisprudence at Tokyo Imperial University. It was after his appointment that he convened a meeting of six professors of the school whom he believed he could trust to work with him. At any rate, he could only hope so, for he was perhaps putting his life in their hands when he told them it was their duty as well as his to do everything possible to conclude a war that, it was then patently obvious, might well annihilate the nation.

Having secured their agreement, Nambara sat down with them to work out a plan of campaign. They decided, first, that the sooner Japan sued for peace the better, but that probably the most appropriate time for such an action would be when Germany finally surrendered. In any case, Japan must attempt to end the war before American forces landed on Okinawa. Further, to facilitate the surrender, Japan should make overtures to the United States directly; if that turned out to be impractical, then some neutral nation (not the Soviet Union) should be asked to proffer its good offices in mediating between the two powers.

Japan, the professors agreed, had no choice but to accept Allied peace terms in their entirety; she must not attempt to make conditions. This would, obviously, be a hard pill to swallow, but Nambara's group could see no alternative.

They decided that the best way to implement their plan was, first, to drive a wedge between the army and the navy, for it was the army which was most intransigent. Once that was done, the leaders of the navy must be persuaded to issue an unequivocal statement, making clear that Japan had been defeated and now had no choice but surrender. Acting upon that statement, the emperor would proclaim an imperial rescript, announcing to the Japanese people as well as to the world at large the fact of Japan's decision to surrender. At the same time, in order to immobilize the leaders of the army, many of whom would fight such a decision tooth and nail, a strong cabinet must be formed under a man like Kazushige Ugaki, a cabinet strong enough to suppress an army revolt.

The professors then turned their attention to the moral and physical chaos that must inevitably follow defeat in a long and bitter war, the first defeat in Japan's history. They considered that, to avoid a national collapse, the emperor in his imperial rescript must assume responsibility for the war and, at an appropriate time, abdicate his throne in favor of a successor. The professors believed that the emperor system should be retained but that measures should be taken to erase the lofty, godlike image of the emperor, making him no more than the constitutional monarch of a democratic nation.

A pipe dream? Perhaps. But the professors felt they had no choice, if their country was to survive, but to bring their plan to the attention of those in authority who were most likely to react favorably to it. They were, after all, men of high standing in the country, and they believed that they could gain access to certain of the senior statesmen, to certain members of the cabinet, and to certain of those in authority at the Imperial Palace. If the plan, in the end, came to nothing, the professors would at least have the somewhat bitter satisfaction of knowing that they had done the very best they could according to their own lights.

Meanwhile, the man around whom so many of their hopes centered announced suddenly that he desired to view personally the bombed-out sections of his capital. Those who attended him opposed the idea, not only because they wanted to spare him the sight of the city's terrible desolation but also because they feared the enemy might raid the city again while he was away from the palace and out of reach of his own air raid shelter. However, it was finally decided that if he made his tour on a Sunday, the enemy would be less likely to strike that day, it being, presumably, a day of rest.

Accordingly, at nine in the morning on Sunday 18 March, the emperor, accompanied by his grand chamberlain and attended by only two guard cars, issued from the palace in his black official car flying a flag with a gold imperial chrysanthemum on a red background. It was a windy day, and clouds of dust rose everywhere from the debris that had not yet been cleared away.

The small procession visited the areas that had been hardest hit.

There the emperor saw piles of charred bodies, he saw survivors scrabbling among the ruins of their dwellings looking for salvageable goods, he saw the stark steel skeletons of factories and plants, he saw hills that had once been green and were now only mounds of dust, and he saw little bits of paper, posted here and there, fluttering in the wind, bearing such messages as "Tokiko, come to the office. Only Father is alive. Mori."

The dusty, ragged, despondent survivors of the raid were, of course, astonished to see their monarch appear suddenly in their midst, so astonished that some of them did not have time even to bow their heads, as they were required by law to do. This may have been the first time that many of his subjects actually saw the emperor, for that too was against the law. It was a sorrowful man they saw, a man deeply touched by the suffering and desolation that surrounded him.

At the ornamental gate of the Tomioka Hachiman Shrine, in Fuka-gawa, the emperor descended from his car. There he was received by Shigeo Ōdachi, the home minister, who spoke to him about the extent of the damage. Somberly the emperor returned to his car and continued his mournful tour of inspection. Finally he told the grand chamberlain that in 1923 after the great earthquake he had visited the scenes of disaster where there was nothing left, but that this time it was much more horrible perhaps because in 1923 there had been few tall buildings in Tokyo. "This seems infinitely more terrible. Tokyo," murmured the emperor, "has become no more than scorched earth, has it not?"

He said no more, returning to the palace at eleven. Less than three hours later an enemy plane bombed Asakusa, an area which he had inspected on his tour. While he was riding through the devastated city, American bombers raided the islands of Kyushu and Shikoku, far to the west; their chief targets were the airfields located there, although nearby cities did not escape. There seemed to be no question that the enemy was preparing to land on Okinawa in the not very distant future. Then, like a giant in seven-league boots, he would stride from one island to another until he had reached the country's heart. Was there no way to stop him? The peace groups said yes; so did the army and the navy; but their methods were different, perhaps irreconcilable.

It was on that same day, 18 March, that an air raid warning sounded in Hiroshima. The radio announced that enemy planes were flying over Okayama, Nada, and Matsuyama. The day was overcast. Antiaircraft guns fired into the cloudy sky. The people of Hiroshima trembled in their shelters, waiting for the bombs to fall. But no bombs fell. The planes passed over the city and disappeared beyond the southern sea. Did Hiroshima, its people wondered, have a charmed life after all?

On 20 March the army formulated a new strategy for fighting the coming "battle of Japan," while the navy, on that same day, finalized plans for an all-out battle to prevent the enemy from landing on Okinawa. The differences of opinion that had separated the two forces were now becoming outright divisiveness; the sister services were turning into rivals. In January, when the army had proposed that the two forces combine their air power in order to attack the enemy fleet in the East China Sea, the navy had been reluctant because it had been unable to repair the damage it had suffered at the Battle of Leyte.

But now, while the army was preparing to repulse an enemy landing on one of the main islands, the navy was concentrating its forces for a final battle for Okinawa. (As events were to turn out, this was also to be the final battle that the Imperial Japanese Navy would ever engage in.) Its *tengo sakusen* (best translated, perhaps, as "divine strategy") called for the deployment of over three thousand planes, of which some two thousand were to be suicide planes. Their aim was to inflict such extensive damage on the enemy fleet that the Americans would eventually decide a landing on Okinawa was proving too costly in both lives and matériel.

Did either the army or the navy believe its own rhetoric? Can men who follow the logic of war ever be persuaded to listen to another logic? On 21 March, the very next day, came a premonition of disaster. The radio announced that a large segment of the Japanese forces defending Iwō Jima had been utterly annihilated and that the commander, General Tadamichi Kuribayashi, had committed suicide a few days earlier. Before his death, he asked his troops, in a moving appeal, to continue the struggle to the last man. The voice of the Japanese radio announcer choked as he reported the commander's last words, and the people who listened found tears coursing down their cheeks. "Our ammunition is exhausted," Kuribayashi said, in part, "and our supply of water has run out. Yet those of our troops who are still alive are resolved to fight the enemy to the end. Remembering the great benevolence of the emperor, I have no regrets."

Then what about the mass of the people? Were they to be allowed to have regrets? Dead men have no regrets, and that windy March day, with a hint of early spring in the air, Death had grown to be so familiar a companion that it seemed the people of Japan were ready, even eager to welcome him. Their leaders kept assuring them that they wanted to fight the final battle on their own soil; perhaps by now the people believed what they had been told so often. The prime minister, Kuniaki Koiso, addressed the nation over the radio, committing his government and the army to the recapture of Iwō Jima, Saipan, and Guadalcanal. "Why," he cried, "do you think our forces continue fighting in the Philippines and Rabaul? Is it merely for purposes of defense? No! Japan is even now preparing for a great offensive!"

On 25 March the government announced the formation of what it called "the people's volunteer corps." All Japanese, both male and female, over the age of thirteen and under sixty, except for sick people and pregnant women, were to be mobilized to work on war production. If, or rather when, the crisis came, they were to take up weapons to battle the invader. But what weapons had they, the people of Japan, with which to counter the machine guns and the tanks of the enemy? They had bamboo spears.

Dutifully, then, they drove stakes into the ground, and around the stakes they wrapped rice straw in the shape of human beings; then they aimed their bamboo spears at the straw figures. Old men and women, weakened by hunger and privation, were hardly able to lift the spears, let alone hurl them at the mock enemy. Then sometimes the old men, enraged by their own weakness, would throw their bodies at those seemingly indomitable figures of straw, trying to knock them over. But the figures remained standing: there was nothing anyone could do.

The people turned away in despair. If they believed that they truly wanted to fight the final battle on their own soil, that does not mean they also believed they had any chance of winning it. Peering up into the skies at the giant, silvery B-29s, looking around them at their ruined cities, they knew in their hearts the war was lost. Yet still they turned back and picked up their bamboo spears, to hurl them once again at the straw men. Had not their leaders told them that that was what they must do? Cold and hungry and deprived of hope, they had no choice, it seemed, but to obey.

On the same day that the Japanese government announced its determination to use bamboo spears, if necessary, against the enemy, Dr. Albert Einstein affixed his name to the memorandum prepared by Professor Leo Szilard recommending that the atomic bomb should not be used against Japan. In this he joined a growing list of scientists who had been instrumental in the development of the bomb and who, now that they knew Germany did not possess it, were opposed to its use. Shortly after that, Niels Bohr expressed the same opinion. Among the scientists who were responsible for the bomb there was an increasing number, then, who believed that Japan was, to all intents and purposes, already defeated and that to drop the bomb was no longer justifiable.

Before the month was out, the Zacharias-Farago plan to depose Japan's prowar leadership had obtained the approval of both Admiral Ernest J. King, chief of naval operations, and James Forrestal, secretary of the navy. Of the background to the plan, Zacharias was later to write that there "were recent intelligence reports disclosing a definite Japanese trend which could be exploited to move the Japanese toward surrender, or at least a termination of hostilities prior to our invasion of Japan proper. Among these was a very significant report given in the utmost secrecy to one of our intelligence officers in a neutral capital. It outlined in great detail the course Japan intended to take and stated that General Koiso would soon resign and permit the appointment as prime minister of Admiral Suzuki, an old confidant of the Emperor and leader of what I even then had come to call the 'peace party.' Moreover, the document indicated that the Emperor himself was leading a group of influential personalities desirous of obtaining peace terms under the most favorable circumstances."[5]

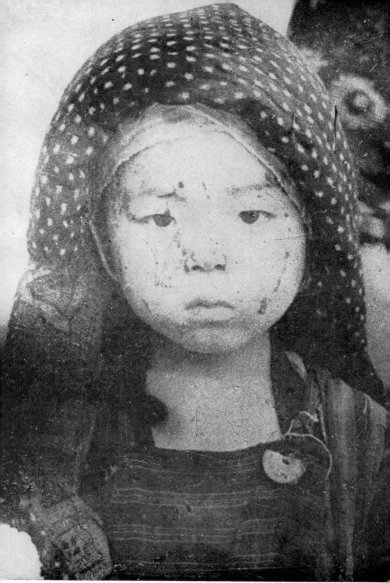

1. A young child of the atomic age.

2. Albert Einstein, who found matter could be converted into energy and estimated how little matter was needed to produce great energy.

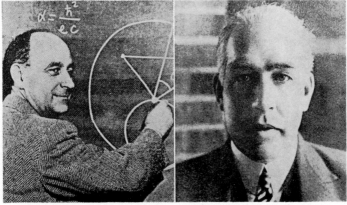

3. Enrico Fermi, who was the first to cause neutrons to penetrate the nucleus of an atom.

4. Niels Bohr of Denmark, whose team was the first to prove that the uranium atom could be split.

5–7. *Left*, James B. Conant, president of Harvard University; *above right*, Karl T. Compton; and, *below right*, Ernest O. Lawrence. Together with Dr. Compton's brother, Arthur Holly Compton, these were three of the scientists most involved in getting the atomic project moving politically.

8. Yoshio Nishina, leader of Japan's nuclear effort.

9. Walt Bothe, one of Heisenberg's most able colleagues in the neglected German attempt to develop nuclear energy.

10. Robert Oppenheimer and Leslie Groves, leaders respectively of the civilian and military personnel in the bomb project. In the foreground are the remains of the tower which had held the first atomic bomb in the New Mexico desert, July 1945.

11, 12. *Above*, George C. Marshall chief of staff of the American army and, *below*, Henry H. Arnold chief of staff of the American air force when the important decisions were taken.

13. Carl Spaatz, commander of the Pacific strategic air forces at the time the bomb was flown to Hiroshima.

14. Ellis Mark Zacharias, who believed that the Japanese could be persuaded to surrender without the dropping of the bomb.

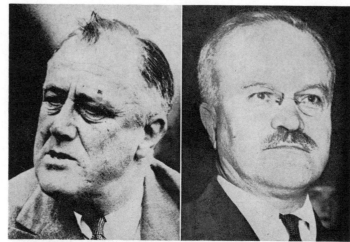

15. Franklin D. Roosevelt, president of the United States during World War II until May, 1945.

16. Vyacheslav Molotov, foreign minister of the Soviet Union 1939–49 and 1953–56.

17. Winston S. Churchill, prime minister of the United Kingdom, and Harry S. Truman, president of the United States; these two men ratified the decision to drop the bomb.

Zacharias hoped that now, with Forrestal's and King's approval, the plan might go all the way up to the president and there be acted on. But Roosevelt was then at Warm Springs, attempting to regain his health. He had little strength to spare, and what little he had he devoted mostly to the draft of a speech in which he restated his belief that war was an unrealistic method of resolving differences of opinion between sovereign states and his hope that it would never again be made use of.

CHAPTER 4 **APRIL 1945**

Suddenly life in Hiroshima seemed to have been altogether transformed. It was not only the work of demolition that continued in the districts of Takeya-chō and Hirataya-chō, where fire prevention belts were being laid out. All the dwellings that had formerly stood there had by now been pulled down; only an occasional earthen warehouse pierced the monotonous desolation. Now middle-school boys and girls, who had been drafted for the work, were clearing away the debris left by the demolished houses.

Another change had overtaken the city. Its former population of some four hundred thousand had dwindled, and to take the place of these vanished civilians there now appeared hordes of soldiers. Patches of khaki became increasingly evident in the streets of the city. What, the people wondered, did this sudden appearance of large numbers of troops portend? Was the long-threatened invasion about to take place at last? Was the "battle of Japan" about to occur here on the streets of Hiroshima? Those who remained there moved uneasily about, amid the confusion and disorder, oblivious to the accustomed beauty of their spring, which, surprisingly, had come that year as it came every year. The peach trees were in blossom, the weeping willows were thick with new foliage; but the people of Hiroshima had almost no time for these happy manifestations of nature's annual reawakening.

Like the people everywhere in Japan that April, they looked about them as though their world was a place they had never seen before. It had been transformed not only by the many physical changes that had occurred, it had been transformed by fear and anxiety, by dread of the future, and by hunger and sleeplessness. The people were exhausted and frightened; yet there was something else to be read in their bloodshot eyes—a kind of dull anger. But against whom was it directed? Against the enemy, which was reducing their beloved country to ashes? Against their own leaders, who had somehow got them into this dreadful predicament? Against a hostile fate? Against themselves? It was a question to which there was no single answer, only many answers; and it was an anger that could not be vented, only frustrated. Straw men offered little release, bamboo spears little hope.

Probably the people of Tokyo were the worst off. In mid-March, five days after the disastrous raid of the tenth, the cabinet decided that the capital must be evacuated; only those who did essential work were to be permitted to remain. Now the evacuation orders were being carried out. The people were to be given only five days in which to leave their dwellings and seek refuge in the surrounding countryside. Everywhere one saw houses on which the simple, stark word "EVAC-UATE" had been chalked up. Those whose dwellings had been condemned now found that their supply of electricity and water had been cut off and their telephones were no longer in operation. They, with their dwellings, had miraculously survived the raids; now a single cabinet order proved to be just as disastrous.

Soldiers, acting under orders, bound huge ropes around the flimsy wooden houses, and the houses came down with a crash. Students helped transport furniture from the condemned dwellings, and long lines of tightly packed vehicles edged slowly away from the center of the city. But of course there was not room for everything. Non-essentials—things like books and pianos, cabinets and braziers—stood piled on the streets, while their disconsolate owners looked for buyers. But it was a buyer's market because the articles that had to be left behind fetched only a small fraction of their value. Some were simply abandoned, left stranded in the rubble-strewn streets. It was hard to believe that this had once been the third largest city in the world; even harder was it to remember that its homeless, hungry people had once been the arrogant conquerors of the Pacific.

In his journal a political commentator, Kiyoshi Kiyosawa, wrote despondently: "Japan's substance has dwindled to what it was before the Sino-Japanese war back in 1894; we have not even had to wait for the Americans to come and dispose of us. The army kept telling us, in its broadsides, that war is the mother of culture, and if we questioned that dictum we were branded as traitors. Say the words over again: war is the mother of culture. If she is, then she is truly a dreadful mother!"

On 1 April this mother gave the world a frightening demonstration of her maternal feelings. On 1 April the Allied forces, having secured the Kerama islands, west of southern Okinawa, landed on beaches around Hagushi, on Okinawa's west coast, under the umbrella of the heaviest barrage of naval gunfire in the history of warfare. A total of 1,317 Allied ships took part in the operation; carrier-based aircraft numbered 1,727; the landing force itself was composed of 180,000 men.

Seventy-seven thousand Japanese troops attempted to defend the island: 69,000 were men of the Thirty-second Army, commanded by Lieutenant General Mitsuru Ushijima and 8,000 were marines under the command of Rear Admiral Minoru Ōta. In addition, some twenty-five thousand Okinawan civilians, between the ages of seventeen and forty-five, had been mobilized; this number included just over two thousand upper-class students, both boys and girls. Thus it will be seen that the invaders were nearly twice as numerous as the defenders, while their fire power was at least ten times greater. Further, they controlled both the sea and the air.

Why then did the Japanese, against such overwhelming odds, even attempt to defend the island? For an answer to that question, one must address oneself to the Imperial Navy, which believed that if it could gain a victory, at whatever cost, on Okinawa, it could turn the tide of war just enough to secure favorable terms from the clearly victorious enemy. It must be noted that in this a majority agreed with the navy: the government itself, many of the senior statesmen, many of the mass of the people. It was chiefly the army which disagreed, for the army was determined to fight the "battle of Japan." But now even the army was glad to have the temporary delay that the battle for Okinawa provided.

As a result, it became one of the fiercest battles of the Pacific. The Allied forces made rapid progress through northern Okinawa, but the Japanese had entrenched themselves in the southern hilly region, which they had no intention of giving up except at tremendous cost. Meanwhile, kamikaze pilots, following the navy's "divine strategy," were inflicting heavy losses on enemy shipping. On 5 April the Imperial Navy ordered the ten remaining warships of the Japanese Combined Fleet, including the dreadnaught *Yamato*, to sail for Okinawa. The navy's rather imaginative, if also rather pathetic, plan was to strand the ships on an Okinawa beach, where they might be used as a fortress against the enemy. But would the Allied fleet permit them to reach Okinawa? It seemed most unlikely. Nonetheless, the ten warships began making preparations to depart for Okinawa.

The fifth of April was not only a crucial day in the history of the Imperial Navy, it was also a decisive one in the life of Japan itself, for on that afternoon the Koiso cabinet resigned en masse. The reason given was that the cabinet was no longer able to conduct the war and that a new and more powerful cabinet was needed.

What was needed, of course, was someone capable of making the decision to surrender; and there was no such person. Just as there had been no single supreme commander in chief for the conduct of the war, there was now no single person who had both the ability to decide that the war was lost and the authority to accept responsibility for that decision. In theory, of course, the emperor was supreme in the country, in fact, he owned the country, it belonged to him personally; and so, of course, he possessed final authority in all matters pertaining to his land, but it was a theoretical authority only, an authority he did not, and was not expected to, exercise.

In practice, the war was conducted by the Supreme Council for the Direction of the War, called the Big Six, which consisted of four cabinet members (the prime minister, the foreign minister, the minister of war, and the minister of the navy) and the two military chiefs of staff. Since the emergence of the army into power, it had insisted that the minister of war be a general in active service, so it was actually he, plus the two chiefs of staff, who had so far wielded the greatest authority. But they seldom agreed amongst themselves, and there had been little unity, throughout the war, of thought and effort. Thus how were these divided leaders to arrive at a consensus favoring surrender? Could a new cabinet achieve what appeared to be, on the face of it, altogether impossible?

Since Koiso, upon tendering his resignation, had suggested a fairly sweeping reorganization of the cabinet, forming what would be in effect a cabinet directly allied with imperial headquarters, Marquess Kido took the initiative of conferring with both the army and the navy. On this subject they were able to reach an immediate consensus: they both disapproved. The selection of the next prime minister, then, was referred, as it had been in the past, to a conclave of the senior statesmen, all former prime ministers.

Here consensus appeared more difficult to achieve, but finally the senior statesmen agreed to suggest to the emperor the nomination of Baron Kantarō Suzuki, a retired admiral of the Imperial Japanese Navy. Suzuki opposed his own nomination on the grounds that he was too old (he was seventy-nine), and Tōjō opposed it because it carried the premiership further away from the army. Nonetheless, it was approved.

After a private conversation with Kido, Suzuki was received by the emperor. The audience occurred shortly after ten o'clock that night of 5 April. After being commanded by the emperor to form a cabinet, Suzuki advanced the reasons he felt would make him unequal to the task: his age, his increasing deafness, and his political inexperience. He added that he would like to follow Emperor Meiji's advice that military men should not become entangled in politics. He respectfully begged, therefore, to be allowed to decline the emperor's mandate.

For the first time in their tense audience the emperor smiled at his former grand chamberlain, a man whom he himself, as well as the rest of the country, deeply respected. He discounted Suzuki's lack of political experience as well as his advanced age and his infirmity. He added that, at this crucial moment in the country's history, he felt there was no one else he could call upon. He paused, then repeated, "No one else." Between the emperor and his former grand chamberlain there existed a special relationship: of deep affection on one side, and of intense loyalty on the other. The tired old man bowed deeply and retired from the presence of his master; it was to be his thankless, exasperating task to form and maintain a wartime government to preside over Japan's first defeat.

Having accepted the imperial mandate, Suzuki set out almost at once to consult with several senior statesmen as to the composition of the new cabinet. It is impossible now to say with certainty whether he realized at the outset from his cryptic private conversation with Kido, from his knowledge of the roles that Konoye and Yoshida were playing behind the scenes, and from the tone of the emperor's voice and his choice of words when he overrode Suzuki's hesitation, that he was to be called upon to end the war. Later, he was to testify that, in view of the gravity of the situation, despite his outward vacillation, he considered it his duty to do his utmost to bring an immediate end to hostilities, and for that reason chose Shigenori Tōgō to be his foreign minister. He believed that Tōgō, who had also been foreign minister at the time of Pearl Harbor, had opposed the war from the very start. Several conversations between the two men were required before Tōgō could be persuaded that Suzuki actually did intend "to do his utmost" to end the war as soon as possible. Finally Tōgō accepted the portfolio that had been offered him, the same one he had held back in December 1941.

Did he realize quite how serious was the news from Moscow that reached Tokyo on the very day the Koiso cabinet fell? He may not have, for the news, although unfavorable, did not appear to be of immediate importance. The Soviet foreign minister had called the Japanese ambassador to the Kremlin to tell him that the Soviet Union, in view of the "altered situation," was abrogating the Neutrality Pact that had existed between the two countries since 13 April 1941. However, according to the terms of the pact, it was to remain in effect for five years, after which it would be renewed unless either signatory gave the other a year's notice that it did not wish to renew the pact. Thus, according to its terms, it would necessarily remain valid until April 1946.

The Japanese were, of course, ignorant of the secret undertaking Stalin had given to Roosevelt and Churchill at Yalta to enter the war against Japan within "two or three months after Germany has surrendered." It is quite possible, then, that the new foreign minister trusted the Soviets to fulfill their obligations. The army, apparently, did not. An entry in the supreme command headquarter's secret journal reads as follows: "Taking into consideration Molotov's unfriendly attitude, we may safely assume that the Soviet Union already regards Japan as an enemy." The army, apparently, had had more experience with duplicity than the foreign ministry.

By 7 April Suzuki had completed the composition of his cabinet, and on that day, while the ceremonies of attestation were being held in the Imperial Palace, Tokyo was raided by over a hundred enemy planes: ninety B-29s and thirty P-51s. Japanese fighters flew up in an attempt to intercept the invaders, and the roar of gunfire reverberated throughout the city, which was hazy with early spring mist.

On the same day the remnants of Japan's once proud and mighty Combined Fleet were sunk off the coast of Bōnomisaki ("Cape of Bō"), in southern Kyushu. The giant battleship *Yamato*, the chief glory of the fleet, drifted to the bottom with some twenty torpedoes embedded in its hull. For all practical purposes, the Imperial Japanese Navy, once all conquering, now ceased to exist. It was no longer a factor in the war.

Undismayed, the army continued imperturbably with its suicidal plans. It still had a force of some two million troops in Japan proper (although only half of them were adequately armed); as transportation it had at its disposal only 70,000 trucks and other types of military vehicles, some ten thousand cars, and under a half million horses. Realizing the inadequacy of its resources, the army was hurriedly inducting maimed men into the service, men with only one arm, men whose legs were crippled. Even such men, by army standards, would be useful in suicide squadrons; they could take the place of the ammunition that was lacking.

If the Suzuki cabinet had been formed to enable Japan to surrender, that fact was not immediately apparent. The new minister of war, General Korechika Anami, presented the cabinet with the army's

demands: all possible measures must be taken to allow Japan to continue the war to the end, including the unification of the army and the
navy. The new prime minister agreed; and, on the very day that his
cabinet was sworn in, he spoke to the people of the nation, saying,
among other things, "Should I die, I hope that you will advance over
my dead body to continue the fight against the enemy." Strange words
to come from a peacemaker! They were not encouraging.

At the same time, General Anami issued directives to his weakened
force, instructing both officers and men to obey the words of the
emperor, for in them lay final victory; to defend the sacred soil of
Japan with their lives; to regard themselves as the advance guard for a
hundred million fellow Japanese. His words, and those of Suzuki,
reassured a fairly sizable group of young army officers who had feared
that Suzuki's cabinet was about to play a role in Japanese history
similar to that played by the Badoglio government in the history of
Italy. If that were so, their intention was to overthrow the new cabinet
by a military coup d'état and replace it with a stronger one headed by
a general on the active list. Having listened to both Suzuki and Anami,
they decided they could wait a little longer: perhaps their beloved
army was not going to be traduced into the treason of surrender.

Others in the country, those who believed that Japan's only hope of
survival lay in accepting the enemy's peace terms immediately, were
less convinced that they could continue waiting. At the same time, the
military police increased their surveillance over what were considered
"dissident elements." Strangely enough, or perhaps not so strangely
when one considers the hysteria rampant in the about-to-be defeated
country, the recently translated memoirs of Georges Clemenceau were
playing a major role in the investigations of the Kempei-tai. For one
thing, the translator of the memoirs was a retired general, Kōji Sakai,
one of whose patrons was Prince Konoye. Konoye's intimacy with
Lieutenant General Binshirō Obata was well known to the Kempei-tai;
equally well known to them was the fact that both Obata and Konoye
opposed the present leadership of the army, favoring a purge that
would make it less blatantly militaristic. There was also the fact that
Shigeru Yoshida, known for his pro-British and pro-American senti-

ments, was a frequent visitor at Konoye's house. All in all, in Kempei-tai eyes, it was an unsavory group.

Of equal interest to the military police, and equally sinister, was the substance of Clemenceau's book. In it he told how, during the First World War, at a critical moment in France's history, he took over the war ministry and purged the army of its corrupt leaders. This action may have been instrumental in bringing the United States into the war and so ensuring Germany's defeat. The fact that the book, in General Sakai's translation, was now being widely read by Japan's politicians and businessmen became a cause for concern to the Kempei-tai. If a purge of this kind had occurred in France during the First World War, might it not also happen in Japan during the second? People who were known to be reading Clemenceau's memoirs became suspect.

Then, early in this same month of April, the Kempei-tai got their hands on something far more tangible and far more sinister. It was a copy of Prince Konoye's memorial to the throne, and it had reached Kempei-tai hands in a roundabout way. Konoye had shown a copy of the memorial to Yoshida; Yoshida had made a copy for his own use; working in Yoshida's residence as a houseboy was an army agent who had got hold of the memorial and made a photographic copy of it; this eventually reached the chief of the defense section of the War Ministry; and from there it was sent on to the headquarters of the military police.

The Kempei-tai now possessed irrefutable proof of Konoye's and Yoshida's "treason"; but what on earth were they to do with their proof? It was like a live but undependable grenade in their hands; if they pulled the pin, who would be blown to bits by the resulting explosion? Both Konoye and Yoshida were men of consequence, and both were associated with the throne: Konoye through his own position in Japanese society, and Yoshida through his father-in-law, Count Makino, a senior statesman. There was the further fact that the emperor himself had read the memorial. This fact alone seemed to rule out any possibility of putting Prince Konoye under restraint; but what about Yoshida? His arrest would be a severe blow to the propeace movement, to be sure; at the same time, however, it might well backfire.

That grenade might explode right there in Kempei-tai headquarters, it might even damage the army itself, and instead of harming the peace movement might give it added impetus.

There was no longer any question that the morale of the people was disintegrating, its confidence in the army diminishing, and its desire for an end, one way or another, to a hopeless war steadily increasing. Criticism grew more outspoken. "The army is putting on a bold front," people said, "but it knows the war is lost." "It claims Japan is winning the war, but how does it explain the increasing number of enemy planes attacking the country?" "The army needs new leaders. . . ."

Indicative of the hysteria that was taking over the country was the vast number of superstitious belief which appeared to arise from no-where and which then spread across the nation with brush fire rapidity. Someone apparently decided, for example, that pickled scallions were an effective defense against the falling bombs; everybody dutifully ate pickled scallions. Then someone else said, "If you want to be safe, you must eat rice with your pickled scallions for breakfast." Then this was further amplified: "You must not only eat pickled scallions with your rice, you must also tell your friends about the power of the charm."

One reported incident led to an equally mad craze. According to the story, a husband and wife escaped unharmed from a direct hit on their house, and after the bombing was over they found two dead goldfish lying on the floor. To give thanks for their escape, the couple laid the fish reverently on a Buddhist altar. In no time at all the whole country was offering prayers to goldfish, as B-29s, virtually unmolested, rained incendiary bombs where they pleased.

In various parts of the nation, shrines sold amulets intended to protect their wearers from bombs. Some amulets were considered more efficacious than others, and among the most powerful had been thought to be those sold by the Ana Hachiman shrine in Waseda. There people used to line up in long queues in order to purchase the shrine's amulets. The fact that it went up in flames during the 10 March raid on Tokyo did nothing to diminish the number of people throughout the country who continued to put their trust in amulets.

Along with the superstitions went the rumors, which passed from mouth to mouth in much the same fashion. One widely held belief was that the great Allied landing on the homeland would be made in August; many people laid plans on the basis of it. Other rumors that swept through a district or a whole city concerned the night's target or targets for Allied raids. On this subject Hyakken Uchida, the author, wrote in his journal: "Today I returned home after hearing a rumor that the Americans were planning to bomb the Nakano district of Suginami Ward tonight. The rumor may be true, but it may equally well be false, and I had been determined not to heed such stories. Deep in my heart, nonetheless, I felt there might be a grain of truth in the report, so I decided that I would be careful tonight. What a pitiful life we lead these days!"

And along with the superstitions and the rumors went the whispers, whispers which were dangerous and had to be kept from the long ears of the Kempei-tai but which slowly, as the desperate days wore on, increased in volume. The whispers were a constant buzz in the background of the life of the people, like the drone of insects over a swampy marsh. "Oh, let's end the war!" people would say. "Let's give in. The Americans are barbarians, to be sure, and their soldiers will commit atrocities against the Japanese, but our life could be no worse under their domination than it is now, with these incessant bombings." "And the invasion to come," another would add. "At least," a third might say, "I can speak English, I could be an interpreter. Perhaps in that case they won't kill me." Then all would fall silent, suddenly fearful that someone within hearing might be a police spy.

Most severely punished, if discovered, were those who spoke against the emperor; almost the worst crime in the Kempei-tai books was lèse-majesté. Yet still, knowing this, people could no longer keep silent. "Soon we will have to admit defeat," one might say, "and then the emperor's future will be black indeed." "Naturally he must assume all responsibility. He has brought this terrible war upon us." "After Japan surrenders, we will not be punished. Only the emperor and his ministers will be put to death." "And rightly too. What's the good of an emperor if Tokyo is to be burnt to ashes?" Then, with a shrug and a glance, the little group would disperse, each with his own thoughts, his own fears and anxieties, his own secret hopes for the future.

Army headquarters, meanwhile, continued to issue communiqués concerning the coming invasion. That dated 8 April began: "The Imperial Army is hereby instructed to intensify preparations to meet and repel the enemy when he attempts to invade Japanese soil." On 10 April Mrs. Aiko Takahashi, a Japanese who was married to an American citizen but who had been caught in Japan by the declaration of war, wrote in her diary: "Today I stood at the window of my Japanese style room upstairs, looking at the cherry blossoms, just as I did last year. I could not help wondering whether I would view the flowers again next year. My mood was a pensive one, and I thought what a short life cherry blossoms have: they come out on the trees and a few days later, even if there is no wind, they flutter to the ground. Tears like falling blossoms began to stream down my cheeks." No doubt the same melancholic thoughts were in the minds of the crowds who, this year like every year, went to the parks to view the ephemeral blossoms. How many of them would see the trees bloom again the following spring?

In the United States the secretary of war flew to Oak Ridge to see for himself how the separation of U-235 was proceeding and to confer with General Groves. Stimson was the first to admit that he knew nothing about physics; but he knew what he liked. And what he liked was to see the atomic bomb completed while he was still secretary of war and to see it dropped on Japan. Nearly eighty at the time, he told Groves that one of the reasons he had remained in office, despite his advanced years, was his strong desire to see that special project succeed. "And should it fail," he added, "I know that the final responsibility is mine."

He was back in Washington in time to hear the upsetting but not unexpected news that President Roosevelt had died suddenly on 12 April at Warm Springs. As is customary, his successor, the former vice-president, was immediately sworn in and within an hour was being briefed by the secretary of war on the "special project." This was the first time he had even heard about the atomic bomb, and now he realized that it was he who would be called upon to make the final decision. That particular buck would stop getting passed, as Harry S. Truman knew very well, only when it reached his own desk.

At Roosevelt's death, there was, naturally enough, much unfinished business before him. One report that he had found time and strength to read but that he had not acted upon was the Zacharias-Farago plan to wage psychological warfare against Japan's leadership. Although Roosevelt had pencilled several notes on the report, he had not, presumably, reached a decision; now the report would have to go through the normal channels again until it reached the new president's desk. And one paper that Roosevelt had not even glanced at was Professor Szilard's memorandum on the use of the atomic bomb. If he had, would it have made any difference to Japan? Would Roosevelt's final decision have been any different from Truman's?

Would a change in the presidency result in any changes in America's war strategy? The people of Japan did not think so. Perhaps they realized that the wheels of the battle wagon must now grind inexorably on, no matter who held the reins; perhaps they were simply so exhausted that no news, not even the death of the American president nor the surrender of Japan itself, could stir them from their lethargy. The fact, however, that the date of Roosevelt's death, by Japan time, was Friday 13 April gave rise to another rumor—a rumor that the date portended ill for the nation.

As it happened, that rumor turned out to be well founded. The month of March, after the great raid of the tenth, had seen some letup in the bombing, but at the beginning of April it had begun to grow increasingly more frequent, while the number of planes taking part in the raids grew ever greater. On 2 April, 50 planes had bombed Tokyo; on 4 April, 150; on 7 April, 100; and on 12 April, again 100. The chief target had been the Nakajima Aircraft Manufacturing Company in Musashino; the central sections of the capital had been left relatively untouched.

On that ominous Friday the thirteenth, the very day that Roosevelt's death was announced, an alert was sounded at 10:40 P.M. Sixteen minutes later it became a full-scale alarm, and in eighteen minutes

160 B-29s swooped down on the capital. For three full hours they dropped both ordinary and incendiary bombs on the center of the city. According to official reports, nearly twenty-five hundred people died in the raid, nearly five thousand were injured, and some six hundred forty thousand were left homeless. Among the buildings that were destroyed was the shrine dedicated to Emperor Meiji, during whose reign modern Japan was founded. It would be grossly unfair to blame Meiji for the jingoism that enveloped the country during the reigns of his son and his grandson; yet perhaps it was not altogether inappropriate that the war which began with Pearl Harbor should have caused the destruction of his shrine.

Among other buildings that were demolished during the raid of the thirteenth were many belonging to the research institute at Koishikawa. Fortunately, as it at first seemed, one of those that did not burn down was Building No. 49, the heart of Japan's N-research project. Here stood Takeuchi's single atomic separator, Japan's last forlorn hope of developing an atomic bomb. Takeuchi himself, that night, was at his house in Zushi, a seaside town near Tokyo; but Fumio Yamasaki and Shinichiro Tomonaga (later a Nobel physics laureate) were both living near the institute, and as soon as the all clear sounded they rushed over to No. 49. It was still standing, amid a sea of fire. The two men pitched in, to help firemen prevent the flames from reaching the building. It was only two-storied, and it was made of wood, but it was vital to N-research, and somehow, by the time morning came and the surrounding conflagrations had been extinguished, it remained undamaged.

Breathing sighs of relief and exhaustion, the men who had fought the flames during the night gathered in Building No. 43, which had also escaped the fiery holocaust, to rest for a bit and to eat their meager wartime breakfast. While they were there, No. 49 suddenly erupted in flame: perhaps a bomb had found its target earlier but had not immediately detonated, perhaps a lick of flame had remained smoldering somewhere and had finally burst into this consuming fire, fanned by a strong wind that had arisen with the dawn. There was nothing the men could do but watch the building burn to the ground, nothing they could salvage of Japan's single, hopelessly inadequate effort to manufacture an atomic bomb. The years of hard work and painstaking effort followed the late American president into history.

And what of the new president? The world knew very little about him. The *New York Times* commented editorially, on 14 April, on his relative obscurity; an Associated Press dispatch from Paris noted that the name of a man unknown to the world was now on everyone's lips; a London newspaper cabled the States for a thousand-word article on this obscure figure who had suddenly become one of the most important men in the world. Truman himself, in a brief twenty-minute address, outlined his future presidential policy. He would follow, he said, the guidelines of his predecessor: unconditional surrender, punishment of war criminals, and the establishment of a universal body to maintain world peace.

It was this "unconditional surrender," as laid down in the Cairo Declaration, that stuck in the craw of Japan's leadership. Would it prove an insurmountable obstacle to the achievement of an orderly surrender? It did indeed seem so. The new prime minister, Baron Suzuki, when he announced the composition of his cabinet gave eloquent expression to the government's sentiments. "The people of Japan," he said, "are the loyal and obedient servants of the imperial house. Should the emperor system be abolished, they would lose all reason for existence. 'Unconditional surrender,' therefore, means death to the hundred million: it leaves us no choice but to go on fighting to the last man."

Discouraging words to come from a "peacemaker"! Then, on 15 April, the peace movement in Japan received its severest blow yet: at six o'clock in the morning, Shigeru Yoshida, Tatsuo Iwabuchi, Shunkichi Ueda, and other so-called traitors were arrested by the Kempeitai. After Yoshida (the prime mover in the peace faction) was taken from his villa in Oiso, the police searched the house, hoping to find a copy of Prince Konoye's memorial to the throne. But Yoshida, having been warned that the military police were closing in, had hidden the memorial in the obi of his concubine, a woman named Korin.

Yoshida was arrested, at least officially, not because of his involvement with the peace movement, but because of his supposed dissemination of dangerous rumors: a rumor concerning the contents of Konoye's memorial, a rumor that the demoralized Imperial Army had lost its confidence in the possibility of winning the war, and a rumor that the Kwantung army had fallen under Communist influence. On the same day, some ten other men in the capital were taken into custody on suspicion of antimilitary and antiwar activities.

The Kempei-tai now contemplated a second wave of arrests, those of Kumao Harada, Aisuke Kabayama, Binshirō Obata, Heisuke Yanagawa, and Kōji Sakai, and then yet a third wave that was to include both Prince Konoye and Count Makino (Yoshida's father-in-law). Once Konoye learned of Yoshida's detention, he realized that he stood in imminent danger of arrest himself, and he is said to have told Marquess Kido that should that happen he would relinquish both his status as a senior statesman and his rank of prince. However, neither he nor Makino was in fact taken into custody. Nonetheless, the series of arrests, especially that of Yoshida, made a peaceful and orderly surrender infinitely more difficult to achieve.

The only body capable of doing so was now the Suzuki cabinet, but a lack of unanimity appeared to prevent it from taking any decisive action. It was also beset by such grave problems as air raid precautions and countermeasures, the relocation of both factories and dwellings, the provision of assistance to those who had suffered from raids, the maintenance of an adequate food supply, the preservation of Japan's transportation and communications networks, and, since the cabinet had not committed itself to peace, the increase in production of vital war material. At the same time, there was the all-important riddle of the Soviet Union to be solved: could her "good offices" be used or were those "good offices" likely to be transformed into a declaration of war?

On this latter point the army was in little doubt. Imperial headquarters noted in its daily journal: "The Soviet Union, according to a consular official posted there, is concentrating a large number of divisions, as well as tanks and aircraft, on its eastern borders. The inference seems obvious that it has decided to participate in the war against Japan.

The immediate question, then, is to decide when it is likely to declare war and what counteraction Japan can and should take."

Here the Soviet Union was acting in accord with the Yalta Agreement, but, as President Truman was discovering in his first days in office, the Soviet and the American interpretations of that agreement were not synonymous. Truman had announced that he intended to follow the policies of his predecessor, but he was soon persuaded that Roosevelt's belief in an enduring understanding between the two nations was both highly unrealistic and potentially dangerous. Roosevelt, as was his custom, had gone his own way; Truman, who realized his own lack of experience in foreign affairs, was more willing to listen.

Almost unanimously they agreed that Russian activities in Eastern Europe posed a threat to the entire continent and, therefore, to America's own security. There was, in particular, dissatisfaction with Stalin's intervention in Poland; but both the American ambassador to the Soviet Union, W. Averell Harriman, and the chief of staff, Admiral William D. Leahy, believed that Stalin, attempting to reconstruct a war-devastated nation, could be pressured without bringing about a serious break in American-Russian relations. On 20 April Truman had a long interview with Harriman on the subject of his coming meeting with the Soviet foreign minister, V. M. Molotov, before the latter continued on his way to San Francisco for the charter meeting of the United Nations. Truman accepted the prevailing view that Roosevelt's "soft line" could and must be stiffened. A few hours before meeting Molotov, Truman affirmed that if the Russians refused to cooperate, "they could go to hell."

It was in this mood that he had his historic showdown with Molotov; his language, according to his own chief of staff, was "not at all diplomatic." At the meeting, which took place on 23 April, Truman "went straight to the point," to use his own words.[6] He told Molotov bluntly that Russia could not hope for American aid unless it accepted the American point of view insofar as the Polish question was concerned. The Russian attempt to institute a pro-Soviet government in Warsaw would make it impossible, in the face of public pressure, for Congress to vote economic aid to the Soviet Union.

Molotov attempted to mollify the president, at the same time putting forward Stalin's view that the United States, Britain, and the Soviet Union could reach an agreement for Poland similar to that which had been attained in the case of Yugoslavia. Truman replied that an agreement *had* been reached: "It was only required to be carried out by the Soviet government." After a further exchange, the president declared curtly that American aid was not to be obtained "on the basis of a one-way street."

"I have never been talked to like that in my life," said Molotov.

Truman answered: "Carry out your agreements and you won't get talked to like that."[7]

Admiral Leahy had not exaggerated when he remarked that Truman's language had been "not at all diplomatic." Churchill was both pleased and impressed by Truman's strong stand, as against Roosevelt's soft one; and so were Truman's advisers. Yet it did not have the desired effect. Stalin replied on the following day with a telegram in which he rejected Truman's attitude. Further inconclusive conversations followed, and by the end of the month the Polish crisis had reached a stalemate.

One of the factors that had persuaded Truman to adopt a stiffer policy toward the Soviet Union was the by then widely held belief in the United States that Soviet intervention in the war against Japan would not actually turn out to be of vital importance. On the day following Truman's meeting with Molotov, the Joint Chiefs of Staff were advised by their planning board that "early Russian entry into the war against Japan is no longer necessary to make the invasion feasible." That excellent but in the end futile advice was tendered on 24 April.

The following day turned out to be one of the most crucial twenty-four hours in contemporary history. Heinrich Himmler, the Gestapo chief, approached Sweden with an offer of Germany's unconditional surrender on the western front. The charter meeting of the United Nations took place at San Francisco. Benito Mussolini was in flight to Milan on, as events were to prove, his final journey. American and Soviet armies met at the Elbe River, where they exchanged their historic handshakes. On Okinawa, Allied forces took the initiative, and it became obvious that victory in that battle was theirs (although Japanese forces were to continue to offer resistance for another two months).

And on 25 April the American president held a long conference with his secretary of war, Henry Stimson, and with General Leslie Groves. Before he became president, Truman had known nothing about the Manhattan Project, although he was aware that there was a gigantic, top secret program in the works. As soon as he assumed office, he was given a short briefing by Stimson, but now was the first time that he was to be told about it in greater detail—in too great detail, as a matter of fact, for Truman kept interrupting, asking the two men to make their reports shorter. They replied that they could not give him a more concise and at the same time accurate account of the atomic bomb. Truman, accordingly, listened to the end, but there seems to be some question whether he understood to the full the responsibilities that possession of the bomb entailed, although the opening sentence of Stimson's report seems clear enough:

"Within four months we shall in all probability have completed the most terrible weapon ever known in human history, one bomb of which could destroy a whole city."

The effect the bomb might have upon American foreign relations, Stimson noted, was not within his province; he was, however, responsible under the president for the use of the bomb against Japan. Should it be used at all? If so, how? When? Where? Further, such immediate considerations aside, there remained the unquestioned fact that possession of the bomb had universal implications. The world, Stimson said, "would be eventually at the mercy of such a weapon. . . . Our leadership in the war and in the development of this weapon has placed a certain moral responsibility upon us which we cannot shirk without very serious responsibility for any disaster to civilization which it would further. On the other hand, if the problem of the proper use of this weapon can be solved we would have the opportunity to bring the world into a pattern in which the peace of the world and our civilization can be saved."

After Truman had heard Groves's report on the development of the bomb and on the probable date of its completion, he gave his approval to Stimson's suggestion that a committee should be formed to study all the implications, both immediate and long-range, that possession and use of the bomb would entail and to make a report to the government on its conclusions. This was to be the famous, and strategically highly important, interim committee. Its composition was soon determined. In Stimson's own words:

"I was its chairman, but the principal labor of guiding its extended deliberations fell to George L. Harrison, who acted as chairman in my absence. . . .[8] Its members were the following, in addition to Mr. Harrison and myself:

"James F. Byrnes (then a private citizen) as personal representative of the President.

"Ralph A. Bard, Under Secretary of the Navy.

"William L. Clayton, Assistant Secretary of State.

"Dr. Vannevar Bush, Director, Office of Scientific Research and Development, and president of the Carnegie Institute of Washington.

"Dr. Karl T. Compton, Chief of the Office of Field Service in the Office of Scientific Research and Development, and president of the Massachusetts Institute of Technology.

"Dr. James B. Conant, Chairman of the National Defense Research Committee, and president of Harvard University."

Both Bush and Conant were unsure whether they were in a position to represent the scientists working on the project who now feared that use of the bomb might result in a worldwide arms race, thus furthering, not the pleasures of peace, but the bitter logic of war. Stimson replied that, in part because of this very fact, consideration was being given to the formation of a scientific advisory panel to the interim committee. The panel, which was formed shortly thereafter, was composed of J. Robert Oppenheimer, Arthur H. Compton, Ernest O. Lawrence, and Enrico Fermi, all of them physicists who had made vital contributions to the production of the bomb.

In Japan, meanwhile, where the Manhattan Project was still a wholly unknown quantity, the army continued to insist that victory was not only inevitable, it was imminent. On 19 April the daily newspapers, with a mysterious—or perhaps not so mysterious—sameness, all ran articles headlined: "THE TIME TO GRASP VICTORY IS NOW!" Once again Clemenceau entered into the calculations of the Imperial Japanese Army, perhaps in its effort to counteract the secret belief, held by many and inspired by his memoirs, that what the army needed was a drastic change in leadership. And not only Clemenceau but Foch also was quoted by the Imperial Army. In fact, Japan, at this stage in its life, was compared to France during the darkest days of the First World War. Did not France, fighting on indomitably, emerge victorious? Then why should not Japan? What the army neglected to point out, in its somewhat specious comparison, was the role played by France's friends, especially the United States, in 1918.

Both the army and the Foreign Office were, in their different ways, thinking about neutral nations. Private and abortive approaches had already been made to both Sweden and Switzerland, but Tōgō knew that standing in the way of any official approach were those two uncompromising words, "unconditional surrender." At the same time, he was well aware that any attempt to approach the Allies directly at this point would bring down upon the government the full wrath of the army, might in fact topple the shaky Suzuki cabinet, and so put an end, for the time being, to any hope of peace.

The Soviet Union was also, at least officially, a neutral country still, although its attitude toward Japan was obviously growing colder and more hostile. This fact was a source of great concern to the army, for if the Soviet Union should suddenly become a belligerent, then the army's plan to wage its final "battle of Japan" would be rendered immediately worthless. Japan was in no position (so much was obvious even to the supreme command) to engage two powerful enemies, one on either side of it. Accordingly, the army concluded, despite its apprehensions, that it must devote its energies to keeping the Soviet Union in a state of neutrality.

On 29 April Colonel Suketaka Tanemura, of the army's staff headquarters, completed the draft of a plan aimed at doing just that. Tanemura's extravagant plan ended: "Japan must, at all costs, avoid war with the Soviet Union, so as to be free to continue the war against the Americans and the British. We must, therefore, be prepared to surrender Manchuria, the Liaotung Peninsula, Southern Karafuto, Taiwan, the Ryukyus, the Northern Kuriles, and Korea. We must accept the fact that we will have to revert to the time of the Meiji Restoration and try to find a new beginning for the reconstruction of our nation."

Forgotten in an instant was the fifteen-year-long struggle since the outbreak of the Manchurian Incident; forgotten also was the oft-repeated battle cry that Japan, in going to war, was only seeking to avenge the blood of the millions who had fallen on the Asian mainland during the wars against China and Russia. In its last forlorn hope, in its desperate resolve to defeat the apparently undefeatable enemy, the army was willing to surrender to another potential enemy all that it had fought so hard to win. It was willing to ignore the mounds of dead that lay piled high in Tokyo and Osaka and the other large cities of the country. It was willing to bear the sufferings of the survivors; it was equally willing, in its final insane strategy, to tranform them into "human bullets."

The twenty-ninth of April was also the official birthday of the emperor. On that day he made his customary pilgrimage to Yasukuni Shrine, where the spirits of Japan's war dead were then, and are now, venerated. As the emperor stood bowed before the symbol of the millions who had perished so that the ambitions of Japan's military-politico-economic establishment might be satisfied, what passed through his mind? Was it a prayer for victory? A prayer for peace? That is a question, presumably, that only the emperor himself and the force to which he bowed his head could answer. Prayers are usually silent.

B-29s are not. On 30 April, the last day of the month, early in the morning, the people of Hiroshima heard one flying over their city, a lone invader. Then they heard the sound of explosions. The bombs had fallen in the center of the city, near Ōtemachi, where large city banks and offices were located. Because it was so early in the morning, only eleven people were killed—Hiroshima's first sacrifices on the altar of war, its first hostages to the future.

CHAPTER 5 **MAY 1945**

By the beginning of May, Hiroshima was awash in a sea of khaki. Two weeks earlier, the Second General Army, under the overall command of Marshal Shunroku Hata, had established its headquarters there, and by now there was a constant coming and going of armed men, from private soldiers all the way up to general officers. The Second General Army, charged with the defense of western Japan should the enemy attempt a landing on its shores, was composed of two distinct armies—the Fifteenth (Kinki, Chūgoku, and Shikoku) and the Sixteenth (Kyushu).

The people of Hiroshima felt that this heavy military traffic boded no good for their city and lived in ever growing dread of a massive Allied raid, particularly since that lone B-29 had inflicted eleven casualties, at the end of the previous month, before casually vanishing into the western skies. At the same time, work on the fire prevention zones was continuing, while a large number of nonessential citizens had been evacuated into the neighboring countryside. The mountains that bordered the city were covered with bright green young leaves; the weather was still fairly cool, and of an evening young couples, as they had for centuries past, could be seen boating on one or another of the city's rivers. The war could not be permitted to banish altogether the immemorial rites of spring.

Even in Tokyo which had, so far, received much harsher treatment from the enemy, people took time to note the arrival of the new season. The author, Hyakken Uchida, observed in his journal: "Swallows have once again this year built their nests under the eaves of the Kōjimachi entrance to Yotsuya Station. When I watched the birds today, they appeared to be brooding. Having half feared they wouldn't come this year, because the whole area around the station is in ruins, I was very pleased to see them."

Swallows were not, of course, the only objects flying through the skies of the capital: B-29s were now almost daily visitors. As of 1 May, the duration of air raid alerts and alarms was reduced, and people were cautioned by their newspapers to take care not to miss the now short-ened warnings. Had the baleful shrieks grown so familiar? In addition to these regular interruptions, interruptions that a man did not know whether he would survive or not, the people still remaining in the capital had to cope with the increased difficulty of simply getting through the day. City blocks that had so far escaped the raids were still supplied with water, but only between ten in the morning and noon. The municipal supply of gas had been altogether stopped; the only fuel available for cooking was charred wood from burnt out houses, but there was no shortage of that.

In front of Shinjuku Station, amid the ruined buildings and the dust-coated trees, stood a huge billboard on which was written in great black characters:

> Our houses may have been burnt down,
> But our spirit has not even been seared.
> Damn LeMay to hell! He'll never conquer us!
> Fellow Japanese, rise up and fight!

Sometimes the characters were obliterated by the spring wind, which carried huge swirling gusts of powdered plaster through the ruined streets of the city. Then people passing Shinjuku Station who had stopped to read the stirring words found that their throats were choked —but not by emotion.

On 2 May came word of the death of Hitler and two days later of the fall of Berlin. Clearly, there had never been a more propitious time for Japan to sue for peace. The Allies, victorious in Europe, would now be inclined to listen to any reasonable offer from Japan, and Japan herself no longer had even the ghost of a reason for continuing to fight. Her 1941 agreement with Germany and Italy, wherein those three powers agreed not to make peace with either the United States or Great Britain save with the consent of all the parties to the agreement, was no longer valid. Italy had previously fallen to the Allies; now Germany was defeated, that Germany with which Japan had planned to share the world. Was Japan now to go on fighting alone?

It appeared that she was. At seven o'clock in the evening of 4 May, the new prime minister, Baron Suzuki, spoke to the nation over the radio. "I am resolved," he said, in the course of his address, "to sacrifice everything in order to continue the war. I fervently hope, my fellow countrymen, that you, like your brothers at the front fighting for the homeland, will now gird up your loins, ready to give your lives for your country. Above us stands the sacred figure of the emperor; protecting us are the spirits of his ancestors. . . ."

But was Suzuki truly so determined as his words would seem to indicate? There is no easy answer to that question, for his role during this period was highly ambiguous. Although he persuaded Tōgō to join his cabinet as foreign minister, although he implied that he was in favor of finding some means to end the war, and although the emperor, in commanding him to form a new cabinet, appeared to be of the same mind, Suzuki continued to play the army's game. Later he was to explain that at that time he felt he had no choice, that continued Allied insistence on "unconditional surrender" remained an insurmountable stumbling block, and that to have sued for peace then would have infuriated the army and plunged the country into civil war.

Perhaps, perhaps not. Perhaps, had the peace faction been stronger, Suzuki might have taken heart and used the German capitulation as a lever with which to dislodge the army from its position of power. The peace faction, however, since the recent arrests by the Kempei-tai, had found itself obliged to work even more secretly than before—so secretly, in fact, that the mass of the Japanese people were quite unaware even of the existence of a peace faction among the country's governing élite.

If Suzuki, however, remained unmoved by the German defeat, two members of the faculty of Tokyo Imperial University who had previously tried to take a step toward peace now were inspired to take another. On the afternoon of 7 May, Professor Nambara and Professor Takagi called on Marquess Kido to try once again to persuade him to use his influence with the emperor to get an imperial rescript issued terminating the war. They pointed out to Kido that, as everyone knew, the chief obstacle to peace was the army, but that, at the same time, the emperor, according to the provisions of the constitution, was supreme commander of the armed forces. If, therefore, the emperor were to

order the army to observe a cease-fire, preparatory to effecting a surrender, the army would have no choice but to obey. But Kido greeted
the academic proposal with reserve. A highly practical man, he knew
full well that the emperor was supreme commander of the armed forces
only in name; the actual power lay with the military, and the military
—should the emperor issue such an order at this point—would simply
ignore it. The power of the emperor was symbolic, it was not real; and
Kido was a realist. He accordingly sent the two professors away with a
noncommittal reply. Had he been less of a realist, had he been more
imaginative, more daring, rasher even, he might have been moved to
action and his country might have been spared great suffering. The
atom bomb might never have been used.

In the United States preparations for dropping the bomb were continuing according to schedule. On 6 May eight hundred technicians
attached to the 509th Composite Group sailed from Seattle aboard the
Cape Victoria; their destination was the newly constructed air base on
the island of Tinian. Test flights of the bombing crew itself had been
virtually completed; the plane that was to carry the big unwieldy bomb
was ready; and a communications network had been set up.

Production of U-235 and plutonium was also continuing according
to schedule at Hanford and at Oak Ridge: the August target dates
would in all probability be met. The sole uncertainty was whether the
bombs would work at all; the scientists were convinced that they
would, but there could be no absolute guarantee until those bombs
were actually dropped.

During the long period between the beginning and the end of construction of the bomb, the plants at Hanford ceased operations only
once. This was caused by a sudden decrease in electric power which
triggered a safety device in the reactors. Little was said at the time about
the cause of this unexpected contretemps, but later it was revealed that
one of Japan's new weapons, the balloon bomb, had been responsible
for it.

The army's artificial leather balloons, some five meters in diameter,
capable of carrying either a fifteen-kilogram conventional bomb or a
five-kilogram incendiary bomb, were finally operational. In all, some

nine thousand such balloons were sent on their way to the American mainland from a Pacific island. The army was counting on the so-called jet air current which flows from west to east over the Pacific during the winter, and apparently two of the balloons actually reached the vicinity of Hanford. One of them fell on the electric wires carrying current to the plants, thus triggering the safety device. Although it took three days to put the plants in full operation again, the Imperial Army can hardly be said to have made any appreciable dent in the Manhattan Project's seemingly inexorable course.

On 7 May, just after dawn, what Lansing Lamont calls "a dress rehearsal of the big test" was carried out at Alamagordo, in New Mexico, which Professor Robert Oppenheimer had given the code name of Trinity. Why Trinity? Was it because, as some say, Oppenheimer saw in his mind's eye a triangle composed of Los Alamos, Alamagordo, and the various plants? Or was it because, as Lamont relates, Oppenheimer, just before being asked to suggest a code name, had been reading a sonnet that began:

> Batter my heart, three-person'd God; for, you
> As yet but knock, breathe, shine, and seek to mend. . . ?[9]

If so, it was a singularly apt, or a singularly inapt, name, depending on one's point of view. In any case, the test was successful, since it provided the scientists with valuable data, but it gave no certainty of success.

Also on 7 May the German armed forces surrendered unconditionally to the Allies. Robert P. Patterson, undersecretary of state, is reported to have asked General Groves whether he thought that, now Germany had surrendered, there would be any change in American plans to use the atomic bomb in Japan. Groves is said to have replied that he could see no reason whatsoever for any changes.

On 8 May, proclaiming V-E day to the American people, President Truman issued an official announcement that began: "This is a solemn but glorious hour. General Eisenhower informs me that the forces of Germany have surrendered to the United Nations. The flags of freedom fly all over Europe."

Of chief interest to Japan was, in Truman's own words, "another statement in which I informed the Japanese what they could expect, and called their attention to the fact that we were now in a position to turn the greatest war machine in the history of the world loose in the Pacific.

" 'The Japanese people,' this statement warned, 'have felt the weight of our land, air, and naval attacks. So long as their leaders and the armed forces continue the war, the striking power and intensity of our blows will steadily increase, and will bring utter destruction to Japan's industrial war production, to its shipping, and to everything that supports its military activity.

" 'The longer the war lasts, the greater will be the suffering and hardships which the people of Japan will undergo—all in vain. Our blows will not cease until the Japanese military and naval forces lay down their arms in *unconditional surrender*.

" 'Just what does the unconditional surrender of the armed forces of Japan mean for the Japanese people?

" 'It means the end of the war.

" 'It means the termination of the influence of the military leaders who brought Japan to the present brink of disaster.

" 'It means provision for the return of soldiers and sailors to their families, their farms, and their jobs.

" 'And it means not prolonging the present agony and suffering of the Japanese in the vain hope of victory.

" 'Unconditional surrender does not mean the extermination or enslavement of the Japanese people.' " [10]

The following day Captain Zacharias, having gained unexpectedly quick approval for his plan, recorded a fifteen-minute speech, *in Japanese*, which was to be sent to San Francisco to be broadcast to Japan. Zacharias echoed President Truman's announcement of the previous day, pointing out that now that Germany had been defeated, Japan's destruction was merely a question of time. The only way, he went on, for Japan to prevent its own destruction was to cease all resistance immediately and to surrender unconditionally. "Your future is in your own hands," he said. "You are the ones who must make the choice— whether to let your soldiers perish in vain or to return once more to prosperity through peace."

Zacharias was to make many more similar broadcasts in the future. Unfortunately, he was unable to offer any assurances about the future of the emperor, and that appeared to be even a greater obstacle to peace than the Allied insistence on unconditional surrender. The question of the future status of the emperor was an awkward one, for in the higher echelons of government in Washington there was no agreement, nor was there agreement among the Allied powers. Joseph C. Grew, who had been American ambassador to Japan before the war and who remained well disposed toward the country, was tireless in stating his view "that the surrender of Japan would be highly unlikely, regardless of military defeat, in the absence of a public undertaking by the President that unconditional surrender would not mean the elimination of the present dynasty if the Japanese people desired its retention." This point of view, unfortunately for Japan, was not shared by all the makers of American war policy; the president offered no such public undertaking; the Japanese military were free to continue their insistence that if the people loved their emperor, they had no choice but to continue the war.

Nor was the news that now reached Japan from Germany encouraging. It may well have been inaccurate, but it too fed the flames of war, for it described the terrible hardships that the Allies intended to inflict upon the defeated nation; or the news may, in fact, have been manipulated by the army for its own purposes. Back in March the Japan Newspaper Corporation had been established under the direct control of the Information Bureau, which meant that all news published in Japanese papers from that point on was censored by the military. Freedom of the press ceased to exist; the newspapers had become no more than propaganda organs of the army.

On 11 May the Supreme Council for the Direction of the War convened for a three-day conference. It was the first such meeting since Suzuki had formed his cabinet, and it differed from previous meetings of the council in that it was attended only by the Big Six themselves. Hitherto the work of the council had been largely done by subordinates, secretaries, and undersecretaries, many of them fire-eating officers of the army and the navy. Now, for the first time, the Big

Six (the prime minister, the foreign minister, the minister of war, the minister of the navy, and the chiefs of staff of both the army and the navy) met in closed session.

Strangely, despite the foreign minister's frank assessment of Japan's perilous situation, the Big Six continued to devote themselves to the problem of how to make use of the Soviet Union. Tōgō insisted that little, probably nothing, could be hoped for in that direction, that in fact the Soviet Union might well have already concluded a secret agreement with the other Allied powers to enter the war against Japan (which was of course the case); but the Big Six, ignoring Tōgō's excellent advice, evolved a chimerical three-fold plan for "dealing" with the Soviet Union. It called for (1) preventing the Soviet Union from entering the war against Japan, (2) persuading the Soviets to maintain an attitude of friendly neutrality toward Japan, and (3) requesting the Soviet Union to use its "good offices" in mediating favorable peace terms.

Tōgō pointed out that Japan would be obliged to offer enormous concessions to Russia if she was to be "bribed" away from adherence to her European wartime allies, who were also no doubt making glowing offers. To this, the Big Six, again strangely in the light of history, agreed. They further agreed that implementation of the first two points should begin at once; as for the third point, they added the proviso that it should be attempted "in due course."

Thus, the two great obstacles to direct negotiation with the United States and Britain: insistence on unconditional surrender and uncertainty about the future status of the emperor, persuaded the supreme council, however unrealistically, that its ancient enemy might now be enveigled into becoming a friend. Playing a part, no doubt, in this obviously absurd decision were rumors of dissension in Eastern Europe between the Soviet Union on one side and her former Allies on the other. And there was indeed growing dissension there.

It played a part also in the final deployment of the bomb. For one thing, opinion was divided in Washington's ruling circles as to whether Stalin should be told about the bomb and, if so, how much he should be told. There seemed to be no question that the Soviet giant, once it recovered from the depredations of the war, would be in a position to produce an atomic bomb. Would the bomb, in that case, be an active force in the maintenance of postwar peace or would it trigger an arms race that might result in a nuclear war?

There was, further, the question of a meeting of the Big Three—Truman, Stalin, and Churchill. Churchill wanted the meeting to take place at once, and furthermore he wanted it to assume the nature of a showdown. He feared Russian hegemony in Eastern Europe, and once American and British troops began to withdraw, the Russian position would be rendered infinitely stronger. Churchill desired the showdown with Stalin to take place while Western troops were still making their presence felt. The American secretary of war, Henry Stimson, argued that the West would have its strongest card to play *after* the test explosion of the bomb, which was scheduled to take place in July. He accordingly counseled Truman to delay the forthcoming meeting of the Big Three, and it was this point of view, agreed to by many other high-ranking members of the American government, which eventually prevailed.

The question of the future role to be played by the Soviet Union was also discussed at numerous meetings held during the month of May by President Truman's interim committee. "On the 16th, Bush distributed to the other members copies of the memo in which he and Conant had advocated a wide exchange of scientific information and the prompt inauguration of a program of international control of the production of atomic weapons. This seems to have been too momentous a proposal for the Committee to examine with care at this meeting. The discussion then and at the next session a few days later became hung up on the question of how long it would take the Soviet Union to produce an atomic weapon."[11]

As to whether the bomb should or should not be dropped upon Japan, neither General Groves nor Professor Oppenheimer appears to have had any doubt. After the fall of Germany, "the fact remains," Groves wrote, "that the original decision to make the project an all-out effort was based upon using it to end the war." And Oppenheimer: "After the collapse of Germany, we understood that it was important to get this ready for the war in Japan. We were told that it would be very important to know the state of affairs before the meeting at Potsdam at which the future conduct of the war in the Far East would be discussed."[12]

On 8 May an advance party of the 509th Composite Group arrived by air in Tinian and settled down to the hardships of life on a green Pacific island, where tall coconut palms shaded white coral beaches. Approaching ever nearer was that day when the bomb, whose production had been begun out of fear that the Germans would produce it first, would also arrive on that small Pacific island, ready to perform the task that had been anticipated some four years and some two billion dollars before. Only the target would be a different one from that which had been originally anticipated: Germany's former ally would reap the harvest that had been sown for Germany herself. The war was progressing by a logic of its own.

In Japan food shortages were becoming increasingly more acute. Such necessities of daily life as bean paste, soy sauce, vinegar, oil, and even sugar and salt were unavailable except to the very rich. The average adult earned some three hundred yen a month, and out of this he had to pay astronomical black market prices for such commodities as eggs or radishes or bamboo shoots if he wanted to save himself and his family from absolute starvation.

An entry in the journal of Musei Tokugawa, dated 20 May, reads: "How many people in Japan are still confident that we will win the war? Aside from the young suicide pilots and other simplehearted youths, I doubt that there is anyone. Admiral Suzuki, our prime minister, Sohō Tokutomi, the dean of our newspaper reporters, and of course the leaders of the army and the navy go on issuing their defiant statements. But what do they truly believe, deep in their hearts? I suppose my own thoughts are not too dissimilar from theirs: one day I feel elated, the next terribly depressed. But of course I dare not believe hat Japan will lose the war; to believe that is forbidden. Nevertheless, in my mind's eye there is a picture of Japan defeated: I see unskilled surgeons performing a major operation on a small child, an operation that results in the child's untimely death."

If Tokugawa was thinking of Japan's leadership wasting precious days as it endlessly considered how best to woo the Soviet Union to its side, then his description is an apt one. But if he believed that it was only the mass of the people who were deceived, then he was himself deceived, for the leadership too was practicing a kind of self-deception on a massive scale. Yet, from the army's obstinate point of view, what alternative was there? Direct negotiation with the enemy could only result in repeated insistence on unconditional surrender, which was not acceptable, nor had the enemy seen fit to provide any assurances in regard to the emperor; no other neutral nation (and the Soviet Union, it must be remembered, was still officially neutral) appeared strong enough to exert sufficient pressure on the Allies to gain more favorable peace terms than had been proposed; at the same time, the growing confrontation in Europe suggested Russia might be persuaded that Japan could be useful in much the same way that Japan hoped to make use of Russia. If it was a pipe dream, it was probably no sillier than that other grand illusion of the military—repelling an enemy invasion, gaining a great victory, and then dictating peace terms to the enemy instead of the other way around.

In its propaganda campaign to maintain the fighting ardor of Japanese civilians as well as soldiers, the army command now made use of rumors of Allied ruthlessness that were trickling out of defeated Germany. The country was to be divided into four occupied zones, with no government of its own; its productive capacity was to be dismantled; so-called war criminals were to be tried and punished; the defeated people were being given hardly enough food to sustain life; those German prisoners of war who were allowed to return to their homeland were forced to walk all the way back; others were being detained like slaves in the victorious nations to help in the work of rehabilitation. There was no end to the accounts of Allied atrocities in defeated Germany, and if the Germans were being treated in that brutal, inhuman fashion, what would happen to the Japanese should they be placed in a similar situation? Clearly, setting aside the problematic "good offices" of the Soviet Union in mediating an acceptable peace, there was no admissible alternative to continuing the war to the end, even though the end of the war might mean the end of Japan as well. To the people of the proud island nation who had never known defeat, death must be preferred to slavery.

Or so, at any rate, the army kept telling them. By 23 May it had mobilized nineteen new divisions and fifteen independent mixed brigades, many of them composed of aged veterans or young untrained recruits, ill-equipped and ill-armed. No matter: they could still give their lives, young and old, in defence of the sacred homeland. On that twenty-third day of May, in the palace, the emperor, wearing the uniform of commander in chief as well as all his decorations, presented each commander with his regimental colors. In March the emperor had conferred a total of sixteen new regimental flags; in April, eight; now in May, forty. Probably never since the Meiji Restoration had a Japanese emperor handed out so many regimental colors on a single day.

A bewildered nation understood that its war aim had now drastically changed from a grandiose dream of establishing a Greater East Asia Coprosperity Sphere to that of defending a beleaguered homeland, but, however bewildered and frightened they might have been, the people continued to play their futile game of follow-the-leader. What else, indeed, could they do? Their role had been clearly established back in 1882, when the Meiji emperor issued his imperial rescript defining the indomitable Japanese spirit (the *yamatodamashii*): the armed forces were not a mere fighting machine, they were men imbued with a great spiritual strength, a strength peculiar to the Japanese that must ultimately lead them to victory. Now the army, while it tirelessly pointed out that modern war was a war of scientific strategy, based on raw material and production, at the same time called on the people to rely upon their unique spiritual strength for final victory. Any contradiction that may have existed between a mid-twentieth-century war and a late nineteenth-century imperial rescript was not apparent to the army.

Its field service code called upon every enlisted man to exert himself to the utmost in the confident belief in final victory, and it was upon this assurance that the army made its plans for the defence of the homeland. "Japan's rise or fall," said the code, "is dependent on victory or defeat. Remembering the illustrious history of the Imperial Armed Forces, which in hundreds of battles have never known defeat, you must continue fighting to the end, for victory is certain."

As for civilians who might be exposed to enemy action during an invasion, the army insisted that they, like the fighting men themselves, were both protected and inspired by *yamatodamashii*. "The enemy," said the high command, in its Decree Concerning the Battle for the Homeland, "may advance using civilians, even women and children, as a shield, so as to dampen the ardor of the armed forces. Should they do so, no soldier must be in doubt that the civilians, men, women, and children, will gladly lay down their lives for the motherland. The armed forces must not hesitate to attack and so defeat the enemy." At the same time, the decree noted that during a battle the injured were not to be cared for; nothing mattered but a remorseless attack upon the enemy.

Such were the premises upon which the army proposed to engage and defeat the enemy when he invaded the home islands. Yet even within the highest echelons of the army itself, it was apparent to many that the most Japan could hope for was a temporary victory. If she succeeded in repelling an Allied invasion, clearly at great cost to both sides, then she would at least be in a position to secure more favorable peace terms. The Allies would think twice before attempting a second, perhaps equally costly invasion. This view was held by the minister of war himself, General Korechika Anami. Thus, at this point in the conduct of the war, a leading faction within the army and the still hopeful peace faction were nearing a rapprochement. Their chief point of difference was that the army faction desired to seek peace only after fighting a battle on Japanese soil; the peace faction desired to seek peace without doing so. It was rather a colossal point of difference, but it demonstrated, nonetheless, that both factions were at least facing in the same direction.

In the United States, meanwhile, on 25 May, the Joint Chiefs of Staff issued directives to the commanders in the Pacific to prepare for an invasion of Japan. Code-named Olympic, the invasion was to begin on 1 November on the island of Kyushu, from which it would then move to the main island, Honshu, on which both Tokyo and Osaka are located. It was anticipated by the Joint Chiefs of Staff that the Japanese would almost certainly put up an extremely stiff resistance, which might well result in staggering American losses.

It was the duty of General Arnold, chief of the United States Air Corps, to soften, so to speak, the home islands, in an attempt to lessen potential American losses in the projected invasion. Based in the Marianas, General Arnold's B-29s were indefatigable. Between 9 March and 16 April they had conducted low-flying raids over Tokyo, Kawasaki, Nagoya, Kobe, and Osaka, destroying large areas of these cities with incendiary bombs and drastically reducing Japan's productive power. During the latter part of April, raids had been directed chiefly at aircraft plants; this may have been due, at least in part, to a temporary shortage of incendiary bombs at the bases. During the first half of May, the B-29s had raided airfields in Kyushu, and by the second half of the month there was no longer, presumably, a shortage of incendiaries, for the superfortresses recommenced their night fire-bombings of the cities.

Tokyo, the prime target, was visited on 24 May by over five hundred planes and once again on 26 May by a similar number. Virtually the whole of the western, northern, and central parts of the city were wiped out. It has been estimated that after those two raids had ended, some fifty-one percent of the capital had been transformed into rubble. The destruction was in fact so thorough that Tokyo was now, at least for the moment, removed from the list of targets for incendiary bombing.

A vast number of the capital's major buildings were hit, including the Imperial Palace itself. The palace, behind its moats and surrounded by trees, consisted of a number of buildings, of which the main one, the chief symbol of the empire, was constructed in October 1888 for the Meiji Emperor, who had moved his capital from Kyoto to Tokyo. Adjacent to it were two other buildings, in the rear one of which the emperor and empress had lived before moving to the more secure concrete dwelling called the Obunko. Beneath it had been built a bomb shelter for the imperial couple, and there, during the night of the twenty-fifth, they took refuge.

Guarding the palace that night were nearly ten thousand soldiers, government workers, and fire-fighters, together with more than forty fire engines. Despite their best efforts, a strong wind fanned the flames, and in less than four hours twenty-seven buildings were destroyed. These included the main building, where the fire apparently started in the roof, as well as the adjacent rear building, which still contained a number of important paintings and other art objects. General Mori, commander of the Imperial Guards Division, who had come immediately to the site, ordered every soldier of the division to grab what he could and carry it to safety. General Tanaka, commander of the Eastern District Army, also rushed to the palace, but the efforts of both generals did little good, although much was salvaged before the buildings burnt down.

Apparently the first reports of the destruction of the palace buildings, which had hitherto seemed immune to enemy action, were telephoned to Sadataka Hisamatsu, the emperor's aide, who in turn reported immediately to the emperor. He paled upon hearing the news; then, after a few moments' silence, so the report goes, he murmured, "So, the palace has burnt down." His tone was sad, although later, again according to report, he said he felt better now that he was sharing the destruction with the rest of his people. In any case, after that one remark, he was silent the rest of the night; the next afternoon he and the empress made their difficult way through the rubble of the buildings. At that time he thanked the many people who had tried to save the vanished structures, and he also expressed his sorrow at the loss of life that had occurred during the bombings and the subsequent fires.

Both General Tanaka and General Umezu (the army chief of staff) sought to assume responsibility for the loss, but the minister of war, General Anami, refused to accept their resignations. He announced that he was responsible for the defense of the country's capital city, and finally the emperor himself was forced to command him not to resign. Anami's resignation at that time might have brought down Suzuki's government and might have made Japan's difficult decision to surrender more difficult still.

A few days later, on 29 March, some eight hundred men of the 509th

Group arrived at Tinian on the *Cape Victoria*, to be welcomed by the advance party that had arrived ten days earlier by air. Of the group's two thousand men, including scientists and technicians, approximately half were now in Tinian. As soon as the new men arrived, they were cordoned off from other fighting units based on the island, and the strictest secrecy was observed. It was, therefore, something of a surprise when the voice of Tokyo Rose was heard welcoming the men to the area and using the group's code number. This somewhat astonishing fact was not, however, thought to compromise the mission of the 509th, which was still what it had been—to drop a single bomb, and then escape. Only the target remained unknown and undecided.

This was one of the questions that challenged President Truman's interim committee on the atomic bomb, which met in the offices of the secretary of war, in Washington, on 31 May and 1 June. On 31 May, in Japan, Kanji Kunieda, the author, made the following entry in his diary: "The great Kanto earthquake of 1923 destroyed more than half of Tokyo, and even the Ginza went up in flames, but during peacetime it was possible to recover from so great a disaster in just a couple of years. Now enemy planes sweep down on Japan, raining death and destruction over all of us. How long will it take us to recover from this disaster? Or will Tokyo be like Hamburg and London? Will it return to the time when the plain of Musashino was still covered with reeds? Though a country may lose a war, its mountains and its rivers continue to exist. How tragic it is that the military led us into this war without foreseeing the might of the enemy! Am I the only one to think so?"

CHAPTER 6 **JUNE 1945**

As the first days of June ushered in the rainy season, the people of Hiroshima were beset by a series of strange and conflicting rumors, rumors so contradictory that the people hardly knew what to believe. For one thing, there no longer seemed to be any question that Field Marshall Shunroku Hata, commander of the Second General Army, had established his headquarters on the city's East Parade Grounds. That presumably meant, then, that Hiroshima was destined to become a front line in the forthcoming battle for Japan and destined also, inevitably, to find itself the target for Allied air raids.

So far there had been only one, that of 30 April, but almost nightly now the people heard B-29s roaring over the city and almost nightly alerts were sounded, but as yet no more bombs had fallen. The planes, dropping mines in the Inland Sea, continued to spare Hiroshima. While its citizens depended, somewhat overoptimistically, on their rivers and their firebreaks to protect them from the worst ravages of incendiary bombings, they continued to listen, in silent horror, to tales whispered by refugees from Tokyo and Osaka.

It was not safe to tell such tales, nor was it safe to listen to them, for the Kempei-tai was everywhere, ready to pounce upon defeatists, pessimists, and traitors, and to arrest and punish them. These are foolish people, said the Kempei-tai, more to be pitied than condemned, but since our only hope of victory is to maintain our undying belief in victory such people must not be allowed to go about, spreading malicious and treasonable rumors.

Another rumor that soon gained currency in the bewildered city was that the United States would never bomb Hiroshima. Why? Because so many of its citizens had emigrated to America before the war, so many of them were now citizens of the United States. For that reason, America held Hiroshima in special esteem and would spare it from destruction. As the rumor moved on, it snowballed, as rumors do, until finally it acquired an explicit and circumstantial detail: President Truman had a relative living in Hiroshima; he would never permit it, therefore, to be bombed.

Would the city be transformed into a battlefield? Would it be devastated by B-29s? Would it be spared on orders of the president himself? No one knew what to believe: despair gave way to optimism, then optimism to despair. And how careful one had to be in discussing these matters! A slip of the tongue might land a man in a military prison. Better to go for walks in the surrounding countryside, where the paddy fields were green with new rice plants; better to admire the mountains in their summer finery or the now clear and placid waters of the Inland Sea; better not even to think about what the future might bring.

By 1 June, President Truman's interim committee had completed its deliberations and was ready to make its report; it had been meeting for two days. Later, Dr. Compton was to write: " 'Gentlemen, it is our responsibility to recommend action that may turn the course of civilization. In our hands we expect soon to have a weapon of wholly unprecedented destructive power. Today's prime fact is war. Our great task is to bring this war to a prompt and successful conclusion. We may assume that our new weapon puts in our hands overwhelming power. It is our obligation to use this power with the best wisdom we can command. To us now the matter of first importance is how our use of this new weapon will appear in the long view of history.'

"This, as accurately as I can recall it, was the statement made by Secretary of War Henry L. Stimson as he presented to the 'Interim Committee' the question of what should be done with the atomic bomb. The place was the Secretary's office in Washington. The date was 31 May 1945."[13]

In Stimson's own words, the committee "held discussions which ranged over the whole field of atomic energy, in its political, military, and scientific aspects. . . . The committee's work included the drafting of the statements which were published immediately after the first bombs were dropped, the drafting of a bill for the domestic control of atomic energy, and recommendations looking toward the international control of atomic energy.

"But the first and greatest problem was the decision on the use of the bomb—should it be used against the Japanese, and if so, in what manner?

"The Interim Committee, on 1 June, recommended that the bomb should be used against Japan, without specific warning, as soon as possible, and against such a target as to make clear its devastating strength. Any other course, in the opinion of the committee, involved serious danger to the major objective of obtaining a prompt surrender from the Japanese. An advisory panel of distinguished atomic physicists reported that 'We can propose no technical demonstration likely to bring an end to the war; we can see no acceptable alternative to direct military use.' "[14]

Both Compton and Stimson explain how this decision was reached. According to Compton's account, "Throughout the morning's discussions it seemed to be a foregone conclusion that the bomb would be used. It was regarding only the details of strategy and tactics that differing views were expressed. At the luncheon following the morning meeting, I was seated at Mr. Stimson's left. In the course of the conversation I asked the Secretary whether it might not be possible to arrange a nonmilitary demonstration of the bomb in such a manner that the Japanese would be so impressed that they would see the uselessness of continuing the war. The Secretary opened this question for general discussion by those at the table. Various possibilities were brought forward. One after the other it seemed necessary that they should be discarded.

"It was evident that everyone would suspect trickery. If a bomb were exploded in Japan with previous notice, the Japanese air power was still adequate to give serious interference. An atomic bomb was an intricate device, still in the developmental stage. Its operation would be far from routine. If during the final adjustments of the bomb the Japanese defenders should attack, a faulty move might easily result in some kind of failure. Such an end to an advertised demonstration of power would be much worse than if the attempt had not been made. It was now evident that when the time came for the bombs to be used we should have only one of them available, followed afterwards by others at all-too-long intervals. We could not afford the chance that one of them might be a dud. If the test were made on some neutral territory, it was hard to believe that Japan's determined and fanatical military men would be impressed. If such an open test were made first and failed to bring surrender, the chance would be gone to give the shock of surprise that proved so effective. On the contrary, it would make the Japanese ready to interfere with an atomic attack if they could. Though the possibility of a demonstration that would not destroy human lives was attractive, no one could suggest a way in which it could be made so convincing that it would be likely to stop the war."[15]

That, then, appeared to be that: the committee was in agreement, and the bomb would be used in Japan. But, once again in Stimson's words, "the committee's function was, of course, entirely advisory. The ultimate responsibility for the recommendation to the President rested upon me, and I have no desire to veil it. The conclusions of the committee were similar to my own, although I reached mine independently. I felt that to extract a genuine surrender from the Emperor and his military advisers, there must be administered a tremendous shock which would carry convincing proof of our power to destroy the Empire. Such an effective shock would save many times the number of lives, both American and Japanese, that it would cost."[16]

Immediately after the committee's decision, James F. Byrnes, who was serving as the president's personal representative, reported to the chief executive, in whose hands ultimate decision lay. Byrnes explained the various considerations that had been taken into account by the committee before reaching its decision, including the high cost in American lives of an invasion of Japan proper. The president then "expressed the opinion that, regrettable as it might be, so far as he could see, the only reasonable conclusion was to use the bomb."[17]

But why "as soon as possible?" The obvious answer, of course, is that the sooner the bomb was dropped, the fewer the American lives that would be lost. That, clearly, must have been a prime consideration for American strategists. Considering, however, the amount of time the committee devoted to a discussion of Soviet capabilities and intentions, the thought may also have been present that the sooner the bomb was used, the less likelihood there was of Soviet armies occupying large areas of the Asian mainland and perhaps even of Japan itself. The Americans were aware, of course, that the Japanese had made, and were still making, overtures to the Russians.

Was there also, perhaps, present in some minds the fear that unless the bomb was used "as soon as possible," the opportunity to use it at all would be lost? In that case, the recommendation was eminently reasonable, for Japan's ability to wage war had already been virtually destroyed. Its precious store of oil was daily being depleted; its munitions and aircraft factories, ravaged by Allied raids, had been unable to recover their former productivity. During the month of September 1944, for example, 2,592 fighter planes had come off Japanese assembly lines; in May 1945, the figure had fallen to 1,592. Intensified Allied raids would, it was estimated, cause that figure to drop to some five hundred a month.

And if the Second World War was, as some have described it, "a war of steel," then Japan was now hopelessly outclassed. No longer permitted, by Allied air and sea activity, to import iron ore from abroad, her production of steel ingots during the period from April to June 1945 was approximately 150,000 tons, a fractional 18 percent of her peak production during the war. Other figures, such as those for production of coal, cement, liquid fuel, and shipping, were equally discouraging. The only wartime commodity that had increased in production was bamboo spears; people were still ordered out, both by day and by night, when air raids permitted, to hurl their spears against defenseless straw enemies.

Public morale was visibly deteriorating; the will to fight was waning fast, diminished by the increasing hardships of everyday life. Air raids took their terrible toll in both lives and dwellings; many of the homeless wandered barefoot through the city's streets. Food shortages grew by leaps and bounds. Under the circumstances, it is not surprising that crime was on the increase, even in so basically orderly a country as Japan. Walking through the center of the city, one might see a man tied to a telephone pole wearing a placard around his neck that read: "This man is a criminal who was caught looting a burnt out house. He is being exposed to public eyes as a warning to others."

Meanwhile, in America, the scientists who had worked so hard on production of the bomb were far from unanimous in feeling that it should now be used in Japan. They foresaw that it would add a new and wholly frightening dimension to the act of war, that the United States could not hope for very long to be the sole possessor of the bomb, and that for the United States to use the bomb now might well turn out, in the long run, to be against its own best interests.

Aware of this feeling on the part of his colleagues in the Chicago laboratories, Dr. Compton, upon his return from Washington, offered to convey these apprehensions to the interim committee in time for its next meeting. Accordingly, a "committee of social and political implications" was formed; its chairman was Professor James O. Franck, but its most active member was Professor Leo Szilard, the refugee scientist who had persuaded Albert Einstein to write his famous letter to President Roosevelt—the letter that had been largely instrumental in the creation of the Manhattan Project.

Even before the 31 May/1 June meeting of the interim committee, Professor Szilard had been campaigning against the use of the bomb in Japan. In his own words: "During the war, while we worked on the bomb, we scientists thought for a while that we were in a neck and neck race with the Germans and that getting the bomb first might make the difference between winning or losing the war. But, when Germany was defeated, many of us became uneasy about the proposed use of the bomb in the war with Japan. Many of us were uneasy about how the existence of the bomb would affect the position of the United States after the war.

"After President Roosevelt's death and six weeks before the bomb was tested in New Mexico, I tried to reach the White House and was directed to call upon Mr. Byrnes. There were three of us who went to see him, and H. C. Urey was one of us. Byrnes was not at that time Secretary of State, but he knew of the bomb and had given some thought to problems of foreign policy. The question of whether the bomb should be used in the war against Japan came up for discussion. Mr. Byrnes did not argue that it was necessary to use the bomb against the cities of Japan in order to win the war. He knew at that time, as the rest of the Government knew, that Japan was essentially defeated and that we could win the war in another six months. At that time Mr. Byrnes was much concerned about the spreading of Russian influence in Europe; Rumania, Bulgaria, Yugoslavia, Czechoslovakia, and Hungary were all living under a shadow cast by Russia. Mr. Byrnes's concern about Russia I fully shared, but his view that our possessing and demonstrating the bomb would make Russia more manageable in Europe I was not able to share. Indeed I could hardly imagine any premise more false or disastrous upon which to base our policy, and I was dismayed when a few weeks later I learned that he was to be our Secretary of State."[18]

Professor Szilard's antipathy was apparently reciprocated by Mr. James Byrnes, who was to write of his meeting with the scientist, "Szilard complained that he and some of his associates did not know enough about the policy of the government with regard to the use of the bomb. He felt that scientists, including himself, should discuss the matter with the Cabinet, which I did not feel desirable. His general demeanor and his desire to participate in policy making made an unfavorable impression on me."[19]

Be that as it may, it was now the task of the so-called Franck committee to marshal sufficient and sufficiently convincing arguments (if it could) to alter the recommendation of the president's interim committee to drop the bomb as soon as possible, without prior warning, on a suitably awe-inspiring target in the Japanese homeland. As to whether the United States should inform the Soviet Union of its imminent possession of the bomb, and of its intention to use it in the war against Japan, the interim committee had come to no final and clear-cut decision, contenting itself with making the recommendation that the United States "should seek an understanding with Russia."

That, of course, was precisely what Japan was trying to do, although in a different context, and whereas the United States would have been dealing from strength, Japan was dealing out of abysmal weakness. Obeying the decision of the Big Six, Foreign Minister Tōgō decided that the best way for Japan to enlist the sympathy, and ultimately the aid, of the Soviet Union was through Kōki Hirota, a former prime minister and a former ambassador to Moscow. Hirota signified his readiness to call on Jacob Malik, the Soviet ambassador to Japan, and explore the possibilities of a nonaggression pact between the two countries leading to outright Soviet aid. Hirota was aware that ultimately he would have to offer fairly drastic concessions, but at the first meetings between the two men, on 3 June and 4 June, the discussions centered mainly about Malik's impression that Japanese sentiment was anti-Soviet and Hirota's attempts to persuade him otherwise. These unofficial discussions, as Tōgō called them, ended inconclusively; although they were to be resumed again and again throughout the month, they were never destined to result in the desired rapprochement.

On 6 June, in Washington, the secretary of war conferred at length with the president on the recommendations of the interim committee; and on 6 June, in Tokyo, the Supreme Council for the Direction of the War met twice: from nine in the morning to twelve noon, and from two in the afternoon to six o'clock. Present at the meeting, in addition to the Big Six themselves, were several bureau chiefs and two cabinet ministers. The chief topic of discussion was a plan, drafted by the army, for the future conduct of the war, which the army wanted to see adopted by the supreme council before being presented to an extraordinary session of the Diet scheduled for the middle of the month.

The army's plan, entitled "Basic Policy for the Future Conduct of the War," contained no surprises. It contemplated the possibility neither of surrender nor defeat; it was concerned only with a final, and ultimately successful, battle on Japanese soil. It pointed out that Japan enjoyed two great advantages: the nature of its geography and the harmony of its people; and that with those advantages the battle might be brought to a victorious conclusion, "thus protecting our national polity, preserving our imperial land, and laying a secure foundation for the future prosperity of our race." High-sounding words for an armed force that was already all but defeated!

In support of the plan, Lieutenant General Torashirō Kawabe, the army's vice chief of staff, pointed out that military operations in the homeland would be "altogether different" from those on such outlying islands as Okinawa, Iwō Jima, and Saipan. When the enemy attempts to invade Japan proper, Kawabe said, "he will be met at the point of landing by an overwhelming Japanese force, which will continue its attack until he is defeated and turned back." Victory was to be achieved by (1) destroying a quarter of the invading forces while they were still at sea through the use of suicide planes, (2) destroying another quarter during the attempted landing, and (3) annihilating the remaining half after they had established a beachhead on Japanese soil.

Only the foreign minister was bold enough, forthright enough, and practical enough to speak out against the army's daydreams. He called the council's attention to a number of hard facts, including Japan's inability to recover its productive capacity and its lack of air supremacy. In the circumstances, he found himself unable to support the army's view that the nearer the enemy approached the homeland the more favorable grew the Japanese position. Questioned about the Soviet Union, Tōgō stated bluntly that he did not believe the Russians intended to become allied with Japan or to supply Japan with vitally needed raw materials.

The army repeated the points it had made, time and again, before: in the battle for the homeland Japan would not have to transport troops overseas, whereas the enemy would, making him extremely vulnerable; Japan still possessed a great number of airfields which had been undamaged by raids and from which Japanese planes could take off to strike at the enemy; the main force of the Imperial Army was still virtually intact; the Japanese terrain favored the defender, not the invader; and, as important as any other consideration, Japan had the will to win. A country is defeated, said the army, only if it believes it has been defeated. Japan may be less well equipped materially than the enemy, but spiritually Japan is incomparably stronger; and while the quantity of matériel available is necessarily limited on both sides, there is no limit to the soaring of the spirit. Spirit must, in the end, conquer!

The foreign minister remained opposed; the minister of the navy, Admiral Yonai, remained silent; all the rest of the supreme council, including the prime minister, favored adoption of the army's "Basic Policy for the Future Conduct of the War." The die had presumably been cast.

The army, accordingly, on the very same day, issued to all troops garrisoned in Japan proper a pamphlet entitled "Quick Way to Learn Tactics for the Battle of the Homeland." After assuring the troops that this battle would be quite different from those fought on isolated islands, the pamphlet pointed out that the key to the engagement would be attack, never defense; that troops should entrench themselves on level ground; that the securing of airfields was of paramount importance; and that body-attack combat tactics must ultimately result in victory.

On 7 June the prime minister secured the approval of the cabinet for the army's "Basic Policy," and on the following day the Big Six, along with seven other officials, appeared before the emperor, ostensibly for him to make the final decision. But in fact the decision had already been made. By tradition, an imperial conference was never held until the emperor's ministers had achieved unanimity. This particular conference began at 10:05 in the morning and ended at 11:55; there could not, obviously, have been much time for discussion.

After a few gloomy words were spoken about the state of the country, the morale of the people, the decline in military productivity, and the almost certain refusal of the Russians to supply raw material, the army repeated its familiar arguments. The prime minister rose. "I believe," he said, "that the policy we adopt should be that which was agreed upon two days ago by the Supreme Council for the Direction of the War. I ask the chief cabinet secretary to read that policy aloud."

The familiar words droned on. When Hisatsune Sakomizu, the chief cabinet secretary, had come to the end, Suzuki rose again. "I ask all those," he said, "who have any opinions on this subject to express them now." There was a long silence. "In that case," said Suzuki, "I take it that all present are in favor." The prime minister then pronounced a few closing words: "Japan's situation at the present moment is indeed critical; she has reached the point where she can, so to speak, pull continued life out of the jaws of death. This cannot be accomplished by either wisdom or skill—we must simply surge forward to our final goal!"

The conference had ended. Everyone rose and bowed deeply; the emperor, who had not spoken a word, retired. His silence was customary. He was never expected to speak, only to lend by his presence the final imperial authority to the decisions that had already been reached by his ministers. He now returned to his study. What he did during the next two hours is not known; he had long since given up golf and riding, and his only exercise was a morning and evening walk in the palace grounds. Perhaps he now walked for a time to help him reach a decision. At all events, two hours after the imperial conference ended, the emperor was speaking about it with his lord privy seal, Marquess Kido. Kido's diary notes only: "I was with the emperor at the Obunko from 1:50 to 2:25." Within those few words there lay hidden an imminent and momentous change in Japan's destiny.

After the war, Kido revealed that this was the first occasion when the emperor told him what had occurred at an imperial conference. His Majesty bade Kido be seated, then pushed some papers across his desk and said, "This is what has been decided." His expression was troubled, his voice was sorrowful, and he seemed deeply tired. After Kido had read the policy statement, he understood that the emperor was thoroughly dissatisfied with it. When Suzuki had taken on the premiership at the emperor's command, there had seemed to be a tacit agreement that he would do everything possible to lead the country to peace; now he appeared to be willing to play, if not the army's game, at least a waiting game which might, in the end, turn out to be the same thing.

Recalling now the peace plan that had been proposed to him by Professor Nambara and his colleagues at Tokyo Imperial University, Kido reached the conclusion that the time had come when the course of the country must be changed. It must be steered in a diametrically opposite direction. He would himself do everything he could, but he was convinced that the only man who could effect so dramatic a change was the emperor himself. But assuming the emperor now desired to take action, there still remained the question of how he was to do so. The safest and surest way would have been to make overtures directly to the United States and Great Britain, but the army controlled all channels of communication; it would never allow such a message to leave the country.

There remained, then, only the Soviet Union, with which the army still hoped to treat. Kido, accordingly, on the following day, suggested to the emperor that he send a personal envoy to Moscow, asking the Kremlin to use its good offices in negotiating an honorable peace. This might well turn out to be no more than an unconditional surrender, but Kido, convinced that it was the only way to save the country from annihilation, was now also convinced that His Majesty agreed. He therefore advised the emperor that Japan must seek the best peace terms she could secure and she must do so *at once*. To wait for the military to decide in favor of peace would mean death for the country. Japan's situation was deteriorating so fast and so devastatingly that perhaps the army might now at last be ousted from the position of supremacy in national affairs that it had held for so many years; and the emperor might now be able to take the almost unthinkable step of commanding the supreme council to revoke its approval of the army's "Basic Policy for the Future Conduct of the War" and approve instead a practical plan to achieve surrender and peace. Feeling that the emperor was in accord, Marquess Kido set to work.

In the United States, meanwhile, the so-called Franck committee, the committee of social and political implications, had prepared a report for the secretary of war, protesting the use of the atomic bomb as recommended by the interim committee. "Scientists," wrote the scientists on the committee, "have often before been accused of providing new weapons for the mutual destruction of nations, instead of improving their well-being. It is undoubtedly true that the discovery of flying, for example, has so far brought much more misery than enjoyment and profit to humanity. However, in the past, scientists could disclaim direct responsibility for the use to which mankind had put their disinterested discoveries. We feel compelled to take a more active stand now because the success which we have achieved in the development of nuclear power is fraught with infinitely greater dangers than were all the inventions of the past."

On the subject of using the bomb against Japan, the report continues: "One possible way to introduce nuclear weapons to the world —which may particularly appeal to those who consider nuclear bombs primarily as a secret weapon developed to help win the present war— is to use them without warning on appropriately selected objects in Japan.

"Although important tactical results undoubtedly can be achieved by a sudden introduction of nuclear weapons, we nevertheless think that the question of the use of the very first available atomic bombs in the Japanese war should be weighed very carefully, not only by military authorities, but by the highest political leadership of this country.

"Russia, and even allied countries which bear less mistrust of our ways and intentions, as well as neutral countries may be deeply shocked by this step. It may be very difficult to persuade the world that a nation which was capable of secretly preparing and suddenly releasing a new weapon, as indiscriminate as the rocket bomb and a thousand times more destructive, is to be trusted in its proclaimed desire of having such weapons abolished by international agreement. . . .

"Thus, from the 'optimistic' point of view—looking forward to an international agreement on the prevention of nuclear warfare—the military advantages and the saving of American lives achieved by the sudden use of atomic bombs against Japan may be outweighed by the ensuing loss of confidence and by a wave of horror and repulsion sweeping over the rest of the world and perhaps even dividing public opinion at home.

"From this point of view, a demonstration of the new weapon might best be made, before the eyes of representatives of all the United Nations, on the desert or a barren island. The best possible atmosphere for the achievement of an international agreement could be achieved if America could say to the world, 'You see what sort of a weapon we had but did not use. We are ready to renounce its use in the future if other nations join us in this renunciation and agree to the establishment of an efficient international control.'

"After such a demonstration the weapon might perhaps be used against Japan if the sanction of the United Nations (and of public opinion at home) were obtained, perhaps after a preliminary ultimatum to Japan to surrender or at least to evacuate certain regions as an alternative to their total destruction. This may sound fantastic, but in nuclear weapons we have something entirely new in order of magnitude of destructive power, and if we want to capitalize fully on the advantage their possession gives us, we must use new and imaginative methods. . . .

"The development of nuclear power," the report concludes, "not only constitutes an important addition to the technological and military power of the United States, but also creates grave political and economic problems for the future of this country.

"Nuclear bombs cannot possibly remain a 'secret weapon' at the exclusive disposal of this country for more than a few years. The scientific facts on which their construction is based are well known to scientists of other countries. Unless an effective international control of nuclear explosives is instituted, a race for nuclear armaments is certain to ensue following the first revelation of our possession of nuclear weapons to the world."[20]

Of the actual writing of the report, Professor Eugene Rabinowitch said, in an interview with the National Broadcasting Company, that Szilard "was responsible for the whole emphasis on the problem of the use of the bomb which really gave the report its historical significance —the attempt to prevent the use of the bomb on Japan. While the authorship of the whole report was mine, the fundamental orientation was due above all to Leo Szilard and James Franck." The committee consisted of seven members in all: three physicists (Franck, Hughes, and Szilard), three chemists (Hogness, Rabinowitch, and Seaborg), and one biologist (Nickson).

On 12 June, Professor Franck brought a copy of the report to Washington, where he was met by Dr. Arthur Compton, who had undertaken to assist him in gaining the direct attention of the secretary of war. Stimson's attention, however, was not to be had, so the two men left their copy of the report with Gordon Arneson, recording secretary of the interim committee, accompanied by a letter from Compton to Stimson. Whether the secretary of war read either the letter or the report itself is not on record. Later Rabinowitch was to say it almost seemed as though the report had been dumped into the waters of Lake Michigan. In fact, as will be seen, the report was not wholly ignored, although it was apparently to have no effect whatsoever on top policy making.

On the same day another report was presented to another authority, where it received closer attention. The scene was the Imperial Palace in Tokyo; the man who made the report was Admiral Kiyoshi Hasegawa, former governor general of Formosa; and the man who received it was the emperor himself. Back in February, His Majesty had commanded Hasegawa to make a personal inspection of naval installations, air bases (including those used by kamikaze units), and arsenals. Now, as he stood in the presence of the emperor, the admiral read his discouraging report: Japan, quite simply, no longer possessed the equipment with which to wage a modern war. Nor had she the power to recover: she lacked raw materials, and production of essential armament had dropped almost to a standstill.

After Hasegawa had finished reading his report, the emperor bade him be seated and then proceeded to question him in greater detail. The admiral's replies only confirmed His Majesty's first dispirited impressions. As the audience came to an end, the emperor said that he had imagined the situation to be much as the admiral had outlined it and that there was no question in his mind about the accuracy of the report. With deep sorrow underlying every word he thanked Hasegawa for all his efforts; and after the admiral had withdrawn, the emperor realized to the full, perhaps for the first time, what utter fantasy was the army's plan to fight a last-ditch battle on the home islands. Now he knew that the illustrious history of the Imperial Army had truly come to an end: there remained no single vestige of hope for any kind of victory. Perhaps because of this realization, His Majesty now, for the first time since the war had started, succumbed to personal anxiety: for two days he lay in bed, prostrated by a stomach disorder.

He was unaware, of course, that the day before he received Hasegawa's discouraging report, fifteen B-29s, marked on their tails with a circle pierced by an arrow, had landed on the island of Tinian. And he was unaware, of course, of what their mission was to be.

While he lay in bed, his lord keeper of the privy seal was extremely busy. Meeting with Prince Konoye, Marquess Kido told the prince that "The time has come when someone must declare clearly and openly that the war has got to be brought to an end. I had hoped that Admiral Yonai might do so, but he hasn't acted. That leaves the task, then, to nonmilitary men. I have decided that I shall be the first to speak out, and if I am assassinated for doing so, that doesn't matter. Then you will have to be the next." It was not, after all, a very cheerful prospect but then these were not, for Japan, very cheerful times.

A practical and experienced man, Kido now began a round of talks with leading government figures who, he anticipated, might be likely to support, or at least tolerate, his plan. On 13 June he met both the prime minister and the minister of the navy in separate and private sessions. Explaining his project for sending a personal envoy to the Kremlin from the emperor, he was unaware that the Big Six had already come to a somewhat similar conclusion during the preceding month; the supreme council had, at any rate, decided that the Soviet Union now offered Japan's best, perhaps its only, hope for the future, although the nature of the Big Six approach was to have been rather different from that envisaged by Kido. In any case, Suzuki, having heard Kido out, told him nothing about the supreme council's decision; the prime minister merely agreed to the plan, saying he considered it sound and by all means worth trying.

Kido then called on Admiral Yonai, the navy minister. After Kido had finished speaking, Yonai smiled sorrowfully. "Yes, certainly I agree," he said. "But I am apprehensive about the belligerent stance taken by the prime minister. He keeps saying Japan must fight to the end. For that reason the cabinet cannot make any decisive move toward peace." Yonai added that because of this he had even been considering tendering his resignation.

Upon hearing this, Kido returned to the prime minister and repeated Yonai's words. Astonished (or pretending to be astonished), Suzuki cried, "Did Yonai say that? I always thought he favored continuing the war—*I* was worried about *him*!"

It seems odd that two members of the same cabinet, the prime minister himself and his minister of the navy, were both in favor of taking so momentous a decision as seeking peace, without either being aware of the other's thoughts. Attempts have been made to explain this apparent anomaly by evoking the Japanese word *haragei*, a word combining two characters—that for *hara* (meaning "belly") and that for *gei* (meaning "art" or "craft"). Together they may be thought of as referring to the political technique of a man, for reasons of expediency, hiding publicly what he privately believes. Thus, if Suzuki and Yonai had bared their minds to each other, neither could have been certain that the other was saying what he truly thought. *Haragei* may, indeed, account for the Japanese tendency to speak around a subject in the hope that a consensus will eventually emerge without anyone actually putting into words the desired decision. It may also account, at least in part, for the fact that Japan, knowing she had lost the war, took a tragically long time doing anything definite about it.

In any case, Kido, having presumably secured the approval of both Suzuki and Yonai, on 15 June (two days later) asked the foreign minister to come to his office at the palace. At that time he related the substance of his two conversations and asked Tōgō's cooperation in accelerating the peace plan.

"Of course," Tōgō replied, "I am in agreement with your project. But how can it be implemented in view of the decision taken the other day by the supreme council in the presence of the emperor? As long as that decision stands, I shall find it very difficult to further any movement directed toward peace."

This was, of course, a highly important point, for a decision reached in the presence of the emperor was considered final and immutable. "Indeed," Kido replied, "that is the purpose behind my present strategy. I shall try to persuade the prime minister to summon another meeting of the supreme council, at which the previous decision may be annulled. At the same time, I shall do my best to lead both the government and the high command in the direction of terminating the war. All this I propose to do myself. You, I hope, will initiate diplomatic moves toward peace as soon as possible."

Kido was a man of courage and conviction, but he could never have taken so decisive a stand had he not known that the emperor was also a man of great courage and conviction and that, once the emperor had made up his mind, he would not vacillate. In this case the emperor had clearly determined that surrender, unconditional or not, was Japan's only hope of salvation, and no one but the emperor had the power to overrule the intransigent military. It was not certain that even he had the power, but what was absolutely certain was that no one else had it. The past history of the Imperial Army was one of unswerving loyalty so long as the views of the emperor coincided, or seemed to coincide, with those of the Imperial Army. When it looked as though his views might differ from those of the army, then the army immediately sought out the "traitors" who had so "misguided" him. Assassination had been the army's ready answer in the past, and it might be the army's answer now. Assassination, invasion, civil war, and annihilation: they were all within the realm of immediate possibility.

On 16 June the scientific panel completed for the interim committee a report which Robert Oppenheimer sent on to George Harrison, the committee's secretary. Whether or not the members of the panel had a copy of the Franck report (Oppenheimer said later that they did not), they were thoroughly familiar with its contents and they came to the reluctant conclusion that they could not agree with it. Their report read, in part:

"The opinions of our scientific colleagues on the initial use of these weapons are not unanimous; they range from the proposal of a purely technical demonstration to that of military application best designed to induce surrender. Those who advocate a purely technical demonstration would wish to outlaw the use of atomic weapons, and have feared that if we use the weapons now our position in future negotiations will be prejudiced. Others emphasize the opportunity of saving American lives by immediate military use, and believe that such use will improve the international prospects, in that they are more concerned with the prevention of war than with the elimination of this special weapon.

"We find ourselves closer to these latter views; we can propose no technical demonstration likely to bring an end to the war; we can see no acceptable alternative to direct military use."[21]

Of this recommendation, Dr. Compton has written: "Ten days later, at Oppenheimer's invitation, Lawrence, Fermi, and I spent a long week end at Los Alamos. We were keenly aware of our responsibility as the scientific advisers to the Interim Committee. Among our colleagues were the scientists who supported Franck in suggesting a nonmilitary demonstration only. We thought of the fighting men who were set for an invasion which would be so very costly in both American and Japanese lives. We were determined to find, if we could, some effective way of demonstrating the power of an atomic bomb without loss of life that would impress Japan's warlords. If only this could be done!

"Ernest Lawrence was the last one of our group to give up hope for finding such a solution. The difficulties of making a purely technical demonstration that would carry its impact effectively into Japan's controlling councils were indeed great. We had to count on every possible effort to distort even obvious facts. Experience with the determination of Japan's fighting men made it evident that the war would not be stopped unless these men themselves were convinced of its futility. . . .

"Our hearts were heavy as on 16 June we turned in this report to the Interim Committee. We were glad and proud to have had a part in making the power of the atom available for the use of man. What a tragedy it was that this power should become available first in time of war and that it must first be used for human destruction."[22]

It was a tragedy also that the members of the scientific panel knew so little about what was happening in Japan. Had they been able to look into the mind of the emperor and measure the extent of his determination, had they known that powerful forces in the Japanese government were now, at last, however slowly, organizing themselves in opposition to the Imperial Army, the panel's recommendation might have been quite different. It might even have had an effect on the top-level planners of American strategy. But, as Oppenheimer was later to testify before the personnel security board, "We didn't know beans about the military situation in Japan. We didn't know whether they could be caused to surrender by other means or whether the invasion was really inevitable. But in the back of our minds was the notion that the invasion was inevitable because we had been told that."

Two days later, on 18 June, the service secretaries and the Joint Chiefs of Staff met in the White House with President Truman to secure his approval for that planned invasion. Code-named Operation Olympic, it was to take place on 1 November on the island of Kyushu. "There had apparently," Truman wrote later, "been some differences of opinion as to the best route to be followed, but these had evidently been reconciled, for when General Marshall had presented his plan for a two-phase invasion of Japan, Admiral King and General Arnold had supported the proposal heartily."

After saying that in view of the diversity of experience in other engagements, it was not sensible to give a precise estimate of numbers of casualties, Marshall predicted that casualties in the first thirty days of combat on Kyushu would not exceed those suffered in Luzon—31,000. He also said American casualties would almost certainly be smaller than those suffered in the Battle of Okinawa.

Admiral King supplemented Marshall's statement and said that, although all predictions were dubious, casualties in Kyushu would probably reach a figure midway between those for casualties suffered in Luzon and those in Okinawa. In Okinawa the landing forces had to make a straight frontal attack, but the assault on Kyushu was to be made on three sides simultaneously and there would be much more room for maneuver.

American deaths on Okinawa were between 42,000 and 44,000. Neither Marshall nor King indicated precise casualty figures but it was estimated that between 30,000 and 40,000 men would be killed. It was on the basis of these figures that the military use of the A-bomb without prior warning was recommended.[23]

Truman summed up: "The Army plan envisaged an amphibious landing in the fall of 1945 on the island of Kyushu, the southernmost of the Japanese home islands. This would be accomplished by our Sixth Army, under the command of General Walter Krueger. The first landing would then be followed approximately four months later by a second great invasion, which would be carried out by our Eighth and Tenth Armies, followed by the First Army transferred from Europe, all of which would go ashore in the Kantō plains area near Tokyo. In all, it had been estimated that it would require until the late fall of 1946 to bring Japan to her knees.

"This was a formidable conception, and all of us realized fully that the fighting would be fierce and the losses heavy. But it was hoped that some of Japan's forces would continue to be preoccupied in China and others would be prevented from reinforcing the home islands if Russia were to enter the war."[24]

Another subject that was discussed at this White House meeting was a proposal put forward by Joseph C. Grew, then acting secretary of state, formerly ambassador to Japan, that President Truman issue a proclamation urging the Japanese to surrender, at the same time assuring "them that we would permit the Emperor to remain as head of the state." Grew, Truman wrote, "favored issuing the proclamation at once, to coincide with the closing of the campaign on Okinawa, while the service chiefs were of the opinion that we should wait until we were ready to follow a Japanese refusal with the actual assault of our invasion forces.

"It was my decision then that the proclamation to Japan should be issued from the forthcoming conference at Potsdam. This, I believed, would clearly demonstrate to Japan and to the world that the Allies were united in their purpose. By that time, also, we might know more about two matters of significance for our future effort: the participation of the Soviet Union and the atomic bomb. We knew that the bomb would receive its first test in mid-July. If the test of the bomb was successful, I wanted to afford Japan a clear chance to end the fighting before we made use of this newly gained power. If the test should fail, then it would be even more important to us to bring about a surrender before we had to make a physical conquest of Japan. General Marshall told me that it might cost half a million American lives to force the enemy's surrender on his home grounds."[25]

On this same eighteenth day of June the Japanese prime minister, returning to Tokyo from a pilgrimage to the Ise Grand Shrines, summoned the Big Six to a conference, where their previous decision to fight the battle for the homeland was not actually revoked, although it was modified to the extent that they agreed that Japan should seek the good offices of the Soviet Union in mediating an end to the war. There was further agreement, however, that if the Allies persisted in their demand for unconditional surrender (which, so far as the Big Six could see, meant an end to the emperor system), then Japan would have no choice but to go on fighting.

In accordance with this decision, Tōgō, on the following day, asked Hirota to resume his talks with the Soviet ambassador, Jacob Malik, changing his tone somewhat so as to coincide with this new concession made by the Big Six. On 29 June, in an audience with the emperor, Tōgō reported on Hirota's activities, hearing at the same time His Majesty's judgment that Japan was no longer in a position to continue the war and that every effort should be made to bring it to an end as soon as possible. To this Tōgō gave his heartfelt consent, although he pointed out that the same conditions that made it impossible for Japan to continue fighting would make the securing of favorable peace terms difficult if not impossible. Sadly the emperor agreed that such was indeed the case.

In America the interim committee met again on 21 June, when it adopted the recommendation of the scientific panel, dismissing the Franck Committee's urgent appeal that the bomb be used as a demonstration rather than as a weapon of destruction. Its final recommendation, then, was that the bomb should be dropped as soon as possible on a suitable Japanese target without prior warning. This recommendation coincided with the personal opinions of both General Groves and the secretary of war, Henry Stimson. The interim committee also expressed its belief that Russia should be informed of America's intentions.

Meanwhile, both Kido and Tōgō were pressing forward in their efforts to bring an end to the war. Kido went so far as to confer with the minister of war himself, General Anami; this he did on 18 June, the same day that saw President Truman's approval of Operation Olympic. Anami had just returned from a tour of inspection of Matsushiro, in Nagano Prefecture, where a new general headquarters was being constructed and a huge bomb shelter was being dug underneath a mountain. It was here that the emperor was to take refuge while his army fought the "battle of Japan."

Bluntly Kido opened the discussion by announcing, "I would like to speak to the minister of war about bringing an end to hostilities." When Anami nodded impassively, Kido continued, "The Battle of Okinawa will end in defeat. Our ability to continue the war is virtually nonexistent. Now is the time, then, for us all to concentrate our efforts on ending it."

The ruddy-faced minister looked steadily at Kido for a time. Then he said: "It seems to me only natural for a man in your position to be of that opinion. But I am a soldier, and as a soldier I believe that we must first defeat the enemy when he invades the homeland. Then, when we negotiate for peace, we will be in a more favorable position."

"And do you," Kido countered quickly, "believe the enemy will be inclined to agree to our peace terms after he has completed his landing on Japan? If he does not, then we shall have no choice but to continue fighting, and that can only mean the utter annihilation of the country. The emperor himself is of the opinion that it would be futile for us to go on with the war, and he is deeply concerned about our plight."

Here was a dilemma for the war minister: as head of the army, he was responsible for its continued success; as a loyal Japanese, he was subject to the will of the emperor. How was he to resolve this dilemma? Much was to depend upon his final decision. Meanwhile, he reiterated his belief in the necessity for a military victory, at the same time signifying that he would not interfere with Kido's efforts.

Two days later, after Tōgō had reported to the emperor on the situation in regard to the Soviet Union, Kido had an audience in which he suggested that the emperor convene another imperial conference with the supreme council and that His Majesty himself take the initiative. There was no other way, said Kido, to revoke a decision already reached in the imperial presence. For a time the emperor was silent. Presumably in his mind was an awareness of the fact that it was wholly unprecedented for a Japanese emperor to convene an imperial conference in order to nullify what had already been decided in a previous imperial conference; and acts without precedent are not to be lightly undertaken in Japan. "Very well," the emperor said finally. "Let it be done."

On 22 June, then, at three o'clock in the afternoon, the Japanese emperor met with his Supreme Council for the Direction of the War and himself uttered the first words. They were not, as might have been expected on so unusual an occasion, imperial in tone, nor were they imperious; they were mild, even conciliatory. Pointing out, quite simply, that the Japanese situation had greatly deteriorated and that further deterioration could be expected in the future, he said that although the imperial conference of 8 June had ended with a determination to fight the war to the end, he now considered it necessary to examine other means for bringing an end to hostilities. He then asked the men sitting around him if they had any opinions on the subject.

They remained silent.

"Very well," said the emperor. "Let us hear first from the prime minister."

The old man got slowly to his feet. "It is indeed a great honor," he said, "to be addressed by His Majesty. In my opinion, although it is essential to continue the war, it is also essential to adopt diplomatic methods to bring an end to hostilities in coordination with the war effort. I will ask the minister of the navy to elaborate further on this point."

With this brief, ambiguous statement, Suzuki sat down again, and Yonai, after a moment, rose. "Although," he said, "I believe it would have been more appropriate for the minister of foreign affairs to reply to His Majesty's question, I will take advantage of this opportunity which has been offered me. Since 11 May the members of the Supreme Council for the Direction of the War have gathered informally several times in order to discuss the question of our relations with the Soviet Union. The conclusions that we reached were three-fold: first, a state of neutrality insofar as the Pacific war is concerned must be maintained; second, friendlier relations with the Soviet Union must be established; and third, the good offices of the Soviet Union should be utilized in an effort to mediate favorable peace terms.

"At that time, on the question of the third point, I expressed my opinion that its implementation should be postponed until a later date, an opinion that was approved by my fellow members of the supreme council. However, on 6 June, when I heard a report on the present strength of the country, I realized that our situation had reached an extremely critical stage. It seemed to me that the future of our country would be highly uncertain if we continued the war, and I felt very strongly that it was necessary for us to take steps to terminate the war. On 18 June, during an informal meeting, the supreme council came to the conclusion that the third point should be implemented as soon as possible but with the utmost caution in regard to the order and method of submission of overtures."

Yonai's somewhat fuller explanation seems, in retrospect, hardly less ambiguous than Suzuki's brief statement. The emperor now indicated that it was time for the foreign minister to speak. In reply, Tōgō repeated what he had already said at previous meetings of the council as well as in private audience with the emperor. In his opinion, he said, Japan now had no alternative but to seek the good offices of the Soviet Union in mediating a peace settlement, despite the ever present and extremely serious risks involved in such an action.

The emperor then asked how soon a diplomatic solution might be expected, and Tōgō replied that a Japanese envoy ought certainly to be in Moscow well before the Russians left for the Potsdam conference early in July. Once again he repeated that the course was a risky one, and that Japan must be prepared to make enormous concessions, yet that she had no real choice in the matter and that she must make peace overtures as soon as possible, before she was utterly defeated.

The emperor was silent for a moment, then turned to the army chief of staff and asked his opinion. Unhesitatingly Umezu replied: "I am in full accord with the statement made by the minister of the navy. However, inasmuch as peace offerings must necessarily result in powerful repercussions, both within and without the country, I advocate that the most extreme caution be used in making approaches to the Soviet Union."

Tenacious in his pursuit of peace, the emperor agreed that of course the utmost caution should be observed, but, he asked Umezu, if Japan is overly cautious, will she not be in danger of missing the opportunity to make peace before she is overwhelmed? Driven into a corner, Umezu had no choice but to agree that Japan should initiate peace overtures as soon as possible.

When the emperor now turned to the minister of war, General Anami rose and announced tersely that he had nothing to add to what had already been stated. With that the meeting came to an end. Unprecedented in the annals of Japanese history, this imperial conference, convened and opened by the emperor himself, had taken in all only thirty-five minutes, but it was Japan's first major step toward the ending of the war and toward the saving of millions of lives.

On this same day the United States officially declared a victorious conclusion to the Battle of Okinawa, although the people of Japan were not informed of the fact until 25 June. In reporting the Japanese defeat, the newspapers this time did not use the all-too-familiar term *gyokusai* ("death with honor," "death but not surrender"); they merely announced that the armed forces as well as the civilians on the island had fought valiantly for three months and that they had mounted their last attack on the main enemy force on 20 June.

Despite the disaster of the Okinawan defeat, the army reiterated its intention to fight and win the final battle on the soil of the Japanese homeland. This ceaseless asseveration, however, no longer had the desired effect; once the Okinawan defeat was announced, the mass of the Japanese people appeared to lose what little confidence they had still retained in the ability of the Imperial Army to defend the nation. A joke was whispered around the country to the effect that if the supreme command was driven by the enemy to the top of Mount Fuji, it would continue to insist that the war situation was still favorable to Japan.

Of course such comment was dangerous; if overheard, it brought swift retribution. Shūhei Hayama, an author who was then a seventeen-year-old student drafted to work in a munitions plant, has in his diary the following entry dated 26 June: "Today we were severely punished because we uttered among ourselves such seditious and unpatriotic statements as 'There is no longer any hope for Japan now that Okinawa has fallen' and 'How are we to fight the battle for the homeland with bamboo spears?' Along with five of our roommates, we were taken to a nearby meadow and made to sit down. Then we were pummeled until far into the night. This was for the good of the country."

Long smoldering friction between the people and the military establishment appeared likely to burst into flame at any moment. Wherever the army commandeered an area, the antagonism of the populace against its high-handed methods mounted. Farmers and fishermen living near strategic coasts who had been ordered to evacuate their land saw soldiers stealing their crops and looting their houses.

In an attempt to quell this growing friction, the government now put into effect two measures that had been passed a few days earlier, on 23 June, by the cabinet. These, known as the Voluntary Military

Service Law and the Wartime Emergency Measures Law, were aimed at placing the entire nation under the control of the supreme command and at mobilizing an enormous army with which to hurl back the invading enemy.

All men between the ages of fifteen and sixty and all women between seventeen and forty were liable to induction into the National Volunteer Battle Corps. The number of such men and women was estimated at twenty-eight million. Their duties were to build bunkers near their houses and to assist the regular armed forces by waging guerilla warfare against the enemy. They were subject to the same harsh rules that governed the conduct of the regularly inducted forces. Each so-called volunteer was given a leaflet that informed him, among other things, that he was of course expected to fight as bravely as possible against the enemy; that if he was so unfortunate as to be captured, he was to choose death rather than the disgrace of becoming a prisoner of war; that no matter how fierce the fighting might come to be, he was under no circumstances to leave his post unless ordered to; and that even though he might be wounded, he was expected to continue fighting as long as he was able.

And with what weapons was he to accomplish all this? During the latter part of the month the army displayed, at the prime minister's official residence, the arms that were to be made available to the volunteer corps. In addition to the familiar bamboo spears, these included bows and arrows, sickles, and old-fashioned rifles that had to be loaded through the barrel with powder or iron rods. Even the prime minister himself, a man who was not easily shocked, was horrified when he viewed this primitive display of armaments.

Nevertheless, his government, on 27 June, issued a proclamation that read, in part: "Japanese operations on Okinawa have not only inflicted great losses on the enemy but have also struck a severe blow at his fighting spirit. The Okinawa operations have paved the way for future action by our armed forces. It is expected that the enemy will intensify his air raids over Japan and may attempt an invasion of the homeland. Faced by a second 'Mongol horde,' we must realize that the time has now come to decide the fate of the Japanese empire." No doubt the army had insisted the government issue the proclamation, but it did nothing to reassure an increasingly apprehensive nation or to whip up its martial ardor. On the contrary, the proclamation dealt a severe blow to already weakening national morale. Was the Suzuki government attempting the impossible task of setting the nation afire and at the same time quenching the flames?

While it ostensibly sought to prepare the people for a last-ditch battle, the government was secretly conducting negotiations aimed at drawing the Soviet Union into the war on the Japanese side; if that failed, at securing Soviet raw material; if that too failed, at ensuring Soviet neutrality; and should that also fail, at securing Soviet good offices in mediating a peace. One might have thought such a program could be attempted only in a world of fantasy: it ignored not only the logic of war, it ignored also the simple realities of politics.

Yet this is precisely what Kōki Hirota, the former prime minister, sought to accomplish in his final talks with the Soviet ambassador, Jacob Malik. On 24 June, at Tōgō's insistence, Hirota told Malik that, in place of the neutrality pact which the Soviet Union had already renounced, Japan hoped for a more binding covenant. Malik replied that in the Soviet view the pact was still in force and would remain so, according to its terms, until April 1946, and that he did not believe his government was in favor of any other agreement. Hirota then attempted to barter Japanese rubber and other materials in return for Soviet oil, for Japan was desperately in need of oil, but once again Malik's reply was negative: the Soviets had no excess of oil to give Japan.

A few days later, on 30 June, Hirota had his final talk with Malik. At this time he suggested that, in return for a nonaggression treaty, Japan was prepared to offer far-reaching concessions. 'Among them were the withdrawal of all Japanese troops from Manchuria and (in return for Soviet oil) the giving up of fishing rights that Japan had previously held. Malik promised to transmit the Japanese proposal to Moscow, not by cable, but by means of a courier traveling by the Trans-Siberian Railroad.

This was hardly what Tōgō had hoped for. He did not, secretly, believe that the Hirota-Malik conversations would result in any concrete advantage for Japan, but he had hoped at least for a speedier reply. As the month of June ended, he realized that very little time remained if Japan was to enlist Soviet good offices before the Potsdam Conference. He could see only one other course that Japan might follow, and that was to send a special envoy to the Kremlin.

Or was it already too late? Japan's cities were a burnt out shambles; her people were hungry, disheartened, and resentful; Operation Olympic was almost through the planning stage; Tinian was a beehive of activity. Some of this was known to Japan's leaders, and some was guessed at; some was known to America's leaders, and some was guessed at; but the peculiar logic of war forbids the exchange of more cogent information that might result in the war's end.

CHAPTER 7 **JULY 1945**

By the beginning of the month, the fleets of B-29s based in the Marianas had bombed a number of Japan's smaller and more remote cities—among them Kagoshima, Ōmuta, Hamamatsu, and Yokkaichi (on 18 June); Shizuoka and Fukuoka (on 20 June); Kure (on 22 June); and Moji, Okayama, and Sasebo (on 29 June). In all, by the time the month of June had come to an end, eighteen cities, composed largely of wood, bamboo, and paper dwellings, had gone up in flames. Nowhere had any effective resistance been offered by Japanese antiaircraft fire. To the people of those cities, the superfortresses, gliding smoothly through the early summer skies, were beautifully awesome objects—and maddeningly hateful, for with their departure centuries of work had vanished in clouds of smoke and flame; left behind were uncountable survivors, now homeless, as well as even more hapless folk who no longer needed homes.

When, on the night of 30 June, until the dawn of 1 July, the prosperous and sheltered port of Kure, on the Inland Sea, was mercilessly bombarded, the people of Hiroshima could hardly avoid wondering when their own turn was coming, for Kure lies only a few miles distant. The towering flames of the burning port were visible on the horizon, while the planes that carried the bombs seemed to be flying over Hiroshima itself as they made their way toward the unlucky city. Hiroshima, convinced that it too would soon be a target for American military might, was almost eager to get its bombing over with. Then, at least, it would know the worst: it could stop living in constant fear and begin trying to cope with inevitable desolation. But still the indomitable B-29s continued to ignore the city.

Army engineers, meanwhile, were dynamiting the neighboring mountains in preparation for the construction of fortifications to be used in the coming battle for the homeland. Yoshio Ōhata, a barber in Hiroshima's Minamisanjo-machi, recalls to this day the continuing explosions that left great gaping holes in the once handsome mountains; and he recalls also watching the red skies over Kure throughout the night of 30 June and wondering how soon Hiroshima was destined for a similar fate. It was all so vivid in his mind that he still remembers how, the following day, his hands trembled so shockingly he was unable to wield the tools of his trade.

As it continued to dynamite the mountains, the army ordered the people of Hiroshima to gather pine needles and pile them into huge stacks around the newly bombed craters. Then, when the B-29s eventually did get around to Hiroshima, the army planned to set fire to the great mounds of pine needles, and the resulting smoke would, so the army claimed, camouflage the fortifications that were being constructed. If such a plan seems, in retrospect, to be almost ludicrously absurd, then one must remember that a drowning man, according to the proverb, will clutch even at a straw. In this case the straw was a pine needle, but was it any more ridiculous than hurling bamboo spears at other bits of straw? In the beginning, people all over Japan had piled bags of sand and buckets of water around their houses to protect them from the bombings. When the people saw how worthless such precautions were, they dug shallow holes under their dwellings as bomb-shelters, holes in which—when their houses were actually hit—they were burned to cinders. Now, in the final act of this tragic comedy, they were being commanded to pile up mounds of pine needles around the army's entrenchments. And dutifully, as always, they obeyed.

Ikuko Kumura, then a fourth-year student at the Hiroshima Prefectural Yamanaka Girls' High School who was living in a dormitory in Senda-machi, was ordered twice to go up into the mountains on such an expedition. This she did willingly, despite the backbreaking nature of the work, because she had been assured by her brother, a scholar at Kyoto Imperial University, that Japan would soon be in possession of that famous matchbox bomb powerful enough to destroy a battleship. It was spoken of, she recalls, as a uranium bomb. Meanwhile, until Japan had actually perfected the bomb, pine needles would have to do —pine needles and bamboo spears and ancient muskets dug out of heaven-knows-what imperial attic. Further action against the enemy consisted of drawing caricatures of Chiang Kai-shek on the streets, so that people could walk on him, or of President Truman on billboards, so that people could throw buckets of water at him. The latter went under the name of air defense drills, for the purpose of which the Truman drawings were metamorphosed into incendiary bombs.

Japanese who had actually experienced the inferno of a fire-bombing knew how tragically useless all this so-called preparation was. Mrs. Michiko Sawamura, for example, aged twenty-nine, who had lost her home in the Tokyo raids and had now returned to her native town of Hiroshima, was well aware that air defense drills were a waste of time, and that ordinary air raid shelters were not able to protect people against the blazing heat of an incendiary bombing. A man's only chance was to run as fast as he could; and if he was very lucky, he might escape. Those he left behind—the stumbling old men, the women with children —would be incinerated like insects in a blazing field. Mrs. Sawamura felt bitterly that the government and the army were making a tragic mistake in letting the people of Hiroshima think that buckets of water might save them when the fire bombs actually started falling. But how could she speak out? To speak out, in that crazed and hysterical time, might mean never to speak again.

Gathering pine needles and sticking bamboo spears into straw, the people of Hiroshima continued to wonder when the fire bombs were going to start falling on their city. They did not know—no one in Japan knew—that apparently as early as 3 July, instructions were sent from Washington to the commanders in the Pacific that the four cities of Kyoto, Hiroshima, Kokura, and Niigata were not to be bombed. The commanders were not told why, but it would seem obvious that these four cities had already been selected as possible targets for the big bomb. General Groves, who appointed the target committee to recommend the final selection, was in favor of Kyoto as "the preferred target," but Secretary Stimson ruled it out absolutely. In President Truman's words the secretary "pointed out that it was a cultural and religious shrine of the Japanese."[26] Nagasaki was eventually to be substituted for Kyoto. The problem was to find a populated area that would provide maximum shock to the Japanese war makers, that was also a military target, and that had not previously been bombed. Few cities satisfied all these requirements.

On 4 July the combined policy committee, made up of American, British, and Canadian representatives, met in Washington. Other members of the governments and their services were also present. Sir Henry Maitland Wilson, head of the British Joint Staff Mission in Washington, conveyed his government's approval of the American intention to use the atomic bomb in Japan; this was in accord with the Quebec agreement of 1943. Wilson also reported that Churchill and Truman might discuss the matter further at Potsdam, a little later in the month; but there would seem never to have been any possibility in the mind of either the president or the prime minister that the bomb would not be used. On this subject, Truman has been likened to a little boy on a toboggan racing downhill. In his own words, "The final decision of where and when to use the atomic bomb was up to me. Let there be no mistake about it."[27] Where and when; not whether—let there be no mistake about that either. To Churchill, perhaps, a consideration equally as important as putting an end to the Pacific war was his belief that America's possession and use of the bomb would make Stalin less rambunctious in both Europe and the Far East.

Had the United States secretary of war known about little Ikuko's older brother and his prediction that Japan would soon have the most lethal matchbox in the world, would he have remained so adamant on the subject of sparing the country's ancient and historic capital? For it was there, now that N-research had come to a fiery end in Tokyo, that Japan was making a frantic, last-minute effort to produce an atomic bomb. This was taking place in one of Kyoto Imperial University's two physics research laboratories.

Kyoto itself was still a strangely peaceful city, a happy anomaly in a war-ravaged country. Although food and clothing, here as elsewhere, were in extremely short supply, and although posters in the show windows of the city's department stores warned its people that air raids might be expected at any time, lights still burned brightly in the shops. Carefree pigeons fluttered among the venerable paulownia trees that lined the city's streets and in the vast compounds of the age-old temples. An historic center for Japan's Buddhist sects, Kyoto remained calm and tranquil, blissfully unaware that General Groves considered it the "preferred target" for his atomic bomb, while Secretary Stimson continued to insist it must be spared.

No doubt most of its citizens were also blissfully unaware that in the research laboratory headed by Professor Bunsaku Arakatsu, work was going on, both by day and by night, in an attempt to separate U-235 through the ultracentrifugal method. The Nishina laboratory in Tokyo, under the auspices of the army, had tried, and failed, to produce U-235 by means of heat diffusion. The Arakatsu project in Kyoto was proceeding under the orders of the navy, which, having lost most of its ships, was now trying to reestablish itself through a new and decisive weapon. When it had first approached Arakatsu, he had replied that producing the bomb would be impossible in time for it to be used during the war. The navy countered blandly that in that case it could be used in the next war; Arakatsu and the scientists who worked under him were ordered to carry out research around the clock. The navy's code name for the project was F-research, "f" for "fission."

Of course Professor Arakatsu was correct in his initial unwillingness to go ahead with it: Japan possessed neither the necessary technology nor the necessary raw material. According to the laboratory's calculations, a machine was needed that would turn at more than one hundred thousand revolutions a second. Japan's technology at that time made it possible to build a machine that did not exceed forty thousand revolutions a minute: a vast, indeed an insuperable difference. It was a splendid challenge to the young brains at the laboratory, but it was a challenge they could not possibly meet within a reasonable length of time. Many ideas were offered; some were accepted and tried out; none succeeded.

Another insurmountable obstacle was the ore itself. Professor Kiichi Kimura, who was in charge of this aspect of the problem, estimated that in order to produce a chain reaction a mass of pure U–235 between ten and twenty centimeters in diameter would be a minimal requirement. But to secure that minimal critical mass, an astronomical amount of uranium ore was needed—and Japan simply did not have it. F-research was destined to be no more successful than N-research had been: Japan had entered the atomic race far too late and with far too little.

The top military and civilian leaders of the country were aware, of course, that such research was still going on and that, as yet, it had met with no success. Assuming that the United States was engaged in similar research, they came to the illusory, wishful conclusion that the production of such a weapon would be as impossible for the enemy as it had been for Japan. The army, accordingly, went on with its fanciful plans to repel the invader, while the pro-peace faction in the government, although assuredly aware that it did not have all the time in the world in which to move, seemed unable to take one step forward without then taking two steps backward.

On 4 July, in Washington, the combined policy committee had agreed that the atomic bomb should be used in Japan; on 5 July President Truman had assented. On those same two days, Japan's military leaders, assembled at Sixth Army Headquarters in Fukuoka, were busy making their plans to engage the Allies when they attempted to land on the island of Kyushu. The plan was the familiar one of battering the enemy both while he was heading toward Kyushu and, while he was seeking to land on its beaches, making use of suicide attacks by planes, submarines, and small craft. Of the sixteen enemy divisions that, it was estimated, would steam toward Miyazaki some time in October, the military believed it could annihilate a third while still at sea and another third during the landing. Against the remaining third the Japanese high command anticipated it could wage the battle for Kyushu on fairly equal terms—and, of course, win it.

On the basis of past experience, the military estimated that one out of ten suicide planes would score a direct hit, which meant that at least four thousand planes (along with their pilots) would have to be expended in order to sink four hundred enemy ships. This was considered a practical plan; the grossly conspicuous consumption of young Japanese lives that would necessarily be involved in the operation was not of interest to the military strategists meeting at Fukuoka.

It was, however, a matter of great concern to their commander in chief, and on 7 July he once again took the initiative, summoning his prime minister to an audience. A national holiday of long tradition in Japan is held on 7 July. Imported from China at least as early as the eighth century, it celebrates the one night of the year in which two loving stars on either side of the Milky Way, Altair and Vega, are permitted to meet. Customarily fruit and sweets made of paper were hung on bamboo poles, along with suitable poems inscribed on paper streamers. It was a festival especially favored by young lovers, but this particular seventh day of the seventh month it was not observed; enemy air raids made festivals seem somehow irrelevant.

The raids did not, however, prevent the emperor from conferring with Baron Suzuki. In sharp, quick tones, His Majesty wanted to know what was happening with regard to the Soviet Union; he made it clear that he considered Japan to be wasting precious moments in these prolonged and inconclusive negotiations through the Japanese ambassador to Moscow. After hearing Suzuki's halting and embarrassed reply, the emperor announced curtly that he desired to send a personal envoy to the Kremlin with a message from the throne. It was obvious that the only purpose of this message could be to secure Soviet good offices in mediating peace between the belligerents.

On that same day the foreign minister left Tokyo to call on Prince Konoye at his villa in Karuizawa, a hill resort some ninety miles from the capital. It was Tōgō's mission to persuade Konoye to serve as the imperial envoy. The two men did not actually meet until the following day, at which time Tōgō explained the situation and Konoye agreed to undertake the mission on condition that his hands should not be tied by the foreign ministry. He must, he said, feel free to treat with the Russians as he deemed best. Tōgō replied that anything short of unconditional surrender would be acceptable; but apparently there was a tacit agreement between the two men that even unconditional surrender would be found acceptable so long as the continued existence of the imperial house was guaranteed.

Here was the crux of the whole matter, and were its results not so tragic, it might now be perceived as the peg on which to hang a whole comedy of errors. Throughout the month, Captain Zacharias continued to record Japanese language broadcasts, to be beamed across the Pacific, in which he attempted to make clear to the Japanese people that those dreaded words "unconditional surrender" meant the laying down of arms; they did not mean the enslavement of the nation. Unfortunately, Zacharias was not empowered to make any statement in regard to the emperor himself, despite the fact that a number of America's high policy makers favored the issuing of just such a statement.

On 2 July the secretary of war "wrote a memorandum for the President," in which he said, among other things, that he believed a statement should be issued assuring the Japanese that Allied troops would be withdrawn from Japan "as soon as there has been established a peacefully inclined government, of a character representative of the masses of the Japanese people. I personally think that if in saying this we should add that we do not exclude a constitutional monarchy under her present dynasty, it would substantially add to the chances of acceptance."[28]

Joseph C. Grew, who had been America's ambassador to Japan before the war and who in 1945 was serving as acting secretary of state, expressed much the same opinion somewhat more forcibly. "Throughout the war," he was to write in 1950, "I took the position that propaganda by any branch of our Government against the Emperor of Japan, or any effort to bomb the Emperor's palace, should be withheld. I knew very well that when the time came for Japan's surrender, the Emperor was the only one who could bring it about, and that by issuing an Imperial Rescript, a document sacred to all Japanese, he alone could put it into effect."[29]

After the Japanese surrender had been effected, Tōgō himself was to write: "It now became clear to members of the cabinet that continuation of the war was no longer possible. The minister of agriculture (Tadaatsu Ishiguro), the minister of education (Kōzō Ōta), and two state ministers (Seizō Sakonji and Hiroshi Shimomura), among others, called on me to express their belief that the war must be brought to an end as quickly as possible. Others who were not members of the government came to me with the same thought in mind. Professor Shigeru Nambara and Professor Hasshaku Takagi of Tokyo Imperial University informed me that they believed the time was now ripe to put an end to hostilities."

Thus, on both sides of the Pacific, men were actively working to achieve an immediate peace that would have rendered the use of the bomb superfluous. Unfortunately, also on both sides of the Pacific, other men were working toward other ends. Many Americans in high positions, as well as many of America's allies, were bitterly opposed to retention of the emperor; some advocated that he be punished for his wholly illusory role in formulating Japanese war policy. Once again in Grew's words, "The Emperor had been charged with responsibility for the war, because he gave his approval to the attack on Pearl Harbor. Only those who are fully conversant with the former Japanese system of government can understand why the Emperor who, from all available evidence was bitterly opposed to the war, could not have stopped the attack. . . . Had the Emperor refused to approve the order for the Pearl Harbor attack, there would seem, in the light of the facts as we now know them, little doubt that he would either have been by-passed by the armed forces, or actually held in restraint, so that the military could have their way."[30]

In Japan the militarists used the Allied failure to guarantee the emperor's status to lend strength to their battle cry that the war must be fought to the end, that only by so doing could Japan hope to preserve her national policy. It was now this same, still intransigent army that had to be informed of Prince Konoye's projected peace mission. So far the mission had been kept secret from the minister of war, General Anami, but it could be kept secret no longer, since Konoye—if he went—would have to fly from Tokyo to Moscow. Marquess Kido had often remarked that he, as well as anyone else who worked for peace, stood in constant danger of assassination by fanatical militarists. Would they now permit Konoye to embark on a mission the purpose of which could only be surrender?

On 10 July the question was tentatively broached at a secret meeting of the Big Six—and only tentatively answered. It was a day of constant harrassment by the enemy; alerts sounded not only in the capital itself but also in the districts of Nagano, Yamanashi, Shizuoka, Chiba, and Saitama. Of that day Professor Rintaro Fukuhara, of Tokyo University of Education, wrote: "The morning was fresh and clear. As early as five o'clock small planes began attacking the city, and the raids continued throughout the day. Apparently the enemy's mobile forces are situated somewhere on the sea east of Tokyo, and the main targets of these carrier-based planes are the airfields in the Kanto district. Because of the raids I was unable to get to the University."

The raids did not, however, prevent the Big Six from meeting, for they used the underground bomb shelter at the prime minister's official residence. Few records have been kept of this meeting, although Admiral Yonai, the navy minister, later jotted down a memorandum of the main points that were discussed. Presumably Suzuki opened the meeting by announcing that on 7 July, in an audience with the emperor, he had been commanded to send an envoy to Moscow with a personal message from the throne as soon as possible. The emperor, according to Suzuki, had added that if the negotiations proved successful, Japan could anticipate peace; if they failed, and if the war had to be fought to the end, then the unity of the people would be strengthened. Suzuki said that the main purpose of this meeting of the Supreme Council for the Direction of the War was to decide on what reply should be made to the emperor's command, a reply that Suzuki had promised to deliver on the following day.

Yonai's memorandum is not altogether satisfactory. "The four ministers and the two chiefs of staff," he wrote, "then offered their

opinions on this point, but I shall refrain from noting them down here."
Yonai did, however, record a summary of the advice that the Big Six
agreed was to be offered to the emperor. They concluded that diplomatic negotiations should be initiated with the Soviet Union with
regard to sending an envoy; they pointed out, however, that time
would be required to select a suitable envoy, to receive permission from
the Soviet Union for him to undertake the mission, and for him to
make the actual journey to the Soviet capital; at the same time, they
came to the rather tenuous conclusion that it would be possible for the
will of the emperor to be communicated to Marshal Stalin before the
envoy was finally sent.

In other words, then, both General Anami and General Umezu had
given, if not open, at least tacit consent to the imperial desire. This
attitude was somewhat clarified after the war when Genki Abe, then
home minister, repeated what he had been told by Admiral Soemu
Toyota, chief of naval operations: "The foreign minister announced
that he personally favored the selection of Prince Konoye as the imperial envoy. No one opposed this opinion, but at the same time no one
approved it." The military, presumably, were still engaging in their
favorite day dream of preserving Soviet neutrality while they prepared
to repel an enemy invasion, paving the way for a more favorable peace.

On the following day, at three in the afternoon, the emperor made
a half hour tour of inspection of the work that was then going on to
reinforce the palace's underground bomb shelter. Although the army
had already completed a hopefully impregnable shelter at Matsushiro,
in Nagano Prefecture, the emperor had refused to indicate that he
would take himself and his family there should Tokyo become even
more unsafe than it already was. There seems to be no question that in
the emperor's mind echoed the realization that if he left the capital he
would lose all control over the army: Japan would then have no choice
but to fight the final battle. In view of the emperor's attitude, the army
had undertaken to make the palace bomb shelter strong enough to
withstand a direct hit by a ten-ton bomb—for that, they were told,
was what the Americans had dropped on Berchtesgaden.

The work of reinforcement, given the name of Operation No. 1, was under the supervision of the commander of the Imperial Guards, Lieutenant General Takeshi Mori. The shelter was located only a hundred yards from the Obunko, where the emperor was living and was camouflaged by a great green net so that it could not be distinguished from the foliage of the palace grounds. On the afternoon, then, of 11 July, the Japanese emperor, with the hope for peace in his heart, inspected the shelter that was to house him while his army fought on and on, while his people were annihilated and his country laid waste. It could not have been a happy half hour for him. While he was there, Commander Mori offered explanations of how the work was proceeding; the emperor's only reply was an occasional "*Ah, sō.*"[31] An officer directing certain technical aspects of the reconstruction work reported later: "I believe the emperor stood on the inspection platform for about twenty minutes. At his appearance, clouds massed overhead and rain threatened but did not actually fall while he was on the platform."

The twelfth of July saw the gathering momentum of Japan's tardy will to peace. Early in the morning, without advance notice, the prime minister called on Marquess Kido, who was then living at the house of his brother, since his own official residence had been destroyed during a raid. Suzuki came to the point at once: he desired Kido to request the emperor to summon Prince Konoye to an audience that very day and appoint him as his special envoy to the Kremlin. Fortunately, Suzuki added as he made an abrupt departure, Konoye had already returned from his villa in Karuizawa.

Reporting as soon as possible to the emperor, Kido repeated the prime minister's request. In his diary for the day, Kido noted: "His Majesty was extremely pleased when he heard Suzuki's plea and gave his immediate approval. He informed me that he would call Konoye to the palace that very afternoon." Not long after Kido left the imperial presence at the Obunko, Suzuki himself appeared and repeated the same request, that the emperor command Prince Konoye to undertake the mission to Moscow.

At three o'clock in the afternoon, accordingly, the emperor— departing from precedent—received Konoye in absolutely private audience. It had become customary for at least one other person (a chamberlain or an aide-de-camp) to be present when the emperor granted an audience; but on this particular occasion the two men were alone: they were free to speak their minds in complete privacy.

The audience itself was a brief one. The emperor asked Konoye point-blank to express his opinions on Japan's present situation. Konoye replied that although the army continued to insist on pursuing the war, he did not find the army's figures accurate, a point of view with which the navy appeared to concur. At the same time, he said, the morale of the people was deteriorating, and they seemed to be eager to see an end to the war. Some even went so far as to criticize the emperor himself. Under the circumstances, he concluded, it was desirable to terminate hostilities as soon as possible.

In that case, the emperor replied at once, he would like the prince to consider undertaking the all-important mission to Moscow. Despite his distrust of the Soviet Union and his oft-expressed fears of a Communist revolution in Japan, Konoye, alerted beforehand by Tōgō, offered his immediate submission to the imperial desire. He would willingly go to Moscow, he said, even though it might cost him his life.

Upon leaving the palace, he hastened at once to the official residence of the prime minister, where he discussed the subject of the mission with both Suzuki and Tōgō. The attitude of the Soviet Union would, of course, be the crucial point. The foreign ministry, up to that time, had followed a policy of keeping secret its intention of requesting Soviet mediation while at the same time it attempted to fathom Russia's true attitude. Suzuki now said he was opposed to that policy; he was in favor of absolute frankness. Tōgō countered with a suggestion that Japan inform the Soviet Union it desired to send an imperial envoy, then—only after it had determined what the Soviet attitude would be —cable the contents of the communication from the throne. Suzuki replied that in his opinion it would not be possible to determine what Soviet intentions were likely to be and that, in any case, Japan was no longer in a position to procrastinate.

At 8:50 that night Tōgō sent a cable to Naotake Satō, Japan's ambassador in Moscow, instructing him to inform Molotov—before the meeting of the three powers at Potsdam—of the desire of the emperor to terminate the war as speedily as possible and to send Prince Konoye as a special envoy to Moscow to further that desire. "His Imperial Majesty," the cable said, in part, "is deeply concerned about the ever increasing sacrifices being made and losses being sustained by the peoples of the countries engaged in the war and fervently hopes for a cessation of hostilities as soon as possible. However, so long as the United States and Great Britain adhere strictly to a policy of unconditional surrender, Japan will have no alternative but to continue to fight on to the very end for her honor and her very existence."

On the following day, Satō requested a meeting with Molotov but was told that the foreign minister, engaged in preparing for the forthcoming Potsdam Conference, was too busy to see him. The ambassador then had no choice but to confer with a deputy foreign commissar, Alexander Lozovsky, to whom he presented a Russian translation of the emperor's desires as they had been outlined in Tōgō's cable. Politely, Lozovsky pointed out that Molotov would not have time to reply to the Japanese suggestion before he left for Berlin but promised to pass the communication on to him immediately. Lozovsky also agreed to Satō's suggestion that Molotov should telephone from Potsdam as soon as possible, in order that Japan might have the necessary time in which to prepare for Prince Konoye's mission. Then, several hours later, Lozovsky telephoned Satō to tell him that the Kremlin's reply would have to be delayed for a few more days.

To the ambassador, Molotov's refusal to see him and Lozovsky's late-night telephone call made it more obvious than ever that the Japanese government, in seeking to avail itself of Soviet good offices to end the war, was pursuing a will-o'-the-wisp. Although he could not, of course, know of Stalin's secret promise to enter the war against Japan within two or three months of Germany's defeat, he was well aware that the Soviet attitude toward Japan was not a friendly one, and he made every possible effort to inform his government of that fact and to persuade it to change its course. But the Japanese foreign minister, although he later admitted that he found the Russian attitude "very peculiar," remained unconvinced by Satō's cabled admonitions. In all,

Tōgō dispatched eleven cables to Satō; Satō sent thirteen official replies and four cables that reflected his own personal opinion; the United States government was aware of the contents of almost all of them.

The messages had been intercepted and decoded, and some had certainly found their way to the desks of the secretary of war and the secretary of the navy and from there to the secretary of state, James F. Byrnes. Forrestal, the navy secretary, noted in his diary for 13 July: "The first real evidence of a Japanese desire to get out of the war came today through intercepted messages from Tōgō."[32] In Byrnes's words, "Ambassador Satō told his Foreign Office that the Soviets had insisted upon the unconditional surrender of Germany and certainly would join the Americans and British in insisting upon the unconditional surrender of Japan. He said he knew his views were not in accord with the communications from His Majesty and even though 'my offense is great,' nevertheless 'I want to preserve the lives of hundreds of thousands of people who are about to go to their death needlessly.' And he stressed that 'Japan has no choice but to accept unconditional surrender.'" This, presumably, was the same advice that Byrnes gave President Truman on the eve of the opening of the crucial Potsdam Conference.

In his published account of the incident, Byrnes added: "Had the Japanese Government listened to Satō and surrendered unconditionally, it would not have been necessary to drop the atomic bomb."[33] Byrnes could have added also that had the Allied governments seen fit to offer some assurance in regard to the emperor, it might not have been necessary to drop the atomic bomb. But such reflections, no doubt, are idle: they ignore the logic of war.

President Truman was having a good time, in any case. Early in the morning of 7 July, he had gone aboard the U.S.S. *Augusta*, the heavy cruiser that was to deposit him on 15 July at Antwerp, whence he was to proceed to Berlin for the Potsdam Conference. "It was a wonderful crossing," he wrote later. "The *Augusta* had a fine band which played during the dinner hour each evening. There were movies every night in Secretary Byrnes's cabin. I was up early every morning to take some exercise on the deck and spent a good deal of time talking with mem-

bers of the crew."[34] But it was not all play and no work: "The office
of the first lieutenant of the *Augusta* had been made over into a communications center which was complete in every detail. . . . Here
messages were received and transmitted in virtually the same volume
and with the same dispatch as at the White House itself."[35]

But how many of those messages did Truman see? Did he read any
of the Tōgō–Satō cables that had been intercepted and decoded by
American military intelligence? He does not, in his memoirs, say. It
would appear, however, that his first inkling of the Japanese initiative
came not from his own secretary of state, who was aware of it, but
from Marshal Stalin, who "had told me, shortly after our arrival in
Potsdam, that the Japanese had asked the Kremlin if it would be
possible for Prince Konoye to come to Moscow. The Russians, so
Stalin had informed me, had replied that they could not answer such a
request until they knew what he wanted to talk about."[36] If Truman
had known what Prince Konoye wanted to talk about, might the
Potsdam Proclamation not have been somewhat differently phrased?
If it had included the kind of assurance in regard to the emperor that
Grew so persistently advocated, then the Suzuki government might
have been able to accept the proclamation without anticipating a civil
war fomented by the army. In that case, the bomb need never have
been used; and in that case, perhaps, the postwar arms race with the
Soviet Union that Szilard so greatly feared could have been avoided.

Was Truman advised, before he listened to that "fine band" every
evening, that many of the scientists who had labored to produce the
bomb were extremely troubled by the American decision to use it in
Japan without prior warning? The answer to that question is that he
almost certainly was not. Nor did he seem to be aware that many of the
men in his own government agreed with the scientists that Japan should
first be given an explicit warning. He was on the toboggan, and it was
racing downhill. The tragedy of errors—of errors in Tokyo, in Washington, in Potsdam—was destined to be played to the end.

Unquestionably he was advised that the 16 July test of the implosion
bomb at Trinity had been a blinding success. Truman was by then
installed in the "Little White House" at Babelsberg, near Potsdam.

Trinity, of course, was to have no great effect on Hiroshima, although it did serve to confirm the army's theory about the height at which the bomb should be dropped. The scientists who had been working on the uranium bomb, the Little Boy, were convinced they knew enough about it to be sure it would work—but it was only a single bomb, and it had almost exhausted America's supply of uranium. Should still a second bomb be required, the Fat Man, the plutonium bomb, was to fill the need; and, on 16 July, any uncertainty about its deadliness vanished in a great ball of fire and radioactive dust.

A few days before, a black truck, guarded by seven truckloads of armed soliders, left Los Alamos for Albuquerque. In the truck nestled a wooden box fifteen feet long and a lead cylinder eighteen feet in diameter. The ultimate destination of what was contained in these objects would turn out to be Hiroshima, but that fact was not, as yet, known to anyone in the world. Meanwhile the objects still had a long way to go. From Albuquerque they were to be flown to San Francisco and then transferred to the naval base at Hunter's Point, where they would be stowed aboard the cruiser *Indianapolis* to make the long journey across the Pacific to the little coral island of Tinian. There Colonel Tibbets and his 509th Composite Group were waiting.

So many nearby towns had already been fire-bombed that the people of Hiroshima were sure their own city must be next on the list. At first, when they heard nighttime enemy air activity in the vicinity, the inhabitants of the city would quickly gather together what food they had, a pot or a pan to cook it in, and some mats to sleep on; these they would sling into a handcart and then they would make their way up-river to spend the night in the open air, perhaps on one or another of the neighboring mountains. Then the people had begun to make their evacuation of the city a nightly routine, even when there were no enemy planes to be heard. Night after night the banks of the rivers were lined with these little carts, with weary, stumbling old men and women, and with crying babies. In the morning, back they would go to the still unscathed city, murmuring among themselves, "We have been saved from death again."

These nightly migrations grew so populous that the authorities feared there would be no one left in the city to fight the fires when the expected raid finally did take place. Accordingly, policemen, bayonets stuck onto their rifles, would station themselves at intersections and on bridges, barring the way of those who were considered essential to the city's defense. "Back!" the police would cry, their bayonets bristling. "Get back! Who's going to fight the fires if you all leave?" Then back they would go, reluctantly but without choice, back to the doomed city.

On 16 July President Truman "met Prime Minister Churchill for the first time. He came to call on me, but I did not feel that I was meeting a stranger. I had seen him on several occasions when he had been in Washington for conferences with Roosevelt, although I had not talked to him then. . . .

"The arrival of Marshal Stalin from Moscow was delayed because of a slight heart attack which he had suffered—this was a well-kept secret. He was due to arrive on the following day. . . .

"The next day I met Stalin for the first time. He came to pay a visit at the Little White House shortly after his arrival at Babelsberg. He was accompanied by Molotov and by Pavlov, who acted as interpreter. Secretary Byrnes was present, and Charles E. Bohlen acted as my interpreter.

"Stalin apologized for being late, saying that his health was not as good as it used to be. It was about eleven o'clock when he came, and I asked him to stay for lunch. He said he could not, but I insisted.

" 'You could if you wanted to,' I told him.

"He stayed. . . .

"I was pleased with my first visit with Stalin. He seemed to be in a good humor. He was extremely polite. . . ."[37]

Back in America, the world's first atomic explosion had taken place in the western desert. "Detailed interpretations of Trinity would take weeks to conclude. But by mid-morning of 16 July it was obvious that the gadget had surpassed all expectations and produced an explosive yield greater than the scientists' most optimistic predictions. It confirmed that implosion was probably the most efficient way to detonate an atomic weapon. It also illustrated for the Hiroshima planners one vital aspect of their mission. The Trinity bomb had emitted a terrific amount of radiation, which had encircled the explosion in a radio-active dust skirt as it rolled across the desert. The radioactivity had created a reverse smothering effect and had actually weakened the blast power of the bomb at great distances. Had the gadget been detonated at a level much higher than 100 feet, the radioactivity would have been far less and the blast power much greater. As the Army desired to kill Japanese by blast rather than radiation, Trinity confirmed their judg-ment that the Hiroshima bomb should be detonated from an extremely high altitude."[38]

These Japanese whom the American army desired to kill "by blast rather than radiation" were now offered the chance to get rich as they contributed to the war effort. Their government began selling lottery tickets at ¥10 each. The first prize was to be ¥100,000; the second, ¥10,000; and the third, ¥1,000. Losers as well as winners, the govern-ment pointed out, would be contributing their best to help Japan win the war.

At the same time, however, rumors had started circulating that this same government was trying to surrender. Seigo Nakamura, a reporter for the *Asahi* newspaper, has the following entry in his journal dated 17 July: "A radio broadcast from Rio de Janeiro announced briefly that Premier Stalin had brought Japan's surrender terms to the Potsdam Conference. A broadcast from San Francisco reported that the Wash-ington correspondent of the *New York Herald Tribune* had written a detailed article on Japan's intention to seek peace. Broadcasts from London also hinted that Japan was suing for peace. According to Reuters, the Soviet Embassy in London said that the Soviet government did not propose to act as mediator in Japan's desire to negotiate a peaceful settlement. At the same time, the embassy declared that any proposals made by the Japanese would be passed on to the Allied powers." Would they? What seemed to emerge, as the Potsdam Conference proceeded, was that Stalin was as off hand in telling Truman about the Japanese proposals as Truman was in telling Stalin about the atomic bomb. In any case, both governments were secretly informed about both developments: the Americans had intercepted the cables between Tokyo and Moscow; the Russians had an indefatigable and competent informer in one of America's atomic scientists, Klaus Fuchs, a German refugee and, perhaps surprisingly, the son of a Lutheran pastor.

In Japan, the government, the military, and the emperor himself anxiously awaited a Soviet reply to the inconclusive overtures that had been made, at the same time listening to radio broadcasts in the hope of getting some indication of which way the winds were blowing at Potsdam. No doubt they knew that Stalin had already mentioned, rather casually, that there had been attempts by the Japanese to secure Soviet mediation. They could not know that Stimson had already heard the news about Trinity. Even if they had intercepted the message sent from Washington to Babelsberg, they could not have understood it: "Operated on this morning. Diagnosis not yet complete but results seem satisfactory and already exceed expectations." Nor could they have known, although it concerned them vitally, that Dr. Arthur Compton had sent on to George Harrison, acting chairman of the interim committee, a petition signed by more than sixty Chicago scientists who had been working on the bomb. The document read, in part:

"We respectfully petition that the use of atomic bombs, particularly against cities, be sanctioned by you as Chief Executive only under the following conditions:

"1. Opportunity has been given to the Japanese to surrender on terms assuring them the possibility of peaceful development in their homeland.

"2. Convincing warnings have been given that refusal to surrender will be followed by the use of a new weapon.

"3. Responsibility for the use of atomic bombs is shared with our allies."

Although the petition was addressed to the president, it seems unlikely that it was forwarded to him in Potsdam in time to have any effect on the wording of the proclamation. It is extremely unlikely, in fact, that Truman ever saw the petition.

The upper age for induction into the regular forces of the Imperial

Japanese Army had been forty, but now it was no uncommon sight to see recruits in uniform who were clearly well past that age. Nor was it unusual for a young officer to have in his company, as a private soldier, a father or an uncle. These overage recruits were sent mainly to the Kanto, Tokai, and Kyushu areas, where they underwent intensive short-term training. Of the arms issued to them, an officer has written:

"There was only one rifle for every ten men and only one bayonet for every eight men. There were no more than seventy rounds of ammunition per rifle, and the rifle had neither breechblock cover, backsight, nor rammer. The scabbard for the bayonet was made of bamboo. Recruits for whom there were no rifles were issued bamboo spears."

In any case, the army's new strategy rendered rifles unnecessary. Daily each new recruit, young or old, was ordered to strap a thirty-five-pound weight to his back and practice digging a foxhole. There, when the enemy landed, he was to hide himself, along with a couple of days' supply of food; by that time, the thirty-five-pound weight would be a thirty-five-pound bomb. When he saw an enemy tank, he was to run forward, release the safety device, and hurl the bomb under the tank. The amount of time between release and detonation was three seconds, so whether the tank was stationary or moving at full speed, the soldier had no chance to avoid death. The men, both young and old, stoically accepted the fact that once this disagreeable daily drill ended, so would their lives.

Their government, however, still hoped to save them, despite the fact that its half-hearted attempts to surrender were meeting with no success. At 10:30 in the morning of 20 July, the foreign office received a cable from Satō, repeating the reply that he had finally got from Lozovsky. It was not encouraging: the Soviet government found the emperor's message too vague and the proposed mission of Prince Konoye too ambiguous. It could not, therefore, "give any definite reply either to the message of the emperor of Japan or to the dispatch of Prince Konoye as special envoy." Forty minutes later came another cable from Satō pointing out that the feeling in Moscow was far different from what Tokyo imagined it to be and that the Japanese government must offer more concrete proposals if it still hoped to make use of Soviet good offices.

At 6:00 that evening, the Big Six, in an emergency meeting, agreed that Japan still had no choice but to seek a negotiated peace rather than accept unconditional surrender, which, in the absence of any Allied guarantee, meant uncertainty in regard to the emperor—and this, in turn, meant that the military would use force in opposing it. The result could only be the fall of the government and perhaps civil war. The supreme council, therefore, decided to repeat its request to send Prince Konoye to the Kremlin, adding that he personally would bring Japan's conditions for a negotiated peace. In addition to these formal instructions, Tōgō sent a second cable to Satō explaining that, because of conditions prevailing within the country as well as outside it, he could make no concrete proposals before Konoye's arrival in Moscow. It was not much of an explanation, but perhaps it was the best that Tōgō could do. The message from the throne that Konoye was to carry to Moscow leaves no doubt that Japan was determined to preserve the emperor system; the utmost concession she was prepared, unwillingly, to make was the abdication of the present emperor and the accession to the throne of another member of the imperial family. If even that were found unacceptable, then Japan would have no choice but to go on fighting, repelling the invading forces if she could.

But on the other side of the world, in Potsdam, it had been decided that there were to be no invading forces. On 22 July Truman met in the morning with his military advisers and heard their views on the use of the atomic bomb; then at noon he heard Churchill's opinion that the bomb should be dropped on the Japanese homeland as soon as possible. Truman agreed. Later, Churchill was to write of the projected invasion: "Now all this nightmare picture had vanished. In its place was the vision—fair and bright indeed it seemed—of the end of the whole war in one or two violent shocks."[39] Perhaps even fairer and brighter to the Russophobic Churchill was the fact that "Moreover, we should not need the Russians. The end of the Japanese war no longer depended upon the pouring in of their armies for the final and perhaps protracted slaughter. We had no need to ask favors of them."[40] What a strange and complex role the Soviet Union had played and was still to play in the destiny of Japan! How impossible it is, even now, to separate the many threads that were woven into the final tragic tapestry!

It was on 20 July that Lieutenant Masataka Hakata, of the army's Central Communications Research Department, first noticed something odd about some of the B-29s that were flying over Japanese soil. For one thing, they bore numbers in 600-range. The department already knew that planes bearing 400 numbers were flying out of Saipan, those in the 500's out of Guam, and those in the 700's out of Tinian. Where were the 600's coming from? Another odd thing was that these planes used only one digit in their signals instead of the customary two; they would radio back to base with such call signs as 2V625, 5V625, and so on. Lieutenant Hakata put them down as newly arrived reinforcements. (In mid-July the air force had changed its frequency from 12,000 kilocycles to 15,200, but Japanese army intelligence soon located the new frequency.)

Then members of the department observed that the one-digit planes were behaving in an unusual manner. Sometimes they flew singly, but more often in a formation of three. Only one bright orange bomb—which the Americans, the Japanese learned later, referred to as a pumpkin—was dropped on each flight; then the planes turned and banked sharply and zoomed away. From the American air force point of view, these flights served two purposes: one was to familiarize the crews with enemy terrain and weather, and the other was to familiarize the Japanese with these unusual sorties. Lieutenant Hakata's department came to the inevitable conclusion that the planes were undertaking some special mission, but no one in Japan could even hazard a guess as to what that mission might possibly be.

At the same time, in a hotel on the banks of Lake Biwa, the nuclear scientists from Kyoto Imperial University conferred with representatives of the navy: it was their first, and last, such meeting. From the university came four professors—Arakatsu, Yukawa (who was later to win a Nobel Prize in physics), Kobayashi, and Sasaki; heading the navy side was Rear Admiral Shigeharu Nitta, attended by Captain

Matao Mitsui, Lieutenant Commander Tetsuzō Kitagawa, and several others. Lake Biwa was then a training ground for the navy's hydroplanes and the buzz of their engines formed a constant background to the conference.

It opened with a general explanation by Professor Arakatsu, which was followed by a discourse by the rear admiral on the structure of a centrifugal separator and then an examination by Professor Kobayashi into the necessary critical mass. After this, Professor Yukawa spoke on "World Atomic Energy." His talk, based on information gleaned from neutral countries, was concerned solely with theoretical aspects of nuclear research. It hardly touched on the actual production of an atomic bomb—beyond Yukawa's prediction that, although such a bomb was theoretically possible, it could not be produced in time to be used in the Pacific war. With this the meeting adjourned; the men who had taken part in it continued to discuss in small groups of twos and threes, as summer breezes from the lake fanned their faces, the theoretical aspects of nuclear energy. Then quietly they dispersed, never to meet again; Professor Yukawa was all too soon to be proven wrong in his optimistic predictions.

The twenty-second of July was the day that President Truman and Prime Minister Churchill agreed, in Potsdam, that the bomb should be dropped on Japan as soon as possible and without prior warning. It was a Sunday, and in Tokyo a quiet one at that: indeed, Tokyo had already been virtually erased from the map of Japan. Those who were left in the capital went outside to enjoy the summer sunshine after the heavy rains of the preceding day. Jun Takami, the writer, described that Sunday in his diary:

"Quilts and clothing were hanging out, to be dried in the sun, beside the flimsy makeshift shacks that had been hurriedly put up on the sites of burnt out dwellings. It was a striking picture. The zinc-roofed shacks must have leaked badly during yesterday's rain. How pitiful it all looked! The devastated areas are full of rusted metal, and the roofs of the shanties are rusted too: indeed, all of Tokyo seems to be rust-colored now."

Another description of the same day has been preserved by Musei

Tokugawa, who wrote: "The sweet oleanders are now in bloom, and young leaves are even sprouting from blackened ginko trees. How brave they looked! On the burnt out site of the Kannon-dō [the main hall of the Temple of the Goddess of Mercy in Asakusa] a temporary shrine is under construction. In the whole quarter, only the amusement center and the green trees are still intact.

"Working people, coming in on street cars and subways that are still running, flood the district every day. Their destination is one or another of the theaters and movie houses of the district. In fact, they seem to go from one to another, spending the whole day there before returning to their homes. It is not a happy sight."

But at least it was peaceful, which could not be said for all of Japan. On the night of that same 22 July a squadron of superfortresses based in the Marianas reduced to ashes the small cities of Ube and Shimomatsu, in Yamaguchi Prefecture. On the following day, Major Chuck Sweeney, who was in command of Crew Number 15 in Tinian and one of the few men in the 509th who had been informed as to the real nature of their mission, flew a B-29—nicknamed the *Great Artiste*— over the marshaling yards of Kobe, where he dropped a "pumpkin," then quickly turned and made his way back to the Marianas. It was this plane that was eventually to drop the plutonium bomb on Nagasaki.

On the morning of 24 July, in Potsdam, the secretary of war showed President Truman a message from George L. Harrison, secretary of the interim committee, suggesting the probable dates when the bombs would be ready for use in Japan. Truman, elated, said that this knowledge was exactly what he needed in order to issue the final warning to Japan. Stimson then repeated his belief that this final warning should include a guarantee that Japan might maintain her imperial house if that was what her people wanted. But the secretary of state, James Byrnes, said that such a guarantee had not been envisaged, and since the text of the proclamation had already been sent to Chiang Kai-shek for his approval, the guarantee could not now be included. Stimson said that in that case it might be transmitted in an oral message; President Truman agreed to consider the matter. The almost inevitable entry of the Russians into the war was also discussed.

In Washington, on 24 July, a courier arrived from Potsdam, bearing General Arnold's opinion that Nagasaki should be included on the list of likely targets for the bomb. Some of the officers present at that day's meeting of the target committee objected that Nagasaki "was not a proper shape and dimension." Messages went back and forth between Washington and Potsdam, but Arnold stood firm. By evening the directive had been concluded and was sent to General Marshall in Potsdam, with a request for his final approval.

Addressed to General Carl A. Spaatz, commanding general of the United States Strategic Air Force, this historic order read:

"1. The 509 Composite Group, 20th Air Force will deliver its first special bomb as soon as weather will permit visual bombing after about 3 August 1945 on one of the targets: Hiroshima, Kokura, Niigata and Nagasaki. To carry military and civilian scientific personnel from the War Department to observe and record the effects of the explosion of the bomb, additional aircraft will accompany the airplane carrying the bomb. The observing planes will stay several miles distant from the point of impact of the bomb.

"2. Additional bombs will be delivered on the above targets as soon as made ready by the project staff. Further instructions will be issued concerning targets other than those listed above.

"3. Dissemination of any and all information concerning the use of the weapon against Japan is reserved to the Secretary of War and the President of the United States. No communiqué on the subject or release of information will be issued by Commanders in the field without specific prior authority. Any news stories will be sent to the War Department for special clearance.

"4. The foregoing directive is issued to you by direction and with the approval of the Secretary of War and the Chief of Staff, USA. It is desired that you personally deliver one copy of this directive to General MacArthur and one copy to Admiral Nimitz for their information."

It was signed by "Thos. T. Handy, General G.S.C., Acting Chief of Staff."

President Truman, who quotes the directive in his memoirs, adds:

"With this order the wheels were set in motion for the first use of an atomic weapon against a military target. I had made the decision." But had he? The directive was similar to the one that had been drafted by General Groves back in May, and it was written, signed, and approved in Washington *before* the ultimatum to Japan was issued in Potsdam. It was, in effect, a definite order to drop the bomb. Although Truman adds in his memoirs, "I also instructed Stimson that the order would stand unless I notified him that the Japanese reply to our ultimatum was acceptable,"[61] no assurance was ever offered in that ultimatum to Japan, either oral or written, concerning the status of the emperor, and one wonders whether it ever occurred to the "little boy on the toboggan," as General Groves described him, that he had any choice but to say yes. Further, the directive hardly suggests, either explicitly or implicitly, that it was the president of the United States who was ordering the use of the bomb. If any chief executive did indeed give the go-ahead signal, then it may have been the lingering ghostly presence of the former president rather than the living, moving presence of the incumbent one.

The Japanese government, meanwhile, continued to pin its hopes on Moscow. What it wanted, what indeed it had to have and still hoped to secure through the good offices of the Kremlin, was an official statement from the Allied powers explaining precisely how unconditional surrender would affect the imperial house—something more, in other words, than was contained in the Japanese-language broadcasts of Captain Zacharias. But in Moscow, representatives of the American Joint Chiefs of Staff met twice with the Russians, on 24 July and 26 July, to discuss plans for the invasion of Japan. The Soviet Union, then, toward whom Japan was still looking for help and with whom her neutrality pact was still in effect, was to all intents and purposes already her enemy.

On 24 July women working in the Soviet embassy in Tokyo, as well as Russian wives and children, sailed for home from the port of Sakata, in Yamagata Prefecture. This move, which ought to have made it abundantly clear to the Suzuki government that the Soviet Union was no longer a friendly power, was optimistically interpreted merely as an attempt to escape from the disastrous American raids. If so, why had it not come earlier?

"On 24 July," writes Truman, "I casually mentioned to Stalin that we had a new weapon of unusual destructive force. The Russian Premier showed no special interest. All he said was that he was glad to hear it and hoped we would make 'good use of it against the Japanese.' "[42] Of this "casual mention," Professor Szilard has written: "One could hardly say that the attempt to inform Stalin was a very vigorous one. Mr. Truman did not say, 'Excuse me, Mr. Stalin, but you do not seem to understand. I am not speaking of just another bomb; I am speaking of something that will get Russia and the United States into the greatest difficulties after the war unless we find a solution to the problem which it poses.' Mr. Truman said nothing of the sort."[43] Both Truman and Stalin may have had their reasons for this strange reticence: Truman, because both the United States and Great Britain hoped to use the bomb as a means of containing Russia; Stalin, because the Soviets already knew a great deal about the bomb and had no special desire, at that point, to find a solution to the problem that it was going to pose.

On the island of Kyushu, the Eighty-sixth Division was working around the clock to complete an extensive network of fortifications surrounding Shibushi Bay, on Ōsumi Peninsula, where the Imperial Army believed that the Allied forces were most likely to attempt their first landing. After the war was over, Lieutenant General Tomotarō Yoshinaka, commander of the division, said, "We were confident that we could wholly destroy the first-wave landing of five American divisions at the water's edge." His troops may have felt less confident: they were being given only one meal a day—a bowl of rice mixed with bean cake —and all of them were suffering from malnutrition and its consequent effects: general debility, stomach disorders, and the like. They were hardly in any condition to repel a well-fed and well-armed invader.

Even so, however, the troops were faring better than the rest of the population. As of 11 July, the already meager ration of staple food had been reduced by 10 percent; and that staple food was no longer the rice upon which the Japanese people traditionally depended but rather a flour made out of sweet potato vines, mulberry leaves, pumpkins, and horse chestnuts. There was little nourishment in it, and most of the people in the country were weakened by fairly constant diarrhea. In the readers' column of the *Yomiuri-Hochi* newspaper for 24 July there appeared the following letter:

"The number of emaciated men and women in the country is conspicuous. Everyone is suffering from diarrhea; everyone has to go to the toilet many times a day. No one can work properly, and production will inevitably decline. The problem is the flour that we are being given. All we ask is flour of a higher quality that we can digest more easily. If we are to win the war, we must be supplied with food that will not make us sick." The Japanese military was still telling the people they must be prepared to fight to the end. The American military was saying much the same thing. "There are no non-combatants in Japan," one officer announced. "Our enemy is the entire population of the country."

On 25 July the War Department in Washington received word from Potsdam that Secretary Stimson and General Marshall had approved the directive to General Spaatz. The order to drop the bomb was now official; only that careering little boy on the toboggan could now prevent the other Little Boy from falling on Hiroshima. And perhaps not even he could do it. If only the Japanese would decide to surrender unconditionally! But with the emperor's fate still unclear, they could not. The tragicomedy continued.

Ironically enough, on that same July day, among the communications handed to General Groves in Washington were the results of a poll taken among the atomic scientists. In the words of Dr. Compton, speaking of the Chicago petition to the president:

"It was difficult from such petitions to get a balanced view of how men were thinking. General Groves accordingly suggested that I supervise an opinion poll among those who knew what was going on. Farrington Daniels, then Director of the Metallurgical Laboratory, took charge of the poll at Chicago. Oppenheimer at Los Alamos and Lawrence at Berkeley used less formal methods of sounding the opinions of their men. . . .

"Daniels asked and received replies from 150 members of the Metallurgical Laboratory at Chicago. His questionnaire had five procedures, graded from no use of the bomb in this war to its military use in the manner most effective in bringing prompt Japanese surrender. There were few who preferred not to use the bomb at all, but 87 percent voted for its military use, at least if after other means were tried this was found necessary to bring surrender."[44]

At least one American study of the poll considers Compton's analysis "biased." According to Giovannitti and Freed, "In fact, only 46 percent voted for a *military* demonstration. It seems to be an obvious misinterpretation to say that the scientists by voting in Point 3 *for* an experimental demonstration were not really *against* the bomb's military use on Japan. They *were* against the military use of the bomb unless two important steps were first taken—a demonstration of the bomb and a demand for surrender. Even those who favored a military demonstration opposed the *unchecked* use of the bomb; and only 15 percent supported the 'military point of view most effective.'

"The circumstances under which the poll at Chicago was conducted were hardly the best. The Groves order to poll the scientists was made hurriedly. One of the scientists polled, Rabinowitch, related the conditions under which the poll was taken:

" 'Now this questionnaire was distributed to the members of the project by people appointed to carry them around. We were not given more than a few minutes to answer the questionnaire. . . .'

". . . Groves turned in the petitions and the poll results to Stimson's office on 1 August—five days before the bomb burst over Hiroshima. As Interim Committee Secretary Arneson pointed out:

" 'I think it would be only frank to say that at that time . . . as far as Secretary Stimson was concerned the issue had been decided and there was no further need for expressions of opinion from the scientists in Chicago or anyone else.'

"On this subject, one matter remains open for conjecture. As far as can be determined, only the Chicago scientists were polled on their opinions yet Compton said that Oppenheimer at Los Alamos and Lawrence at Berkeley sounded out 'the opinions of their men.' How

18. Reijirō Wakatsuki, who was with the emperor when news of the American landing on Iwō Jima reached Tokyo. He advocated fighting on till the Allies realized the futility of war.

19. Kōki Hirota, an ex-premier whose chief concern was to prevent Russia from joining the war against Japan.

20. Hideki Tōjō, the wartime prime minister in Japan.

21. Kantarō Suzuki, who was prime minister at the time of the decision to surrender.

22. Kōichi Kido, lord keeper of the privy seal and a major influence during the war and at the time of the surrender.

23. Shigenori Tōgō, foreign minister at the end of the war, who had opposed the war and tried to end it quickly.

24. Shigeru Yoshida, originally in favor of the war in Southeast Asia but opposed to war with the United States, he later argued for an early peace. He served as prime minister several times during the postwar perod.

25. Shunichi Matsumoto, deputy foreign minister and one of Shigenori Tōgō's chief helpers.

26. Shigeru Nanbara, later president of Tokyo University, who was an early advocate of a quick peace.

27. Tokyo, an aerial view of Chūō ward at the end of the war.

28. Yokohama after a bombing raid.

29. Osaka in summer 1945.

30. Kobe after being bombed on 5 June 1945.

31. Okinawa: Japanese prisoners march to a dock for transfer to another island.

32. An American air base on Guam similar to that at Tinian.

33. Winston Churchill, Harry Truman, and Joseph Stalin at Potsdam.

34. Clouds bursting upward after the explosion of the bomb.

5. The Little Boy before the damage was done.

6. Hiroshima, 6 August 1945.

37. Like the preceding picture this photograph was taken near Miyuki Bridge, 2,500 yards from the hypocenter, soon after the explosion.

38. The *Enola Gay* lands on her return from Hiroshima, 6 August 1945.

. The Industry Promotion Hall, 150 yards from the hypocenter.

. Aioi Bridge, nearly 300 yards from the hypocenter.

41. A panoramic view of Hiroshima after it was destroyed.

42. The hypocenter, showing the remains of Shima Hospital.

43. The scene 100 yards from the hypocenter.

44. A building about 230 yards from the hypocenter.

45. The remains of Kokutaiji Temple, about 170 yards from the hypocenter.

6. The remains of a well-known clock shop about 670 yards from the hypocenter.

7. A scene 1,400 yards from the hypocenter.

48. About 1,700 yards from the hypocenter.
49. The temporary headquarters of the Hiroshima military district set up after th
explosion.

did they sound them out and what were the results? Did Oppenheimer and Lawrence make a report to Compton on their findings or on their failure to conduct any survey of opinion? A search of the record fails to indicate the existence of such a report. Why? It cannot be because there was unanimity of opinion for the military use of the bomb, which in itself is a result worth recording."[45]

After the war had ended, according to the same authors, George Kistiakowsky, the chemist who was in charge of the explosives section at Los Alamos, "learned that American Intelligence had not been accurate in its estimate of the Japanese condition to fight on. 'The Japanese were far nearer to surrender than the estimates indicated,' he said, 'and had I known that, *I would have certainly joined a number of other people in Los Alamos arguing against the use of the bomb.*'

"Oppenheimer did not feel qualified to question the intelligence reports he had been given. He had been told 'that an invasion was planned. *It would be necessary* and it would be terribly costly.' He accepted this analysis and persuaded Kistiakowsky and others to accept it. And, in the last analysis, Oppenheimer, whose influence on his colleagues was enormous, fully endorsed the use of the bomb:

" 'On the whole you are inclined to think if it was needed to put an end to the war and had a chance of so doing, we thought that was the right thing to do.' "[46]

The italics are the authors', and they are intended to emphasize the points that the authors desired to make.

On this same July day, the vice chiefs of staff of the various armies garrisoned in the Japanese home islands met at imperial headquarters to implement further their plans for a last-ditch battle. Their directives, which had already been stated and restated, were all too familiar; what they came down to was that Japan must stage an initial all-out attack as soon as the enemy attempted to land, paying no heed to what that attack might cost in lives.

The government, meanwhile, still awaited some sort of word from its ambassador in Moscow. Its secret desire to send an imperial envoy to the Kremlin was, however, no longer secret: rumors had spread throughout the country, and many people fiercely opposed the plan, calling for the resignation of the cabinet. Rumors were flying about also concerning the emperor. Did he intend to remain in Tokyo? Was he going to take sanctuary in the newly built shelter at Matsushiro? Were the three sacred treasures—the mirror, the sword, and the jewels—that constitute the imperial regalia of Japan also to be given sanctuary at Matsushiro? If so, this clearly meant that Japan intended to fight on.

The peace faction in the government, its eyes on Potsdam, knew that for the time being the conference was recessed because of general elections in Britain. The Japanese decided to take advantage of this by pressing the Soviets once again to use their good offices. At 7:00 that evening (25 July in Japan) Tōgō cabled Satō: "Utilize this opportunity to meet Molotov at any place he designates. Explain to him the imperial Japanese government's true intentions. On 19 July Captain Zacharias said that Japan had but two alternatives: one was to accept a dictated peace after defeat, the other was to agree to unconditional surrender and so derive the benefits stipulated in the Atlantic Charter. This statement cannot be taken as mere propaganda. Obviously it is intended to persuade us to surrender, but at the same time it is highly worthy of note that the United States has now referred to the Atlantic Charter. It is absolutely impossible for Japan to accept unconditional surrender, but we have no objection to a peace based on the Atlantic Charter. You are instructed to communicate our position through the appropriate channels. . . "

The "appropriate channels" already existed: American military intelligence was still reading the exchange of messages between Tōgō and Satō. But nothing came of it. The decision to drop the bomb had already been made, and on the following morning, 26 July, the necessary fissionable materials arrived at Tinian aboard the cruiser *Indianapolis*. On the afternoon of the same day, the last components of the bomb were flown to Santa Fe and then transported by truck to Albuquerque, where three B-29s of the 509th Composite Group were waiting.

On the evening before (Moscow time), Alexander Lozovsky, Molotov's deputy commissar for foreign affairs, received the Japanese ambassador. For the first time the Russian appeared to realize that Japan was actually seeking the good offices of the Soviet Union. Satō agreed that that was what Japan was seeking, repeating the desire of his government to send Prince Konoye to Moscow as an imperial envoy. Lozovsky wanted to know whether the proposals that Konoye would be bringing referred solely to relations with the Soviet Union or did they refer also to a termination of hostilities? Satō replied that they referred to both. Lozovsky then assured Satō that he would soon have an answer.

He did indeed soon have an answer, and it was no great surprise to Satō although apparently it was a considerable shock to the blinkered Suzuki government; but first came an event of major proportions that had to be dealt with on both sides of the Atlantic as well as on both sides of the Pacific. Late in the afternoon of 26 July, in Potsdam, a message was received from Chiang Kai-shek approving the text of the proclamation demanding Japan's surrender. Accordingly, copies were handed out at seven o'clock to reporters, who were told they might release the news at 9:20 P.M. At the same time, American information bureaus were ordered to make the contents of the proclamation known to the Japanese people in every way possible. This released a flurry of activity in Washington. By Washington time, the word was received at 3:10 P.M., and fifty minutes later English-language broadcasts were being sent by shortwave from the west coast. A few minutes afterwards, the salient points were being transmitted in Japanese. Then the entire proclamation was translated into Japanese, and, after being checked carefully by Japanese-language experts, was broadcast in its entirety from San Francisco at six o'clock.

This, by Japan time, was 7:00 in the morning of 27 July.

Apparently the broadcast was first picked up by a monitoring station in Chōfu, a Tokyo suburb. After the war, Seiichiro Katsuyama, who was working in the station, was to describe the event in the following terms: "The potato fields around the station were already glistening under the hot, early morning sun. Suddenly the words 'Potsdam Proclamation'—the proclamation of the three powers—sounded in my earphones. The broadcast was emanating from San Francisco. I had heard the words 'unconditional surrender' so often in the Zacharias broadcasts that I was hardly surprised to hear them again in the proclamation broadcast. However, this seemed to be a communication of considerable importance, so I made six recordings of it. Then, after checking it carefully, I typed it out, jumped on my motorcycle, and made my way as fast as I could to the foreign ministry."

The communication that he carried was dated 26 July 1945 and began with the following words: "We, the President of the United States, the President of the National Government of the Republic of China, and the Prime Minister of Great Britain, representing the hundreds of millions of our countrymen, have conferred and agree that Japan shall be given an opportunity to end this war." In all, the proclamation contained thirteen paragraphs. Tōgō immediately summoned his deputy foreign minister (Shunichi Matsumoto), the director of the treaties bureau (Shinichi Shibusawa), and other top bureaucrats of the ministry for an exchange of views.

Three points in the proclamation seemed of immediate and paramount importance. The first was the fact that the future status of the emperor had been left ambiguous. Paragraph 12 stated, "The occupying forces of the Allies shall be withdrawn from Japan as soon as these objectives have been accomplished and there has been established in accordance with the freely expressed will of the Japanese people a peacefully inclined and responsible government." This did not, apparently, mean that the emperor system would necessarily be abolished; at the same time, it gave no assurance that the system would be maintained. Without such an assurance, the men meeting at the foreign office agreed, unconditional surrender would be difficult, if not altogether impossible, to accept. In the original draft of the proclamation, as it had been drawn up by Joseph Grew and revised by Judge Samuel Rosenman, this particular paragraph had continued: "This may include a constitutional monarchy under the present dynasty if the peace-loving nations can be convinced of the genuine determination of such a government to follow policies which will render impossible the future development of aggressive militarism in Japan."[47] Had this statement been retained in the final draft, Tōgō's task in bringing the war to an immediate end would obviously have been rendered infinitely easier.

The second point to be considered was a more auspicious one. It was contained in the final paragraph, which read: "We call upon the government of Japan to proclaim now the unconditional surrender of all Japanese armed forces, and to provide proper and adequate assurances of their good faith in such action. The alternative for Japan is prompt and utter destruction." Despite the menacing tone of the last statement, the fact that the proclamation now called only for the unconditional surrender of the armed forces rather than, as in the Cairo Declaration of 1943, for the unconditional surrender of Japan seemed to offer room for maneuver. Perhaps even the army might be persuaded to accept it.

Finally, the foreign ministry was relieved by the fact that the Soviet Union had not subscribed to the proclamation. This seemed to indicate that the Kremlin would remain in a state of neutrality. This, too, was interpreted as a hopeful sign that the Allied powers would eventually accept something less than unconditional surrender.

The foreign office, accordingly, came to the decision that, although the proclamation ought, and indeed must, ultimately be agreed to, it should not be agreed to immediately. Negotiations with the Soviet Union might still result in more favorable terms, terms that the Imperial Army could accept and still save face. Thus, despite the ominous words of Paragraph 5 ("Following are our terms. We will not deviate from them. There are no alternatives. We shall brook no delay."), the ministry came to the conclusion that Japan could still afford to wait a little longer. Tōgō recommended to Suzuki that the government continue to await the Soviet reply to the Japanese proposal to send Prince Konoye to Moscow, or elsewhere, with a message from the throne.

He offered the same advice that night to the emperor, to whom he gave the original English text of the proclamation, along with a Japanese translation, pointing out to him that since it did not bear the Soviet premier's signature, the foreign office believed that Japan should go on holding out for the Soviet reply before accepting the proclamation. The emperor himself apparently agreed, still hoping for encouraging word from the Kremlin and not overly impressed by the proclamation, despite its categorical tone. Nevertheless, after Tōgō left, His Majesty spent quite some time with his chamberlains, poring over both the English text and the Japanese translation.

Half an hour after his audience with the emperor, Tōgō attended the regularly scheduled meeting of the Supreme Council for the Direction of the War. It is interesting to note that this was not considered an emergency session, and, with the exception of Tōgō, the Big Six did not regard the proclamation as an actual ultimatum. Even the final phrase—"The alternative for Japan is prompt and utter destruction"—failed to persuade them, for Japan had already been visited with nearly utter destruction. Between 17 July and 24 July, British and American planes had bombarded cities, airfields, and warships anchored in the Inland Sea. How, the Big Six wondered, could devastation be more prompt or utter? They were destined, unfortunately, to find out.

That same day also the cabinet met, and they too decided to adopt a wait-and-see attitude. Their chief concern remained the status of the emperor, and so long as that was unclarified, they agreed that Japan must continue to procrastinate until the Soviet Union tendered its reply. Had Stalin subscribed to the proclamation, the Japanese government might have realized that it no longer had time for procrastination; but the Soviet Union, according to the terms of the earlier pact, was still in a state of neutrality. This was soon, with American assistance, to be circumvented, but for the moment the Japanese decision to delay its decision served Stalin's purposes well. With great astuteness, he was playing a cat-and-mouse game, a game in which he himself was the cat—while the mice were the Japanese government as well as the governments of his wartime allies.

At that same cabinet meeting, it had been decided that the government would not attempt to withhold the *fact* of the proclamation from the people—this, indeed, would have been impossible—but instead would release the text in an expurgated version, instructing the newspapers to play it down as much as possible and to refrain from editorial comment. In an attempt to counter this anticipated move, the Americans, that same day, rained tens of thousands of leaflets onto Japan's twelve major cities, explaining the proclamation and pointing out that the Allied powers did not consider the Japanese people to be their enemies but rather the military that had plunged the country into this · disastrous war. The surrender that the Allies were calling for, the leaflet said, would free the people from the army's stranglehold and create the opportunity for building a new and better Japan.

But, the leaflet continued, unless the country agreed to immediate surrender, the bombings would continue. On the back of the leaflet, along with a photograph of a superfortress, were listed the cities destined for destruction: Otaru, Akita, Hachinohe, Fukushima, Urawa, Takayama, Iwakuni, Tottori, Imabaru, Yawata, Miyakonojō, and Saga. Hiroshima, it will be noted, was absent from the list; so were Nagasaki, Kokura, and Niigata.

That same evening, in Potsdam, word was received that Churchill had been defeated in the general election and that the new prime minister, Clement Attlee, would take his place. The conference remained in recess pending the arrival of Attlee and his foreign minister, Ernest Bevin.

By 27 July, in Hiroshima, evacuation to the nearby countryside of some twenty-five thousand primary school children above the third grade had been virtually completed. This process had been begun back in April, while as far back as November of the preceding year the construction of fire prevention zones had been initiated. So far over eight thousand dwellings had been demolished, but now the municipal authorities decided that the number was insufficient and that an additional 2,500 had still to go. Resigned householders removed what goods they could and then sadly watched their cherished homes being pulled down with a tremendous clatter, in clouds of dust and powder, to the ground.

On 28 July, the last components of the atomic bomb, which had been transported from Los Alamos to Sacramento, were about to be flown to Tinian. A slight accident occurred: at takeoff, a faulty door flew open, shattering a wing of one of the planes. It was not serious; nothing was damaged; no one was hurt; it merely meant a slight delay. Perhaps the atomic bombings of Japan would not take place quite so soon as had been anticipated.

Unfortunately, the government, which of course knew nothing of either the projected bombings or the delay, made no move to take advantage of this slight contretemps. On the contrary, it succeeded—perhaps inadvertently—in making matters worse. In accordance with the cabinet decision, the newspapers of 28 July had done their best to make the proclamation seem a minor matter. Brief headlines in the *Yomiuri-Hochi*, the *Asahi*, and the *Mainichi* newspapers all declared the proclamation to be "absurd," while short stories listed some, but not all, of the points that it contained. Omitted were both Paragraph 9, which stated that "The Japanese military forces, after being completely disarmed, shall be permitted to return to their homes with the opportunity to lead peaceful and productive lives," and Paragraph 10, which began, "We do not intend that the Japanese shall be enslaved as a race or destroyed as a nation. . . ." The military were, of course, fearful that such declarations would weaken still further the popular will to continue the war.

The military were, in fact, dissatisfied with the cabinet decision to do nothing for the moment. Accordingly, they persuaded the prime minister to hold a press conference in which he would make the "unofficial" rejection of the proclamation by the newspapers somewhat more official. This the aged premier did at three o'clock in the afternoon of 28 July (Japan time). He did it without the knowledge of his foreign minister, and the results of it—no doubt unintentionally—could not have been more disastrous for Japan.

When the reporters asked Suzuki to explain the government's attitude toward the proclamation, he said his government considered it to be nothing more than a restatement of the Cairo Declaration and so of little importance. Then he used the now famous word *mokusatsu*. It is not a common word, and in making use of it Suzuki may have meant to do no more than repeat the cabinet's decision to wait a little longer. Unfortunately, *mokusatsu* is a word susceptible of various interpretations. *Moku* means "to keep silent"; *satsu* means "to kill"; taken together, they are defined by Kenkyusha's *New Japanese-English Dictionary* as "take no notice of; treat (anything) with silent contempt; ignore [by keeping silence]; remain in a wise and masterly inactivity."

It is hard to guess what the old admiral had in mind when he threw that word out to the reporters. To ignore the proclamation *for the time being*? To treat it with contempt? Perhaps even "to remain in a wise and masterly inactivity?" It was, in any case, a wholly disastrous word, for to the Americans it meant only that Japan had now officially "rejected" their ultimatum. The *New York Times* for 30 July carried on its front page a story headlined by the words: "JAPAN OFFICIALLY TURNS DOWN ALLIED SURRENDER ULTIMATUM." It had been a long sad month for the Japanese—they were hungry, they were worried about how they were to get through the coming winter without adequate clothing—and now it was even sadder that the month was about to end on that calamitous word *mokusatsu*. For the Americans, it could have but one result: Japan, having rejected the Allied ultimatum, must now be subjected to the "prompt and utter destruction" that the Potsdam Proclamation had threatened. "The bomb," in the words of Secretary Stimson, already quoted, "seemed to me to furnish a unique instrument for that purpose." On that same day, Stimson, Groves, and Harrison completed the draft of a declaration to be issued by the president of the United States immediately after the first atomic bomb had been dropped on Japan.

In Tokyo, the new bomb shelter for the emperor in the Imperial Palace grounds had been completed. The compound within the wide moats had resumed its traditional quiet. Officers and men had withdrawn, after being given presents by His Majesty. Private soldiers had been presented with cigarettes embossed with the emblem of the imperial chrysanthemum, and officers, with cuff links bearing the same emblem. Although the links were made of porcelain, because of the shortage of metal, they were encased in splendid paulownia boxes. On 30 July the air defense room was formally handed over by the First Imperial Guards Division to the Imperial Household Ministry. The ceremony was an extremely brief one, curtailed by the fact that Tokyo was in the process of being raided by 180 American planes.

On that same day, Colonel Suenari Shiraki, head of the fifth section of the second department of the supreme command of the Imperial Japanese Army, which was in charge of collecting and analyzing information about the Soviet Union, spoke to the operations section of general staff headquarters. The Soviets, Shiraki said, have been transporting a large number of vehicles to the eastern front by means of the Trans-Siberian Railroad. That means, he said, that transportation of troops to the frontier has already begun. It was believed that the Soviets had concentrated nearly a million and a half men there, as well as five thousand planes and three thousand tanks. The demoralized and depleted Kwantung Army could hardly hope to cope with so vast an array. Colonel Shiraki predicted that the Soviet Union would declare war on Japan around 10 August. His prediction was not welcomed by the Imperial Army, which, like the government itself, still hoped to maintain Soviet neutrality.

On 30 July, also, the Japanese ambassador in Moscow repeated to his government that in his opinion its view of the Soviet situation was unrealistic. Satō reported further that he had spoken again to Lozovsky, repeating Japan's fervent hope that the Potsdam Proclamation would not prevent the Soviet Union from receiving Prince Konoye and acting as mediator to bring an end to hostilities. Any formula short of unconditional surrender, any formula that guaranteed Japan's national polity, would be acceptable. Lozovsky gave no reply; both Molotov and Stalin were still in Potsdam.

The question of how Stalin, despite his previous undertakings to the Allies, was to declare war on a country with which he was still in a state of neutrality, remained unanswered. Molotov had indicated that Stalin would like the United States and Great Britain to "request" Russia's aid. Truman, after conferring with his aides and his allies, declared that he "did not like this proposal." He found it "cynical." Instead, he and his secretary of state, James Byrnes, evolved another formula, based on the Charter of the United Nations, whereby Russia might evade her formal commitment to Japan to maintain a state of neutrality until the following April.

"On 31 July," Truman tells us, "I wrote Stalin as follows: 'In response to your suggestion that I write you a letter as to the Far Eastern situation, I am attaching a form letter which I propose to send you at your convenience after you notify me you have reached an agreement with the

Government of China. . . . If you decide to use it, it will be all right. However, if you decide to issue a statement basing your action on other ground or for any other reason prefer not to use this letter, it will be satisfactory to me. I leave it to your good judgment.' "

In his "form letter," as he calls it, Truman, after quoting from the declaration signed at Moscow on 30 October 1943 and from the proposed Charter of the United Nations, concludes: "It seems to me that under the terms of the Moscow Declaration and the provisions of the Charter, above referred to, it would be proper for the Soviet Union to indicate its willingness to consult and cooperate with other great powers now at war with Japan with a view to joint action on behalf of the community of nations to maintain peace and security."[48] This solution, it would seem, was not considered cynical.

On 30 July, also, American planes dropped leaflets over the city of Hiroshima. They read: "If the war goes on, Japan will be destroyed. This is certain. The longer the war goes on, the more Japan will be crippled and the harder will be the task of post-war reconstruction. It is not difficult for a man to give up his life for his country, but true loyalty now means the termination of the war and the concentration of the national effort on the rehabilitation of the country."

On the following day, Brigadier General Thomas F. Farrell, deputy director of the Manhattan Project, who was then on the island of Tinian, informed General Groves in Washington that the bomb was ready, the planes were ready, and the men were ready. His understanding of the 25 July directive was that the bomb might now be dropped as soon as weather conditions permitted. Groves presumably agreed: the authority to carry out the order to drop the atomic bomb on Japan was now in the hands of the field commander. The only reason it was not dropped immediately, then, was that weather conditions, for a few days, did not permit it.

But it was, after all, to make no difference. Japan continued to waste the precious moments that remained; everyone appeared to be in a state of immobility, awaiting the good word from Moscow. Even the emperor, at least for the time being, had his mind elsewhere. On the last day of the month, he summoned Marquess Kido and told him that he wanted the Three Sacred Treasures to be brought to the Imperial Palace. The emperor said that he would protect them with his own person, and should enemy forces parachute into Tokyo in the battle for the homeland, he desired no alternative but to share the fate of the treasures themselves. The mirror, the sword, and the jewels had been presented by Amaterasu-o-Mikami, known as the Sun Goddess, to her grandson when he descended from heaven to rule the earth—and had ever since, according to Japanese legend and history, been the sacred symbols of imperial rule, for the imperial house was still considered to be in the line of direct descent from the goddess herself.

CHAPTER 8   AUGUST 1945

In Hiroshima, as the fateful month began, rumors of all sorts multiplied with remarkable fecundity and spread with scarcely believable speed along the grapevines of the still untouched city. *Why* was it still untouched? That was what everyone wanted to know, the question everyone tried to find an answer to—and one answer seemed as credible as another. Often the answers were contradictory, but that seemed to make little or no difference: like Alice when she was in Wonderland, the people of Hiroshima had learned to believe any number of impossible things before breakfast. That is, if there *was* any breakfast; frequently there was not.

One of the most agreeable rumors that scampered about the city ran to the effect that the Americans had left, and would leave, it unscathed because of its beauty: once they had won the war, they would transform it into a resort town. That was a happy rumor to believe, either before or after or even without breakfast. A rather less happy one had it that the Americans were saving Hiroshima for some terrible fate, a fate more terrible than any that had yet struck the cities of Japan.

Still another rumor reached the ears of many, including Kōichi Okitsu, a thirty-six-year-old bank clerk. He heard, in his own words, that "the Americans were planning to bomb the great dam that had been built in one of the northern mountains, thus releasing an enormous flood of water that would inundate the whole city and carry all its inhabitants to a watery death in the Inland Sea."

Okitsu's house in Shiroshima Kita-chō (about a mile and a quarter from the center of the atomic explosion) stood beside the Ōta River, the mainstream of Hiroshima's seven delta rivers. Often, when he climbed to the top of the riverbank on his side and looked across to the opposite bank, which stood so much higher and seemed so much stronger than his own, he would recall that in older days, when Hiroshima was still a feudal town, the samurai dwelt on the far side while members of the lower classes, merchants, and artisans, had their houses on the less protected side. Okitsu had been told that the bank on his side of the river had been made deliberately low, so that if ever its waters overflowed, the merchants and the artisans—not the samurai— would be carried away by the flood. One could hardly help remembering such things when one kept hearing the persistent story that the Americans were planning to bomb the great dam.

The rumor, in fact, gained such wide credence that the municipal authorities distributed life-rafts to some two hundred thousand people. These were not very sophisticated affairs, merely four bamboo stems tied together by straw ropes, but the authorities assured the people who received them that all they had to do to be saved, if the Americans carried out their diabolical plot, was to strap the little bamboo raft to their backs: then they would remain afloat. Since there were not enough of these so-called life-savers for every member of a household, those who remained without were told to make rafts for themselves. Okitsu was one of the people who was given one.

Another was Mrs. Shinobu Hizume, the forty-four-year-old wife of a man who worked in the Deposit Bureau of the Hiroshima municipal government. But Mrs. Hizume had four children; and she still recalls, to this day, her trip up into the mountains to cut down enough bamboo to make five more little rafts—four for her children and one for her husband. Like most of the people of Hiroshima, she believed that they would indeed serve as life-savers in the event of emergency.

Another such believer was Wataru Sasaguri, also forty-four, the president of a poultrymen's association, who lived in Hiratsuka-chō, not far from one of the city's seven rivers. He had been told that the raft would save his life either in the event of flood or in case of an incendiary bombing. Should the latter occur, all he had to do, to escape the billowing flames that might engulf the city, was to jump into the river with his life-saver strapped to his back. Thus, he considered himself safe in either event. Anyway (for the rumor of course grew as it traveled), even when the Americans did bomb the dam, the great tide of water that was released could not possibly reach Hiroshima for at least eight hours—plenty of time in which to escape.

Everyone wanted his life raft; no one bothered to give much thought to the realities of the situation. There were a number of dams in the vicinity of Hiroshima. The great one in the north, called Taishakukyō, was situated some thirty miles from the city proper. Even should it, as well as half a dozen others of equal size and distance, be bombed, to what extent would the waters of the city's rivers rise? If the people had been more rational, in those few days before the bomb fell, if they had been less thoroughly conditioned to believe everything the authorities told them, they would have realized that their life rafts would be unnecessary in the event the Americans did bomb all the dams in the vicinity and useless if they fire-bombed the city itself. But now everyone, before retiring for the night, made sure that his life-saver lay beside his pillow.

The flames of rumor were further fanned by two American prisoners of war who had been captured when their plane was shot down on 30 April in Hiroshima's only preatomic bombing. Haruo Masumoto, a twenty-four-year-old private first-class in the medical corps of Hiroshima's Western Second Army, who had been detailed to attend to their injuries, remembers the incident. "The only medicine I had," he recalls, "was tincture of iodine, so I had no choice but to paint iodine over their wounds. Then I stood in the background as they were being interrogated. One, who seemed to be about twenty-three or twenty-four, frequently murmured, 'Awful, awful.' When asked what was awful, he replied, 'Not that I've been captured. But soon a terrible bomb will be dropped on Hiroshima, and the whole city will be wiped out. And I'll be wiped out with it—that's what's so awful.' None of us really took in what the prisoner was saying. We all thought his ravings about that 'terrible bomb' absurd, and laughed at his fears."

But the prisoner kept muttering, "Awful, awful," and Masumoto, who was treating his wounds, began to believe, almost against his own will, that there was something to what the young American was saying. Masumoto had been in the army some two years, and he was aware how greatly its morale had deteriorated in that time. Now, as he watched the prisoner refuse all food save potatoes, as he heard him repeat again and again his dire prediction, Masumoto was finally persuaded that Hiroshima had indeed been preserved so far only so that it might be the target for that "terrible bomb." To his buddy, another private first-class, Masumoto whispered, "You know, I don't think it's at all unlikely that we'll be the next."

Meanwhile, the city lay under darkened skies, for a typhoon was racing across western Japan toward Korea. In the gusty winds and the typhoon rains, the city's sixth and last demolition plan was being carried out. The authorities had decided that another 2,500 houses had to go, and now, one after another, they were collapsing into rubble. Hiroshima was not to be free of the typhoon's effects until 4 August; many who complained adout it could hardly have realized that it was that very typhoon which was granting them a few extra days of life. For on Tinian, by 2 August, everything was in readiness—everything except the weather necessary for sight-bombing. At 12:15 P.M. (Mariana time) the last components of the atomic bomb were put into the hands of the 509th Composite Group.

At Potsdam, on 1 August, the three powers held their last two meetings, most of which were devoted to wrangling over European problems—zones of occupation, trials of war criminals, German reparations, territorial demarcation, and the like. Presumably Japan was no longer a subject for discussion, although the new British prime minister, Clement Attlee, did suggest a private conversation with Truman following the afternoon session. No record of this talk has ever been made public, but it is to be supposed that the question of the "new weapon to be used on Japan" (in Attlee's words) certainly came up. Attlee was later to write: "Agreement for the dropping of the bomb by the United States had already been given by Sir Winston Churchill on behalf of Britain. I was, therefore, not called upon to make a decision, but if I had been I should have agreed with President Truman."[49]

"It was three o'clock in the morning [of 2 August]," Truman records, "when the Potsdam conference formally adjourned. The delegates from the three nations spent some time in saying good-bys, and at 4 A.M. I left Cecilienhof with my party and returned to the Little White House. Shortly thereafter I left Babelsberg for the airport at Gatow on the first leg of my journey home."[50] Truman was to fly to England, to meet King George, and then to return to the United States as he had left it, aboard that happy ship, the *Augusta,* with its fine band and its nightly movies.

It is interesting to note that immediately upon the closing of the Potsdam Conference, he made the following observation: "At Potsdam the Russians had pledged their signature on a document that promised co-operation and peaceful development in Europe. I had already seen that the Russians were relentless bargainers, forever pressing for every advantage for themselves. . . .

"Anxious as we were to have Russia in the war against Japan, the experience at Potsdam now made me determined that I would not allow Russians any part in the control of Japan. . . . As I reflected on the situation during my trip home, I made up my mind that General MacArthur would be given complete command and control after victory in Japan. We were not going to be disturbed by Russian tactics in the Pacific.

"Force is the only thing the Russians understand. And while I was hopeful that Russia might someday be persuaded to work in co-operation for peace, I knew that the Russians should not be allowed to get into any control of Japan."[51]

Then why, one cannot but wonder, was Truman so anxious "to have Russia in the war against Japan"? When the Potsdam Conference opened, he had been told by many of his advisers that the Pacific war could be won without the Russians, that no concessions need be made to entice them in, and that the problem would be, rather, to keep them out. Nevertheless, "There were many reasons," he writes, "for my going to Potsdam, but the most urgent, to my mind, was to get from Stalin a personal reaffirmation of Russia's entry into the war against Japan, a matter which our military chiefs were most anxious to clinch. This I was able to get from Stalin in the very first days of the conference. We were at war, and all military arrangements had to be kept secret, and for this reason it was omitted from the official communiqué at the end of the conference. This was the only secret arrangement made at Potsdam."[52]

America's "military chiefs" were, in that case, as blind as Japan's, almost as blind as the Japanese foreign office, which persisted in ignoring its ambassador's recommendations and admonitions, and which continued to pin its failing hopes on the Soviets. On 2 August Tōgō repeated his optimistic belief that Satō would soon have an affirmative reply. "The war situation has become desperate," he cabled. "We have only a few days in which to arrange to end the war. The emperor is deeply troubled about this. . . ." Tōgō went on to ask Satō to make every effort to persuade Molotov to receive the imperial envoy. "To miss one day now," he concluded, "may mean a thousand years of regret. . . ."

But Molotov and Stalin, preparing to leave Potsdam, were to return to Moscow by train; they would not arrive back until 5 August (Moscow time).

On 2 August air force headquarters on Guam sent a directive to the 509th Composite Group on Tinian giving the date of the "special attack": it was to be 6 August. The first target was to be Hiroshima, weather permitting; if not, the second was to be Kokura; the third, Nagasaki. The method of attack was to be sight-bombing from the familiar high altitude. Planes other than those engaged in the mission were not to enter within fifty miles of the target area either four hours before or six hours after the attack.

On 3 August Professor Nambara and Professor Takagi once again urged Marquess Kido to make every effort to put an immediate end to hostilities. Hachiro Arita, a former foreign minister, wrote Admiral Yonai, the navy minister, on that same day, saying: "In my opinion, the moment has come for you to take some drastic measure. Should you miss this opportunity, Japan may well be precipitated into a situation from which she may not be able to recover. At the same time, you will have lost forever the chance to requite the emperor's magnanimity."

But all was in vain. The impetus that had, for a time, inspired the emperor and the men around him to move in the direction of peace now appeared stagnant; everyone was still waiting for a reply from the Kremlin; no one seemed able to credit that the Potsdam Proclamation meant exactly what it said: "We shall brook no delay. . . . The alternative for Japan is prompt and utter destruction."

The military continued to issue optimistic communiqués; it was still prepared, even anxious, to fight the final battle. But the people who had to stand in line for over an hour in order to buy their evening newspaper found themselves increasingly unable to believe those communiqués. Japan—they knew it in their hearts—had already lost the war; the will to fight was vanishing fast. The young men, however, who had been drafted into kamikaze units had to believe in something; they could not, otherwise, have gone on. "We believe," wrote one of them, a twenty-three-year-old student, "that our death will not have been in vain if it has made at least some contribution to the well-being of our fathers and mothers, of our sisters and brothers and sweethearts."

The fifth of August was a Sunday. The typhoon had passed; the skies over Hiroshima were clear and the sun was hot and strong, with only a slight southwesterly breeze. The thermometer had risen to 32.2°C. (90.0°F.) and humidity was 77 percent.

Mrs. Hizume, the housewife with four children who had gone up into the mountains to get bamboo for her family's life rafts, decided to take her twelve-year-old son, Tadaaki, out to dig for clams. They went to nearby Miyuki Bridge, and there, while her son swam in the river, Mrs. Hizume thought about Hiroshima. Herself a native of Niigata, she had come to Hiroshima two years before with her husband and family. Before coming, she had been told what a beautiful city it was, but now she decided she did not like it very well. For one thing, she thought, as a menacing whine sounded in her ear, there were far too many mosquitoes.

Akira Fujihira was a seventeen-year-old boy from Tochigi Prefecture who had come to Hiroshima only a few days before (on 27 July, to be exact) to enroll in Hiroshima Higher Normal School, whose entrance examinations he had just passed. However, he had not been allowed to join the school but had been drafted instead into the so-called Volunteer Corps to work at the factory of the Tōyō Kōgyō company. Like many Japanese at that time, he assiduously kept a diary. "Today," he wrote, "is 5 August, a Sunday, but we are not permitted to leave our factory dormitory. What boredom the whole day long! I kept wondering, 'Why am I here?' It seems I am always thinking about home these days. I wonder if I could study in this frame of mind! And I wonder why my thoughts keep going back to Tochigi. Is it because I have not really separated myself from home? My farewell to my mother, to whom I owe so much for bringing me up, was only a brief one. How I should like to go home once more to say a longer goodbye!"

Not everyone who was supposedly confined to quarters remained there. P.F.C. Haruo Masumoto, of the medical corps, went AWOL for that one day, along with two other soldiers, in order to visit the house of his friend, P.F.C. Kawamoto, in Gion-machi. He was glad he had gone, because he was given a lot of saké to drink and, incredibly, a whole chicken to eat. He was even gladder later on, when he learned that his being absent without leave had inadvertently saved his life.

At 9:20 that night an air raid warning was sounded in the Hiroshima district, and seven minutes later the warning became a full-scale alarm. But it turned out, after all, to be only a single B-29, which soon veered around and disappeared. No harm was done. What the people of the city could not know was that it was a reconnaissance plane, sent to observe the weather conditions over Hiroshima; nor could they know that the plane reported back to base predicting good weather for an early morning flight on the morrow.

On 5 August in Moscow the Japanese ambassador, having learned that Molotov had returned, asked for an interview with the foreign commissar. Satō was not to get a reply to that request for two days, at which time the meeting would be fixed for 8 August at 8 P.M. It was later on to be changed to 5 P.M.

That evening, as soon as the sun went down, the people of Hiroshima

ate for supper what food they had and then crawled onto their bedrolls
to get some sleep before the air raid warnings aroused them. Alongside
them lay their bamboo rafts, their first aid kits, and an emergency bag
of clothing and a little food. Since 1 August, it seemed to them that
their nights had been a constant flurry of warnings and alarms; they
had not been able to get much rest.

By 5 August, on Tinian, the crews of the three planes that were to
fly the Little Boy to Hiroshima had already been briefed by Captain
William Parsons and Colonel Paul Tibbets. The crews had seen a film
of the Trinity explosion: they understood at last why they had been
trained to drop only one bomb, then bank sharply. On that same day
the Little Boy itself, now completely assembled, was carefully packed
into the plane that was to deliver it to Hiroshima, the *Enola Gay*. With
its body an inconspicuous dull gray bronze and its tungstite head shining
like a mirror, it gave little indication of the skills, the man-hours, and
the dollars that had gone into the making of it.

Around ten o'clock that night Colonel Tibbets held another conference with the men who were to fly to Hiroshima; then everything
was given a final, last-minute recheck, while the crews of the three
planes that were to carry out the mission heard a last and perhaps
repetitive briefing. The *Enola Gay* was to carry the bomb itself; Chuck
Sweeney, with his Crew 15, three scientists, and a great many instruments, was to fly nearby; the third plane, commanded by George
Marquardt, was to carry a number of cameras.

At 2:27 A.M. Colonel Tibbets taxied the *Enola Gay* (named for his
mother) onto runway A, turned the nose of the plane in the direction
of Japan, and took off, exactly as scheduled, at 2:45. He was followed
by the two other planes. They rendezvoused over Guam and then
headed, in formation, for Hiroshima.

PART III
6 AUGUST 1945

PART III
6 AUGUST 1945

CHAPTER I   8:00 A.M.

M rs. Hizume was usually awake by six, and this hot, clear Monday morning was no exception. Like everyone else in Hiroshima, she was still sleepy, for two air raid warnings had shrilled during the night, one at nine o'clock and another at eleven, and both times she had got ready to leave the house with her family, but on neither occasion did the warning siren turn into a full-scale alarm. Still, her sleep had been disturbed, and now, as she began to prepare breakfast for her family, she realized how tired she was.

The familiar morning smell of the salty waters of the Inland Sea mingled with the equally familiar morning smell of the bean paste soup that she was about to bring to a boil. The Ōta River, which rises in the Chūgoku mountain range, branches into four smaller streams as it approaches the center of the city, and then the largest of these forks again, so most of Hiroshima lies on six deltaic islands washed by these estuarial streams. Where the fresh waters flow into the Inland Sea, tidal currents carry the salt waters up into the rivers. Thus, although one may live some distance from the sea itself, the smell of the sea is a familiar one to everybody in the city.

Mrs. Hizume's house in Minami-machi stood near the mouth of one of the seven rivers, the Kyōbashi. Moving about her small kitchen, Mrs. Hizume thought wearily what a skimpy breakfast her family was to get for the start of a long hot day: a tiny bit of rice mixed with a lot of barley and a soup that, in addition to the bean paste, contained only some sweet potato stems. There were also a very few pieces of pickled vegetable. The first member of the family to join Mrs. Hizume was her elder son, twelve-year-old Tadaaki. Rubbing his still sleepy eyes, he sat at the low table in traditional Japanese style.

Mrs. Hizume, as she watched him gulp down his breakfast, remembered how he had romped about in the river the day before and wondered how this meager breakfast could keep him going. He was already getting tall, but he had a clearly undernourished look. She sighed. Few people in the city were faring any better, and there was nothing she could do. Just as Tadaaki was finishing, the rest of the family came in and knelt around the table. Tadayoshi, the master of the house, was fifty years old; his two daughters, Kazuko and Masumi, were eighteen and fourteen. The younger son, Tadaatsu, who was only seven, had been sent away to live in the country.

Having finished his breakfast, Tadaaki was about to go off to do his work for the day. His school, a municipal middle school in which he was in the first grade, was closed for the summer, and Tadaaki, like other boys and girls in middle and higher schools, had been drafted to help with the new wave of demolition that was going on to create additional fire prevention zones. "Where are my leggings? Do you know?" Tadaaki called, for he was always forgetting what he had done with his things.

As Mrs. Hizume was about to go to the *genkan* ("Japanese vestibule"), where the family always put its shoes before entering the house proper, Mr. Hizume shouted angrily, "Why can't you remember where you put your things? What a sloppy boy!"

Mrs. Hizume, who had been unable to find Tadaaki's leggings, asked, "Don't you remember what you did with them yesterday?"

"Never mind," the boy replied. "I won't wear them today."

As Mrs. Hizume watched her young son trudging off to work, she decided it was no great matter, since no one expected an air raid that day, although the absence of leggings would make the demolition work a little harder for the boy.

She then returned to the table, to join the rest of her family. They were all, as it happens, working at the same place, the Hiroshima Deposit Bureau, but they seldom left the house at the same time. Tadayoshi was a fairly senior employee, Kazuko had been working there for only a couple of months, while Masumi, a second-year student at the Shintoku Girls' High School, had, quite coincidentally, been drafted to put in some work there during the summer holiday.

Her breakfast soon finished, Kazuko was about to leave. Just as she opened the door, however, an air raid warning sounded. The time was 7:09. There were no planes to be seen, however, so Kazuko left at 7:15, saying she didn't want to be late for work. At 7:31 an all-clear sounded.

Major General Shūitsu Matsumura, chief of staff of the Fifty-ninth Army (Chūgoku Military District), was living in quarters near the center of the city. He had been transferred to Hiroshima from Tokyo only a month before, and he found the still untouched city, with its seven sparkling rivers, a delightful change from the desolation of the bombed out capital.

That Monday morning, sitting in the shade in a wicker chair on the verandah, watching the elderly caretaker water the garden, he was thinking that this city which he had grown to like in so short a time could not long escape the attentions of the American bombers. Nearby Kure, which had been an important naval base, was already in ruins, and certainly the Americans knew that Hiroshima was the military center of western Japan as well as the headquarters of the Second General Army. The battle for the homeland, he thought, will soon be on us. How long can this lovely city continue to evade the bombers? Day by day its people grow more apprehensive.

After morning roll call, P.F.C. Haruo Masumoto, who was attached to the Western Second Corps in the West Parade Ground, was summoned to the surgeon's office. There he found the two friends with whom he had gone AWOL the day before. Uneasily they realized that their misconduct had been found out. After being reprimanded by the surgeon, they were told that their punishment was to go to divisional headquarters and ask for instructions to dig a bomb shelter. When they reached headquarters, they were told to wait outside, so they stood at attention in the broiling hot sun. Soon they felt beads of sweat rolling down their foreheads into their eyes; but they continued to stand at attention, waiting.

At the east entrance of Hiroshima Station, one of a long queue of people waiting for a streetcar was Fumio Shigetō, deputy director of the Hiroshima Red Cross Hospital. He had been shifted to Hiroshima from Yamaguchi only two weeks before, but already he had established his routine and would normally, by this time, have been in his office, drinking a morning cup of tea. Today, however, he was late because he had gone to pay a courtesy call on a section chief of the prefectural government. The sun was already extremely hot and there was still no sign of the streetcar, so Shigetō stepped out of the queue to take shelter under the eaves of the station entrance.

Near the center of the city, where the Ōta River forks into the Hongawa and the Motoyasu, stands the island of Nakajima. Just before the fork, the Ōta is spanned by the Aioi Bridge, which in turn is connected with another bridge that crosses to Nakajima. Aioi Bridge, then, is shaped very like the letter T. Over a hundred yards downstream from the bridge, along the banks of the Motoyasu, stood the headquarters of the prefecture's Fuel Distribution and Control Cooperative. A three-story building with a basement, it was known as the *Nenryō Kaikan* ("the Fuel Hall").

At eight o'clock thirty-seven employees of the cooperative gathered, as was customary, in a room on the second floor in order to make their morning obeisance to the emperor. After bowing deeply in the direction of the Imperial Palace, they dispersed to their various desks and offices. One of the employees, Eizō Nomura, saw that a document which was usually kept on his desk and which he now needed was missing. Nomura decided that his section chief had forgotten to bring the paper up from the basement that morning; he would have to go down to get it. He put his spectacles and his wallet on his desk as well as his watch, which he had unchained from his belt, and then made his way down a steep concrete stairway to the basement. About a hundred square feet in area, it was only dimly lit by a naked electric light bulb hanging from the center of the ceiling. To Nomura, entering from the brightly lit rooms above, it seemed almost wholly unilluminated. He began to fumble around in the dark, looking for the missing document.

The Young Men's Hall in Yokogawa-chō, in the northern section of Hiroshima, had been converted temporarily into a primary school, the reason being that the municipal authorities feared the regular schoolhouse would be too conspicuous an object to marauding bombers. Most of the city's children who normally attended primary schools had already been evacuated; only a relatively small number still remained, and even these were not given the instruction they would have had ordinarily. Instead, they were being taught how to make semaphore signals.

Shortly before eight o'clock the school's fourth-grade pupils began their lessons, but soon an air raid warning sounded, and their teacher ordered them to stop. One of them, Noboru Shigemichi whose home was not far from the school, went into a nearby shelter. As soon as the all clear sounded, Noboru, who had been lying crouched in the dark shelter, ran out into the sunlight and then headed back toward his classroom in the Young Men's Hall. On the way, he met two of his fellow pupils. When the three got to the school, however, they found it empty. Opening a window that faced onto the school yard, they entered their classroom and stood for a time discussing whether they should put their things away in their desks and go outside to play.

It has been estimated that, on that Monday morning in August, there were some four hundred thousand people in Hiroshima: two hundred forty thousand of the city's regular inhabitants still remained; another sixty thousand had fled there from other parts of the country; military personnel numbered about ninety thousand; "national volunteers" and students drafted for work of various kinds totaled around ten thousand.

Of these, some were at their desks, occupied with the endless paper work that the logic of war entails; some were working at munitions factories by the sea; some were getting ready to go into the country to try to find food for their families; some were out on the rivers in boats, fishing; some were engaged in the sad labor of pulling down their own or others' houses so as to create additional fire free lanes; some were gathered in public areas, such as school playgrounds, listening to officers of the Imperial Japanese Army assure them in ringing tones that ultimate victory was still within their grasp; and some, happening to glance upward to the east, caught sight of three B-29s winging their way toward the city through the clear blue sky.

After her two daughters had left for the Deposit Bureau, Mrs. Hizume stood for a moment in the *genkan* to say goodbye to her husband, Tadayoshi. He was wearing the national wartime work uniform (called a *kokumin fuku*), with a field service cap on his head. Over his shoulder was slung a first aid kit. At ten minutes to eight he closed the front door behind him. Mrs. Hizume was now alone in the house.

She cleared away the breakfast things, then put some soy beans in a pot to soak in preparation for her family's evening meal. That finished, she went upstairs to hang out the laundry that she had done the previous evening. It was a hot clear day, with a slight breeze; the clothes, she thought as she stepped onto the wooden balcony, would not take long to dry.

The next thing she was aware of was a sudden blinding flash that seemed to sear her eyeballs; at the same time, her whole body felt as though a silvery current was flowing through it, and she heard a slight rushing sound, as of falling sand. Within a split second the current that she had felt passing through her body became a sensation of intense heat. Then she heard the crackle of burning hair. As she put her hands to her head, it seemed to her that every part of her was on fire. Without conscious thought, she ran inside and began to roll on the tatami, the straw mats that covered the floor, in an attempt to put out the flames that she felt were devouring her.

Then the whole house began to quiver. Rising from the floor, she now saw that countless bits of jagged glass had pierced her body; her arms and legs were bleeding; she could even feel the sharp fragments of glass in her face. Hardly knowing what she was doing, she crept downstairs, where the family kept an emergency first aid kit. The stairs too were strewn with broken glass. Then she saw that the walls of her house had caved in; the doors had been blown off; the house no longer had a roof. Outside, it was as dark as though the city had been enveloped in a heavy dust storm. What had happened?

At eight seconds past 8:16, the Little Boy had exploded. Fifty-one seconds previously it had been dropped from the bomb bay of the

Enola Gay at a height of almost six miles. The three B-29s—the bomb carrier itself and the two observation planes—had turned sharply, as their pilots had been trained to do, and had fled the scene of imminent disaster. The explosion occurred at a height of 1,850 feet and less than two hundred yards from the target point, the T-shaped Aioi Bridge that spanned the widest of the seven streams. The huge fireball that formed afterwards possessed, for a fraction of a second, a temperature of a million degrees. To many of the people who saw it, the fireball looked like a tremendous bluish white flash that blazed for about three seconds. The Little Boy had released the equivalent of 13,500 tons of TNT over the center of the city.

The point of explosion in the air is generally referred to as the epicenter; the point directly below it, on the ground, as the hypocenter. This latter was later determined to lie in the courtyard of Shima Hospital, in Saiku-machi. The intense heat of this man-made sun incinerated virtually everything within a radius of some five hundred yards of the hypocenter. Within a three-hundred-yard radius the heat waves travelled at a speed of around twelve hundred feet a second. Buildings as distant from the hypocenter as two miles or more were set ablaze. A thick cloud of smoke mushroomed into the sky to a height of forty thousand feet. The shock wave that followed immediately upon the explosion was felt well over a mile away from the hypocenter. Radioactivity within half a mile of the hypocenter was so intense that almost everyone who managed to survive both the heat and the blast was doomed to eventual death from the effects of the radiation. Death, for some, was so sudden, so swift, they did not even have time to cry out in pain and shock; for others, who were badly burned or injured in other ways, death came more painfully, in a matter of minutes or hours or days; for still others, who were damaged internally by the radiation, death was a lingering affair. Some of the people who were in Hiroshima that morning are still, a quarter of a century later, suffering from the effects of "radiation sickness."

But at the time the bomb fell, no one in the city had any idea what had actually happened. Those who did not die immediately were in a state of shock. Naturally enough, accounts by eyewitnesses of what happened when the bomb exploded differ widely. Most of those who survived, however, seem agreed that people within the city did not hear the bomb: they only saw its blinding flash and suffered its devastating effects; people who lived outside the city heard the boom. For that reason, there were, for a time, two words in use to describe what had happened. Those who did not hear the bomb called it the *pika*— "the flash"; those who did hear it called it the *pikadon*—"the flash-boom." The latter is now the generally accepted term in Japanese to describe what happened during that split second when a city of nearly half a million souls was subjected to an atomic explosion.

In Nobori-machi (some four thousand feet from the hypocenter), Michimasa Kitamura, a fuel merchant, was talking on the telephone to the proprietress of a Japanese inn in Nakajima-honmachi. She had called to ask Kitamura to help her find some girls to work as maids at the inn. He replied that he could think of only one at the moment but that he would be glad to take her over to the inn in a day or two.

"Thank you," said the owner of the inn. "Please bring her whenever it's convenient. An incendiary bomb may destroy my hotel any moment, but I would like to see her all the same."

Kitamura did not have time to reply. There was a blinding flash, and the telephone line went dead instantly. "Hello!" cried Kitamura, but he was unable to say any more. The floor quivered; the walls of his house crumbled in. The woman he had been talking to was already dead: her inn was only a few hundred feet from the hypocenter, and the bomb had exploded almost directly over her head.

The Fuel Hall, as it was called, was also almost immediately below the epicenter. Eizō Nomura, still in the basement of the building, seeking that elusive document, suddenly felt as though a great quake had shaken the earth beneath him. The light bulb hanging from the center of the ceiling went out. An instant later, something fell on him, and he felt a warm trickle on his forehead. He knew instinctively that it was his own blood, but he did not know anything else. The basement was plunged in darkness. He could see nothing.

He groped his way toward the stairs, but when he reached the right spot he found that they were no longer there. There was only a rubble of broken boards and tiles and powdered plaster. As he put his hands in the rubble, he felt something soft; investigating a little further in the blackness, he realized that what he had felt was a human being and that the human being was dead. From somewhere above him he heard cries for help; then the cries became sobs. Frantically he tried to climb the mound of rubble that had once been a stairway, but his way seemed to be blocked by a wall of concrete. Once again some falling object struck him. Now he became aware of the sound of rushing water; obviously, the pipes had been smashed.

He decided that a bomb had made a direct hit on the building and that if he did not get out of the basement he would be either buried beneath the rubble or drowned by rising water. But how was he to get out? It seemed hopeless. The faces of his four children appeared vividly before his eyes, and then he recalls nothing more until he found himself standing dazed on the first floor of the building. Strangely, it was almost as dark as the basement had been.

Then he saw the dim shape of a man standing by one of the windows.

"Who is it?" he called.

"Hirose," came the reply.

Still disoriented, Nomura asked, "What's outside the window?"

"It's a street."

"Then let's jump out," said Nomura.

Once the two men were outside, they saw that the whole area was wrapped in thick black smoke. They ran toward the Motoyasu Bridge. As they started across it, they saw a naked man lying in their path. His legs and arms, pointing toward the sky, were twitching convulsively; his left armpit was burning. They turned and ran down the stone steps to the river.

There they looked back, through the thick gray cloud that enveloped them, toward the building they had just left. As they watched, tongues of flame seemed to appear from nowhere. The wooden window frames were the first things to burst into blaze; soon the whole building was on fire. Now they saw that the buildings nearby were also burning— the dome-shaped Industry Promotion Hall, the building that housed the chamber of commerce, and the post office were all engulfed in crackling flames. Not until then did Nomura realize that seven other people who had escaped from the Fuel Hall, four women and three men, were sitting on the stone steps of the bridge.

The shock wave of the bomb had apparently first moved outward from the hypocenter, forming concentric circles. Then the blast reversed itself, and the air began to move back in, toward the center. This directional charge created a kind of whirlwind that invaded buildings within a radius of over a mile from the hypocenter and that hurled people as well as heavy objects against the walls and floors. All buildings within well over a mile of the hypocenter, except for a few ferroconcrete structures, were totally destroyed. In some cases, the roofs of houses over five miles away were blown off.

Major General Matsumura, in his quarters three thousand feet from the hypocenter, was flung up into the air by the blast. When he landed, he seemed to see a great ball of fire just beyond his garden. P.F.C. Haruo Masumoto, standing at attention some twenty-seven hundred feet from the hypocenter, was thrown fully thirty yards. Noboru Shigemichi, in his classroom at the Young Men's Hall just under a mile from the hypocenter, dropped to the floor when he heard terrifying sounds that could only mean the building was falling apart; as he did, he felt something heavy strike him on the back. Kazuko, Mrs. Hizume's elder daughter, was walking on the street in front of the Fukuya Department Store, about two thousand feet from the hypocenter, when the blast struck her without warning and she immediately fell unconscious to the ground.

Almost everyone who saw the explosion's blinding flash experienced the overwhelming shock wave a few seconds later. For a moment or two after the explosion, the whole city seemed to have fallen into a trance; it was as silent as a city of the dead. Then the grievously hurt began to moan and stir, if they were able, and to seek help. But where, at a quarter past eight on the morning of 6 August, were they to find it?

CHAPTER 2   8:17–12:00 NOON

Investigation has revealed that within that fatal circle around the hypocenter—a circle with a radius of some fifteen hundred feet—there were 3,483 people at the moment of the explosion. Of these, 88 percent were either killed immediately or died that same day. Only 53 of them are still alive today. One is Eizō Nomura, the man who had gone down into the basement of the Fuel Hall to look for a missing paper.

By the time he encountered his fellow workers on the stone steps beside the Motoyasu River, he was in a shocking state. His hair had all been burnt away, and his skin was so damaged that large areas of the flesh beneath lay exposed. Blood was oozing from the many wounds he had sustained on both face and body. His clothing hung in shreds. For a time, neither he nor his fellow workers uttered a word; like phantoms, they stared blankly ahead. But now that the fires around them had begun to spread, the gray cloud in which they had been immersed lifted somewhat. Feeling the growing heat on his torn body, Nomura slithered two steps downward, closer to the river. Since the water seemed to be sinking, he descended one step more.

All around him, flames leapt into the sky, and from the burning buildings billowed great clouds of thick black smoke. Shards of red-hot metal and bits of burning wood rained down upon the nine people who had sought refuge beside the river. Their instinct was to look upward, in the hope of evading the fiery downpour; but when they did, they found that the billowing smoke was extremely painful to their already scorched eyes. Suddenly the water in the river began to swirl, as in a whirlpool, and then it shot upward, to form a giant, uncanny tower of water. As the eight watched, numbed and terrified, the whirlpool seemed to move downstream. By now the fires had spread still further; the showers of flaming objects seemed to be coming from everywhere.

Then great drops of rain began to fall; it was not like ordinary rain at all— it was dark and heavy and extremely cold. In no time at all, the nine men and women were drenched and chilled. Shivering, they mounted the steps and cautiously approached one of the blazing buildings. In about half an hour they began to feel somewhat warmer, and then they realized that they had better try to escape from the fiery inferno around them. They got as far as the Aioi Bridge, but the situation there was no better. The smoke from the burning buildings was so dense they could hardly see to move any further.

Nomura decided, nonetheless, that he would try to get away and, if possible, find help for the others. He picked up a small sheet of tin, soaked it in the river for a time, then—holding it over his head as a shield—began walking toward Koi, at the far western edge of the city. Shocked and injured, he could not move very fast, and he had to make constant detours to avoid the blazing buildings. He did not reach Koi until the afternoon.

That walk through Hiroshima was like taking a stroll through the lowest reaches of hell. The whole city seemed to be on fire. Wherever he walked, clouds of stinking black smoke belched out at him. Dead bodies lay sprawled where they had fallen. Now and then a silent, ghostly figure would cross his path. All the people he saw were injured —burnt or bleeding or both—and all were nearly naked. Their clothing had been burned away or literally torn from their backs by the blast.

When finally he reached Koi, he tried to persuade a soldier to send help to his fellow workers by the river, but as soon as he began to describe their plight he realized how hopeless his request was. All over the city tens of thousands of people were dead or about to die. Numbly, Nomura continued on into Koi, away from the inferno of the ruined city. He was never to see those eight people again. Only later did the realization come to him that he had been one of the few lucky ones.

Nomura had fled from the center of the city; Keisaku Enami took the opposite course. A student at the Sanyo Commercial High School, Enami had been drafted to work at the Mitsubishi shipyard, which stood nearly two miles from the hypocenter. When the bomb exploded, Enami had received only a slight injury on his arm. The head of the student work force, Professor Moritaki of Hiroshima Higher Normal School, had been so badly burnt in both eyes that for over a week he was unable to open them. Another of the men at the Mitsubishi shipyard, Professor Ishihara, had been far more seriously injured. Enami strapped him to a bicycle and in that way got him to a hospital.

Then the young student climbed onto the same bicycle and tried to make his way to his family's house at Nakajima-honmachi, which, although he did not then know it, lay within the doomed circle around the hypocenter. On the opposite side of the bridge across the Ōta River that was called the Shin-ōhashi ("the Great New Bridge"), he saw lying beside the bank of the river a number of girls whom he took to be students. Some, devoured by thirst, were crawling toward the water's edge; then, even as he watched, they lost their balance and tumbled headlong into the swirling stream.

Not until around two o'clock in the afternoon did he get as far as the Motoyasu Bridge; at its foot he saw a swaying figure, a gaunt man who appeared to have fallen into some kind of cataleptic state. Enami continued on to his house—but it was no longer there. It had vanished, and where it had stood was only a desolate empty space, with a few still smoldering fragments. Not knowing what to do or where to go, he began simply to wander about. Like so many others that day, he was in a state of shock, but he still recalls the disgusting stench that was being carried by the south wind. He remembers looking into the Fuel Hall, where he saw seven or eight people huddled together; he could not tell whether they were sleeping or dead. He remembers also noting, with a kind of numbed surprise, that the fine Jisenji Temple, at the foot of Aioi Bridge, had—like his own house—vanished into air.

The fourth son of the chief priest of Jisenji was named Tetsuo Kaji-yama. A fifth-grader in Nakajima Primary School, he was in the school auditorium on the second floor at the moment that the bomb exploded. Although the school was less than a mile from the hypocenter, several of the children managed to escape, more or less unhurt, from the collapsing building. Among them were Tetsuo and his friend, Masami Kumagawa, who was boarding at Tetsuo's house in the temple compound. Quickly the children discussed the catastrophe and decided that the best thing they could do was seek refuge at the house of one of their classmates in Funairi-chō.

After they had rested there for a short while, Tetsuo and Masami thought they should now try to get to the temple. They followed the Tenma River until they came to a railway bridge; they knew that by following the tracks of the railroad they would eventually reach Aioi Bridge. On the way, they stopped at a house that was still standing; there, after being given a couple of little rice balls, the two boys fell into a short, deep sleep.

Not until past noon did they finally reach Aioi Bridge. The whole district was still wrapped in a thick gray cloud, and the temple itself appeared to be surrounded by burning buildings. The boys decided to try to get to it across the dry riverbed of the Ōta. As they walked on, they were splattered by huge drops of black rain.

When they got to the riverbed, they saw a tattered human figure, hardly able even to stand, swaying back and forth as it supported itself with a piece of wood. The boys could not even tell whether it was a man or a woman. Fearfully they approached.

Then they heard, from somewhere inside the figure, the words: "Is it Tetsuo?"

The boy recognized the voice of his mother.

CHAPTER 3   **MORNING**

The fate of Hiroshima's young people was especially grievous, for while most primary school children had been evacuated to the country-side, older students (those in middle and high schools) had been drafted into "volunteer" labor corps. The more fortunate ones were working in offices or factories; the less fortunate were engaged in the demolition work essential for the creation of additional firebreaks. These, consequently, were working outdoors within fatal range of the hypocenter: most of them were killed by the exploding bomb. In at least six instances, working parties consisting of more than two hundred young people were annihilated on the spot. Still older students (those attending higher schools, colleges, and universities) fared somewhat better, for most of them had been drafted for factory work; thus, they were inside fairly sturdy structures at the moment of the explosion, and as a result relatively few of them were killed.

Osamu Kataoka, a first-grader in the Hiroshima Prefectural Daiichi Middle School in Zakoba-machi (some three thousand feet from the hypocenter), happened to be in his classroom, talking to a group of his schoolmates, at the moment of the explosion. (Half of the first-graders in the school were, in fact, supposed to be helping with the demolition work). As they chattered amongst themselves, they were momentarily blinded by the flash; then almost at once the ceiling started to fall in on them. Osamu, along with four or five others, managed to escape from the collapsing building and ran out into the school yard, where he and the others gathered beside a willow tree. Outside, the world was dark, and there was a strange, sharp smell in the air. Suddenly one of the group started to recite the familiar imperial rescript to the armed forces: "A military man must always be loyal to the emperor. He must at all times be courteous, he must honor courage. . . ."

The recitation stopped. Flames from the burning school building grew hotter; embers began to fall. The boys ran to a nearby swimming pool, where they found a number of others already in the water. For some the blindness had been more than momentary, and some had sustained fairly serious leg injuries; these their schoolmates helped to reach the pool. In the water, along with the still living, floated dead bodies—bodies of those who had been so badly burnt they had not been able to survive, together with bodies of others so grievously hurt they had been unable to move their limbs in order to stay afloat. Some still sat beside the pool, too shocked or too damaged to move. The faces of many of the boys had been swollen to twice normal size by the intense heat of the explosion. Osamu led a blind friend away from the now brightly burning building and from the pool that had become a wallow of death. Together, the two disappeared into the smoke and the dust of the city.

Another first-grader, Issaku Watanabe, was walking with a friend to their place of work at the instant of explosion. Shocked and numbed, they turned in their tracks and started back to Issaku's house. On the way Issaku's friend died. He himself, his face inflated like a grotesque balloon, somehow managed to get home. The only clothes left on his body were a tattered pair of underpants: even his shoes had disappeared. By the time he reached his house, he was trembling all over.

When his mother ran to take him in her arms, he cried, "Don't touch me! Everything hurts so! Just let me sleep." Within the house, the blast had turned everything upside down. Issaku's mother managed to push two sofas together in the guest room, and there the boy lay down for a time. He could tell that the skin on the palms of his hands had by now peeled completely away; he knew that his head was badly burnt, his eyes and mouth grossly swollen.

As Mrs. Watanabe stood sadly over him, wondering what she could do for him, he muttered, "Mother, I can't see your face."

"Open your eyes slowly," she said. "Then you'll be able to see me."

At this he nodded and then said yes, now he could see her; but she wondered whether he was telling the truth.

"Oh, Mother," he cried, "let's go back to Ube!"

"Yes," she said soothingly, "that's what we'll do as soon as you're well." Still wondering what she could do for the boy, Mrs. Watanabe got out a precious tin of mandarin oranges from the family pantry that had been turned into a shambles by the blast. Finally she found the can opener and began to put segments of the oranges into the boy's mouth. "Isn't that delicious?" she said.

But by now Issaku's pain had grown much worse. In obvious agony, he writhed on the bed and then threw up all the bits of orange that he had just eaten.

"What is it?" she cried. "What hurts you worst?"

"My arms and legs," he muttered, his words hardly audible.

What was she to do? There was no medicine in the house that would assuage such severe burns. In stricken silence, she sat down beside her suffering son; she was too saddened even to be able to cry. Her husband had gone off on a trip to his native town of Ube, in Yamaguchi Prefecture. Some time later, with the help of neighbors, Issaku was put on a wooden trestle and carried to a reception center in the clothing depot.

All of the 150 first-graders of the Hiroshima Prefectural Daiichi

Middle School who happened to be outdoors at the moment of explosion were killed; of the same number who were indoors, 133 also died.

More than a score of girls from one of the city's high schools were working at the Central Telephone Exchange. When the bomb exploded, the roof of the building fell in, burying the girls beneath piles of debris. Badly burned and badly injured, they began to cry out in the darkness. Suddenly they heard the shrill voice of their homeroom teacher, Mrs. Wakita: "Get up, all of you! Get up! We must fight on until the final victory."

With Mrs. Wakita's help, one of the girls, Taeko Nakamae, managed to extricate herself from the debris that pinned her to the floor. Taeko saw that others were also struggling to their feet. Trying to make their way out of the building, they kept bumping into overturned desks and chairs, and into smoldering bits and pieces hurled inward from the walls and roof. Among all this mountain of rubble could be seen the motionless bodies of a few girls, obviously dead, their heads cracked and bloody.

Taeko managed to get through one of the windows. Outside, she saw scorched trees, fallen telephone and electric poles, and collapsed houses, all licked by tongues of living flame. Joining a host of others, all as black as the scorched trees, she began to run in the direction of Mount Hiji, but after a little while she had to stop: she had no breath left. Numbly, she watched two children—a boy of about ten and a girl of six. "Mako! Mako!" she heard the boy cry. "Please don't die! Mako, are you dead?" The little girl made no reply. As Taeko watched, the weeping boy took the corpse of his little sister into his arms. No one else paid any attention to the scene. Flames were closing in; everyone in the area who could still move, however slowly or painfully, was trying to escape.

Taeko moved on. At last she was in sight of Tsurumi Bridge, beyond which lay Mount Hiji. As she approached, she saw a vast number of people sitting on the bridge. Most of them were completely naked; a few still wore shreds of tattered clothing. All were burnt. Their bodies were as black as though they had been coated with soot, except where patches of open wound showed red. With some, the skin of their backs had simply fallen away and flapped about in the wind like fluttering shirttails. Faces were swollen, with their features distorted beyond recognition. As Taeko stood there for a moment, she realized that the number of refugees fleeing from the stricken center of the city was growing ever greater.

Among them she saw some of her fellow workers from the Telephone Exchange Bureau, as well as one of the department heads. Looking at Taeko, he said: "You seem to be the worst hurt. We'll have to do something for you." Taeko put her hands to her face, where she could feel blood oozing from the injuries; only then did she realize that she must be as disfigured as many of the others on the bridge. The department head took out a cigarette, crushed it, and pasted the tobacco over the worst of her wounds to staunch the flow of blood.

The fires kept coming closer; the air was growing ominously hot; flames had already begun to lick at the bridge itself. To wait here any longer would be fatal. The bridge was crowded with refugees, tottering, creeping, or crawling across, impeded by the bodies of those who had already died.

"Let's try to swim across the river," Taeko said to her little circle of friends from the bureau.

They all nodded their agreement; but the tide from the Inland Sea was flowing in, and the river was deep and dangerous. Although Taeko was a good swimmer, one of the girls told her she ought not to try it because of her injuries. Mrs. Wakita, who had by now rejoined the group, said, "Hold onto me—we'll get across the river together."

In midstream, however, Taeko's strength gave out. She could no longer move either arms or legs; she felt herself drifting into unconsciousness, and it seemed to her that she was already dead. But Mrs. Wakita was still holding onto her. "Take courage, child," she said. "You can't die here."

Just then a boat approached the struggling girl and woman. A man's sturdy pair of arms reached down and helped to pull Taeko into the boat; Mrs. Wakita followed. When they reached the opposite bank, they carefully thanked their savior and then began to walk, with many others, toward a reception center. After they reached it, Mrs. Wakita murmured, "Wait here just for a few minutes. I'll go and get the others."

Taeko could hardly see Mrs. Wakita as she began to walk in the direction of a group of people in the road; Taeko's eyesight was already beginning to fail. All about her, in the gathering darkness, she heard cries of pain and shouts for help. Everyone seemed to be begging for water. Water, water, water, water—the word was a constant theme amid the cacophony of cries and groans.

By that time it was mid-afternoon, and the remorseless August sun beat down onto the victims of the explosion who had taken refuge on Mount Hiji, at the eastern end of the city. One of these, Taeko Naka-mae, overcome by all that had happened to her since 8:15 that morning, with the blistering sun now pouring relentlessly over her torn body, sank into merciful unconsciousness.

Pupils of the Hiroshima Municipal Daiichi Girls' High School were helping to evacuate buildings in the vicinity of Zaimoku-chō, some two thousand feet from the hypocenter. When the explosion occurred, 277 girls in the first grade and 264 girls in the second grade were killed. All had been working outdoors. Some died instantly, some lingered a few moments longer, some (unable to move) were soon burned to death by the fast-encroaching fires. A very few survived. For a short while, one thirteen-year-old girl, buried beneath dead bodies, could be heard crying for water. The headmaster of the school, who had been overseeing the work of his pupils, tried to reach her but, before he succeeded, her cries stopped and she too was dead. He begged pas-sers-by to call for a doctor, to send some kind of help, but the shocked and blackened passers-by were in those first moments motivated only by instinct, the instinct toward self-preservation. Not until later would they begin to think of other people, and then it would be those who were nearest to them. No one came to help the headmaster of the Hiroshima Municipal Daiichi Girls' High School as he tried to dig out his burnt and wounded pupils.

The temporary school in the Young Men's Hall in Yokogawa-chō (some five thousand feet from the hypocenter) was almost a total sham-bles. After ten-year-old Noboru Shigemichi had managed to extricate himself from the wreckage, he fled out to the nearby road, where he saw a group of men who belonged to the civilian Air Defense Corps. "Please!" he called to them. "Many of my classmates are still in that building. I heard them crying. Help them, please!"

Once he had seen the men head toward the building, he turned and started walking. Two days before, his mother and his two younger brothers had gone to Kabe, some ten miles distant from Yokogawa-chō. He had been to Kabe frequently with his father, helping to transport furniture and other household goods, and in that direction he now set off. When he reached one of the main streets, where a streetcar line had formerly run, he saw a throng of nearly naked people, both men and women, all of them as bald as eggs, many with great patches of burnt skin hanging from their bodies. One woman, her face horribly seared, was dashing about aimlessly, as though she had lost her wits.

Terrified, he started running toward Yokogawa Station but found his way blocked by a great crowd of refugees. However, he began trying to push his way through them and, though jostled about, managed to make a little headway. When he reached Shinjō Bridge, a great wall of torn and frightened human flesh blocked his way entirely. He paused, wondering if he could somehow go around them and get onto the other side of the burning buildings. While he still hesitated, afraid to try it, he saw a man plunge into the flames and emerge on the other side. Then he decided he must do the same. He shut his eyes, and in a few seconds he was through. Although he had not been burnt, he had stepped on broken glass, jagged fragments of which had pierced the soles of his naked feet; but Noboru was too shocked and frightened even to feel the pain.

He continued on. As he passed a partly destroyed dwelling, he was stopped by an older woman, who said to him, "Poor boy, your feet must be giving you great pain. Here, take this pair of slippers—they'll help a bit." Courteously, Noboru thanked her, grateful for this unexpected kindness.

As he walked on along the street, he encountered some people coming in the opposite direction. "You better go back," one of them said to him. "The fires are spreading—you can't get through this way."

But young Noboru had his mind set on getting to Kabe and to his mother. Beyond some nearby paddy fields he could see the embankment of the Kabe railway line. If he followed its tracks, he decided, he must eventually reach the village, and this he now set out to do. But it was not easy going because the tracks were scorching hot, heated by the burning sun overhead and the burning wooden ties beneath. The boy began to run, keeping as far away from the tracks and the smoldering ties as he could, and after about a mile and a half he reached a country road where he could see neither fires nor wounded refugees. He recognized the neighborhood. He had reached the suburb of Gion.

Soon his head began to throb. When he put his hand to the aching places, he felt patches of dried blood. At once he went into a house by the side of the road and asked the people living there if they knew of a doctor nearby. They gave him directions, but when he reached the dispensary a nurse told him that the doctor was out. He resolved that, with or without medical aid, he would somehow manage to get to Kabe. But soon, as he stumbled on, he heard a man shout: "All injured come this way." He went, and by the bank of the river he found an emergency first aid station.

When he arrived, he discovered that he was the only person who had come for treatment. A doctor examined his bruises, cleaned them, and put some antiseptic on them, then bandaged his head. As he was about to take off again, he saw half a dozen men carried in on stretchers, all so horribly burnt Noboru thought they must be dead. As he stood for a moment and watched, he saw that streams of injured refugees were now pouring in. For the first time he realized to the full how lucky he had been.

He left the first aid station and headed on toward Kabe; his only goal was to reach the haven of safety represented by his mother and his two brothers. As he walked, the sky turned suddenly dark; swollen, discolored clouds had gathered, and soon rain began to fall. It was not, as one might have expected, a clean summer shower; it was a downpour of heavy black raindrops. In no time Noboru felt cold and soaked to the skin, and his once white bandage was blotched and dirty. He had been through a great deal already that day, and the black rain seemed to be just another hazard. He did not let it stop him from continuing on to Kabe.

Accounts of the black rain differ widely, for both its extent and its duration varied according to the locality. It began in the districts nearest the hypocenter, then gradually began to spread out. For some it lasted only a short time, for others it seemed to go on for hours. It appeared to be caused by the ascending air currents of the blast and the great fires, and it brought with it, as it fell, the radioactive dust that had risen with the mushroom cloud.

This rain was twice cursed, for it not only fell on open wounds, bringing with it radioactive contamination, but also brought with it freezing chill and extreme discomfort. To little Noboru it had seemed to be only an additional hazard, but to many it was a rain of death.

For those who had sought relief in the Tenma River, just under a mile from the hypocenter, the drops seemed to be as large as a man's little finger. They began to fall about ten o'clock and mercilessly pelted the heads of the wounded. One little girl, who could not have been more than seven and who was clinging to a raft in the river, soon began to cry out for help; in a couple of hours, by the time the rain ended, neither she nor the raft were anywhere to be seen: they had been carried out to sea.

In Yokogawa-machi, some five thousand feet from the hypocenter, Katsutoshi Oka, an instructor, escaped with his pupils from the burning school building down to the dried bed of the Ōta River. There, their faces swollen and burnt and with raw red flesh gaping from open wounds, the boys gathered at the foot of the Sanjo Bridge. The bridge, they now realized, had been so badly damaged as to be unusable and the whole district seemed to be in flames; they would be quite unable to return to their houses. Since it seemed they were destined to remain, for the time being, where they were, they began to gather straw mats that had been blown from houses and planks of unburned wood out of which to build makeshift beds.

Everywhere swirling, irresistible windspouts formed, and great columns of flame leapt a hundred feet into the air. The dead and the dying were sucked by the wind into the fire. The seven streams were in turmoil; many who had sought refuge in the water were carried away. Then, just as the fires seemed to be dying down, the heavy black downpour began. Those who were not subjected to its merciless flogging had to bear with the broiling hot summer sun, which seemed to inflame their agonizing wounds.

Suddenly Oka and his pupils saw great purple clouds above them; then the black rain buffeted their burnt and swollen faces. Quickly they covered their throbbing heads with the mats and boards they had just gathered. The downpour, which ended in a few minutes, had been so heavy it had quite extinguished the burning school building. Everything in the vicinity had been turned black; it no longer even looked like the same place. The boys, their tattered remnants of clothing drenched and blackened, began to shiver with the cold. They stripped, wrung the black water out of the bits and pieces of their clothes as best they could, then put them in the sun to dry. The only medicine Oka had was a bottle of tincture of iodine; with it he painted the worst of the open wounds. Moaning with pain, the boys had no choice but to stay where they were.

Some people said that the black stains left by the rain were actually drops of oil; they contended that the Americans had drenched the city with gasoline and that people who did not cleanse themselves of the black stains would soon burst into flame. But the black stains seemed ineradicable; water would not wash them away.

No one in Hiroshima that day, or for many days afterward, had any sense of time. Almost all watches and clocks had been destroyed. But the people seldom bothered to ask themselves or others what hour of the day it might be. Since the atomic bomb fell, the people of Hiroshima had had a different sense of time: all that day of 6 August they wondered how soon they would die and how soon the people around them would die. That was the only sense of time that remained for them. Toward evening, those who had taken refuge in the eastern hills saw an ominous black cloud gather over the western section of the city. They heard the rumble of thunder, and they saw a fierce shower, the last of the day, fall over the tuins of what had once been Hiroshima.

CHAPTER 4 **ALL DAY: THE CITIZENS**

Mrs. Hizume, still stunned, sat for a time alone in her living room. All the windows and doors of her house in Minami-machi had been shattered by the blast, while the house itself leaned precariously at a sharp angle: it seemed as though it was about to fall at any moment. Finally Mrs. Hizume roused herself and, searching among the rubble, found the family's first aid kit. The only disinfectant it contained was mercurochrome. Carefully she removed what slivers of glass she could from her wounds, then painted them with the medicine.

While she was doing this, one of her neighbors looked in. "But you're very badly hurt!" he exclaimed. "I'll try to get you to a hospital." He found a stretcher, summoned another neighbor, and together, with great caution, they laid Mrs. Hizume on it. Then they started off toward Kyōsai Hospital.

"Thank you very much," murmured Mrs. Hizume weakly.

She heard her bearers say that Minami Primary School had been completely demolished. Then suddenly she was aware of a couple of young students from Hiroshima Higher School. They had recognized her and now, both uninjured, they offered to carry the stretcher to the hospital in place of the two older men.

As Mrs. Hizume, with her two new bearers, approached Miyuki Bridge, they encountered a large group of badly hurt victims of the bomb. From the back of one man, who had lost all his hair, gushed great streams of blood. A young mother, her hair burnt to a frizzle, was walking on, as though in a trance, holding the hand of her young child. The little boy was completely naked; from one of his eyes blood coursed down his cheek. The blackened faces of all the injured seemed devoid of expression, as though they had no emotion left; their bits of clothing were all in tatters. From some came groans and cries; others muttered over and over, "Oh, how it hurts! It hurts so terribly!"

One of the men, who had been walking very slowly, now suddenly stopped in his tracks; he swayed for a moment, then fell to the ground.

It seemed clear that he was on the point of death. "What has happened to us all?" Mrs. Hizume kept wondering. "What on earth has happened?" Now, for the first time, she became aware of the fact that she was clad only in her underclothing; the baggy, wartime trousers she had been wearing had utterly vanished. She felt ashamed to be seen like that; but what could she do?

When they reached the hospital, the students laid the stretcher down gently in the crowded yard. All around her Mrs. Hizume could see people more badly hurt than she. Some sat motionless on the ground, unable to stop vomiting; but all that came out was a thin, yellowish liquid. Others sat or lay moaning in pain. No one appeared to have an ounce of strength left. Mrs. Hizume felt her own small store of strength leaving her. "Just rest here for a while," said the students who had brought her to the hospital yard, "We'll try to get some help for you."

For over an hour, Mrs. Hizume lay without moving. She closed her eyes. The most she could do was to go on breathing. Suddenly a familiar voice sounded in her ears. "Mother!" cried the voice. "Are you all right, Mother?" She looked up: the face beside her was that of Masumi, her younger daughter.

"Oh, yes, I'm all right," murmured Mrs. Hizume, "though there are still a lot of pieces of glass in my body. But, Masumi, how did you manage to get here so quickly?" The girl explained that, at the moment the bomb fell, she had been in front of the Hiroshima branch of the Japan Red Cross Society (some five thousand feet from the hypocenter). The blast had knocked her out for a time, but when she recovered consciousness, she discovered she was unhurt. She rushed home. There she had found spots of blood on the tatami in the living room. Realizing that her mother must have been hurt, she asked around among the neighbors until someone told her that Mrs. Hizume had been taken to the Kyōsai Hospital. Masumi returned to the precariously tilting house, found a tin of preserved fruit and some clean clothes, then rushed to the hospital.

After she had helped her mother put on fresh clothes, she went inside to find assistance. Soon she returned with a nurse, but all the nurse could do was repeat what Mrs. Hizume had already done: paint the wounds with mercurochrome. There was no other medicine available. Having done this, the nurse abruptly left the wounded woman; Masumi felt a surge of anger but realized that there was nothing more, for the moment, that could be done. Her thoughts, as she sat beside her mother, were now on the rest of the family. What had happened to her father, her sister, her brother? What had happened to Hiroshima?

After a little while, she rose. "I'm going to see what I can find out," she said. Weakly Mrs. Hizume nodded and, once her daughter had left her, fell into a deep sleep. She was awakened by an air raid warning. Masumi, she saw, had by now returned, and with her help Mrs. Hizume got to the nearby bomb shelter. It was already unbelievably crowded; the foul stench within the shelter could only be that of the already dead.

No bombs fell, and when the all clear sounded, the two women returned to the hospital yard. Then Masumi told her mother that she had learned from a friend that her father had been seriously injured. The friend had given him some water and told him that his wife had been taken to the Kyōsai Hospital. Hardly able to walk, Mr. Hizume had nonetheless headed for the hospital.

"Mother," said Masumi, "just stay here and rest. I'll go and look for Papa." Alone again, Mrs. Hizume fell asleep once more. This time she was awakened by the arrival of a truckload of injured middle school boys. All had darkened and swollen faces; some were still bleeding; none had any clothes. They begged for water. Thinking of her own son, Tadaaki, who had gone off to work so nonchalantly early that morning, Mrs. Hizume felt tears in her eyes. Was the boy alive or dead?

When Masumi came back, she had to report a lack of success. She had wandered about in the neighborhood of their house but had neither seen nor heard any trace of the other members of the family. By now, it was beginning to grow dark. Masumi managed to persuade the hospital authorities to give her mother a bed in one of the wards. The pain had grown worse, but the hospital had no medicine with which to ease it. Neither the mother nor the daughter could face the thought of eating. The young girl lay down on the floor beside the bed, and after a time both women fell asleep.

Although the people of Hiroshima had frequently carried out air raid drills, each family had taken the added precaution of arranging a meeting place outside the densely populated center, as near as possible to the quarter in which they lived. And, of course, when the atomic bomb fell, the frequent drills availed nothing, nor—for those who were within the lethal radius of the hypocenter—did the pre-arranged meeting places. Most either died on the spot or were too badly hurt to walk.

One who did get away, though seriously injured, was twenty-one-year-old Miss Sadako Doi who was working for the army supplies bureau, temporarily situated on the second floor of the Fukuya Department Store (some two thousand feet from the hypocenter). With the help of a couple of her fellow workers, she headed toward the large green park that surrounded the Sentei residence of the Asano family. Later she was to describe that journey: "Streetcars were lying on their sides or even wholly upside down. Electric wires were twisted into grotesque tangles. Rocks, tiles, wooden beams, and every other sort of rubble lay piled in great mounds; underneath we could see the mangled bodies of the dead. We joined the long line of injured people making their way toward Sentei. Their hair was gone, their faces blackened, their exposed bodies red with dried and still flowing blood. One woman clutched the dead body of her child to her bosom. Other children were laughing hysterically, as though they had lost their minds."

The barracks of the Eleventh Infantry Regiment had been wholly destroyed. The soldiers who escaped, their uniforms gone, could be seen hobbling along, also on their way to Sentei; they were using their swords as walking sticks. One of the officers paused. In between bouts of vomiting the now familiar yellow liquid, he was heard to mutter: "Military men must be resigned to any fate! But the sight of so many mangled civilians is not to be tolerated!" As he spoke, a horse galloped by frantically, its hindquarters flaming.

The Asano Park, by the time Miss Doi and her two friends reached it, was no longer a safe refuge. Its beautiful garden had been built by Nagakira Asano, a daimyo of the Edo period who had been given a fief in Hiroshima by the Tokugawa shogun. It stood on the banks of the Kyōbashi River. The house itself—officially known as the Shukkei-en but generally called Sentei by the people of Hiroshima— had already burst into flame, and tongues of fire were licking at the tall old trees and thick shrubs of the garden.

The three girls fled down to the river, its banks thick with the injured. Some had hoped to ease the pain of their burns by immersing themselves in the water, but the swift current was carrying many of them away, down to the sea. Miss Doi and her friends decided their best hope was to try to swim across to the other bank. This they eventually succeeded in doing, but the effort had drained away what little strength remained in Miss Doi's torn body. Once she had reached the temporary haven of the other bank, without a further thought she fell unconscious to the ground.

Among others who had sought sanctuary in Asano Park was Hideo Yasaka, fifty-six years old, whose house was three thousand feet from the hypocenter and who had been critically wounded. However, with the help of his wife, he also succeeded in reaching Sentei; and he also, for a few moments, lapsed into unconsciousness. As the fires began closing in, his wife shook him out of it, and together they plunged into the pond in the center of the garden.

From there they could see a scene of indescribable chaos. Many of the giant trees had already caught fire and a copse of burning bamboo was exploding like a chain of firecrackers. Many who had begun running toward the relative safety of the pond failed to reach it—the mounting flames engulfed them. From all sides came the piercing screams of people who were being devoured by the fire. No one was any longer able to help others; each could only try to help himself. By now fragments of flaming wood had begun to fall upon those within the pond; everywhere floated the bodies of the dead.

Tamiki Hara, a forty-year-old author, also managed to reach the Sentei, along with his family, and from the park they fled down to the banks of the river. There Hara saw a wooden box floating downstream, full of green onions; Hara retrieved it and handed it to someone on the bank, then dived into the river to rescue a young girl who was being carried away by the current.

He and his family stayed by the river until evening. By that time, little of the once handsome garden was left, although a few of the giant old trees were still smouldering. Hara and his brother decided to walk upstream. "All along the banks," he recalls, "were people with faces so distended and bodies so burnt and misshapen, I could not tell even whether they were men or women. Eyes were little more than enflamed slits; wounds were already festering; many of those we saw were clearly on the point of death. When we passed them, they called softly for water. 'Just a little water,' they pleaded. 'Try to help us. . .' "

The stories told by survivors of that August day are numerous—and awesomely repetitive. Put together, like bits of a very big jigsaw puzzle, they form a picture that people who did not experience the catastrophe would like to forget, but that those who were unlucky enough to be in Hiroshima that day can never erase from their minds so long as they live. For many, that period between holocaust and death was very short; for some, it was a long and infinitely wearisome time; and for others, it has not ended yet.

Yasuo Kawano, who survived the explosion although he was only two thousand feet from the hypocenter, heard cries for help from beneath a collapsed dwelling near Kokutaiji-machi. He saw a middle-aged woman trapped beneath the rubble. "Please help me try to free my legs," she pleaded. Kawano did his best but, single-handed, was unable to free her. Then he saw that other people, men and women both, were pinned beneath the debris: some were clearly dead, others begged weakly for help. There was nothing Kawano could do for them.

Hachirōyasutaka Atago, a student at the Hiroshima Higher Normal School, reported that, as he passed by Senda-machi, he saw burning houses toppling over, one after the other, like rows of tenpins. "Fire seemed to be rampaging through the whole city. One boy, seared by the heat, lay on the ground, his eyes open, his hands and feet twitching. Another, also lying on the ground, was simply staring up at the sky. I spoke to him, but he made no reply. Nearby, a young man, his body terribly burned, was rolling on the scorched earth. 'Kill me!' he kept screaming. 'Will somebody please kill me?' Off to one side, in a ditch, floated a great number of bodies. I saw that at least one person in the ditch was still alive. He was trying to climb out. I grabbed hold of his wrists, in an attempt to help him, but the skin just peeled off in my hands. Beneath lay exposed the naked, bleeding flesh."

Other eyewitnesses have supplied descriptions of electric trains that were derailed near Shiroshima (about five thousand feet from the hypocenter). The passengers in the coaches were all dead; some still had their charred and blackened hands wrapped around the straps they had been clinging to when the bomb exploded. Other survivors have reported seeing a large number of horses lying dead on the West Parade Ground; the heat was so intense that their exposed entrails seemed to be bubbling as though in some macabre stew pot.

Students brought in from the suburbs in a truck, to render what assistance they could, tell about being accosted by an elderly woman, whose head was a mass of wounds and most of whose clothes had been ripped from her body. Yet by that time she was no longer thinking only of herself. Standing near a flaming building, she told the students that a number of children had been trapped inside, and she begged the students to try to help rescue them. But rescue was no longer possible because the building was already an impenetrable pyre.

In the Korean quarter of Yokogawa-machi lived some of the more than eighty thousand Koreans transported to Hiroshima from their Japanese-occupied country to work in the city's munitions plants. Crying for help but ignored by the Japanese, some of the Koreans succeeded in reaching the banks of the Ōta River; the rest perished. No accurate record is available of how many of the city's forced Korean laborers survived.

City Hall, situated some three thousand feet from the hypocenter, was a three-story building that burst into flame when the bomb fell. Mrs. Teruko Kita, thirty-five, escaped from the building only to find herself in a sea of fire from which there seemed to be no hope of escape. Her arms were bleeding copiously. She thought of her children, then resigned herself to her fate. Nearby she saw a large empty drum; she decided to climb into it and there meet her death. But the shock of the blast and the loss of blood had so weakened her that she could not lift her body over the edge of the drum. Am I not, she asked herself, even to be allowed to die in privacy?

Then, from somewhere in the chaos about her, she heard an authoritative voice ordering her to make for the Community Center pond. Hardly knowing what she was doing, she staggered toward it, then joined the fifty or sixty people who were already huddled in the shallow, dirty water of the pond. Some, she noted with astonishment, had brought their bicycles in with them.

Among the people in the pond was Hakuzō Iwamoto, a forty-six-year-old taxi driver. The surface of the pond seemed to be blazing, for the fierceness of the nearby fires had given rise to a strong current of air that swept the flames across the water. Iwamoto, who felt as though his head was about to burst from his body, thought to himself that if this was not a nightmare he was in, then it could be nothing but hell itself. Supposing his death to be only a matter of moments, he began to recite the Japanese words of one of the Buddhist sutras: *Namu-miyoho-renge-kyo . . . Namu-miyoho-renge-kyo. . . .* ("Glory to the Sutra of the Lotus of the Supreme Law! . . . Glory to the Sutra of the Lotus of the Supreme Law! . . .")

After about an hour, the fires around the pond began to subside. Those who were still alive climbed out of the foul-smelling, filthy water. Mrs. Kita, once she was on the ground, simply lay there, unable to move any further. Mr. Iwamoto, on the other hand, felt the pangs not only of thirst but of hunger as well. It must be about two in the afternoon, he thought, as he climbed out of the pond.

His first desire was for water, a desire that was easily satisfied, for the broken fire hydrant in front of City Hall was gushing a steady stream of drinking water. His second desire was also soon satisfied. A few yards away from the hydrant lay the body of a policeman, and beside the body was a lunch box. With an almost unconscious bow to its dead owner and perhaps a fleeting memory of his invocation to the Buddha, Iwamoto picked up the box and sat down on the Community Center steps. There he ate the dead man's lunch—some rice mixed with barley, some small dried fish, and some pickled plums—and then he started off toward his house in Ōte-machi.

Fumio Shigetō, the deputy director of the Hiroshima Red Cross Hospital who had been fortunate enough to find himself under the projecting eaves of Hiroshima Station when the bomb went off, was now trying to find his way to the hospital. Having been in Hiroshima only a couple of weeks, he was not yet very familiar with the city's streets, and many of them, he now found as he started off in what he hoped was the direction of the hospital, were simply walls of fire. Shigetō seemed to be the only one, out of all the people around him, who was trying to get to the city's center; the rest were doing their best to flee it.

He was stopped by a military policeman. "Where do you think you're going?" the man asked.

Shigetō explained his position in the hospital and said he wanted to get to it as soon as possible, to render what assistance he could.

"But it's impossible," said the policeman. "Look at those fires. You can't get through."

"It's my duty to get through," Shigetō replied firmly.

The policeman was equally firm. "You just can't do it," he said, and ordered the deputy director not to attempt to go any further.

Young Ikuko Kumura had been in her classroom at the Yamanaka Girls' High School (about a mile from the hypocenter) at the moment of explosion. When she regained consciousness, she found herself lying on the ground near the school. A straw mat had been laid over her, presumably by someone who had assumed she was dead. Once she recovered from her initial bewilderment, she threw the mat aside. She found that she had suffered only minor burns on her face and arms, and so she began trying to help those of her schoolmates who were lying nearby and who were far more seriously hurt.

Soon the school building burst into billowing flame. Ikuko and two other girls fled down toward the banks of the Motoyasu River, but after she had walked about fifteen hundred feet she realized she could go no further. She fell unconscious to the ground, and it was not until around three in the afternoon that she revived. Looking back at the still smoldering school, then looking down at the turbulent river, she decided that the air raid which had devastated Hiroshima could not have been an ordinary one. She recalled what her elder brother had told her about a bomb the size of a matchbox that was powerful enough to blow up an entire city. "Was this it?" she wondered.

Wataru Sasaguri also came to the conclusion that the bomb must have been a wholly new weapon. When he had been working at the Kure naval yard, before it was destroyed, he had heard one of the officers talking about a new type of bomb that exploded in midair. "Was this it?" he wondered.

He himself had been at his house in Hiratsuka-machi (about five thousand feet from the hypocenter). Relatively uninjured, he had made his way to Tsurumi Bridge, where he watched the dense clouds of black smoke that seemed to hang over the entire city. Soon the wounded refugees started coming, their number always increasing. Trying to reach the safety of Mount Hiji, they staggered along as though they were drunk, crying out for water. Sasaguri led them to a freshwater pond. While they were drinking, drinking as though they had a thirst no water could quench, Sasaguri saw little tongues of flame lapping at the wooden railings of the bridge. If the bridge went, with it would go all hope of escape. "Put out the fire!" he cried. "Come and help put out the fire!" But the wounded, the burnt, and the bleeding, merely stared at him; they seemed incapable of movement. Sasaguri ran to the point where the flames had begun to attack the bridge and scooped up handfuls of earth which he frantically threw on the fire. He succeeded in putting it out.

Now a group of about thirty middle school boys got as far as the bridge. All were injured, many quite seriously, and all were crying out for water. Since they seemed unable to move any further—some, in fact, were rolling in agony on the sandy bank, which only increased their pain, for the irritating sand got into the open wounds—Sasaguri found some broken bottles, carried them to the pond, filled them with water, and brought them back to the students. He asked a young man standing nearby, who seemed relatively uninjured, to do the same, handing him an already filled bottle. But the young man too was suffering from thirst, and as soon as he had the bottle in his hand he raised it to his lips and drained it dry. "What the hell do you think you're doing?" cried a military policeman who had witnessed the act. "Try that again and I'll cut you to pieces!" By this time, it was past noon; a vast number of grossly bloated bodies were floating down the river toward the sea.

Haruko Okidoi, twenty-eight, was one of many in the city that morning who were blinded, some only temporarily, some permanently, by flying fragments of glass and metal. Mrs. Okidoi, who lived in Dote-machi (about five thousand feet from the hypocenter), happened to be sitting, at eight seconds past 8:16, in front of a large mirror. It shattered within instants, and the flying glass hit her full in the face. Darkness closed in on her.

Later, she was to write an account of what happened to her that day: "I was living with my grandmother, who was seventy-seven, and my eight-year-old daughter, but at the time of the explosion my daughter had already left for school so I was alone in the house with my grandmother. Immediately after the blast, I heard my grandmother calling weakly for me. 'I'm in here, Grandma,' I called back.

"When she came into the room and saw me, she cried out in horror. 'My poor child,' she moaned, 'what a dreadful sight you are! Come quickly, I must get you to a hospital.' Our next door neighbor helped bandage my face and arms, and then my grandmother and I—I holding her shoulder—made our way to the road below Mount Hiji. My mind was still alert, and I was well aware that I had lost the vision of both eyes.

"My grandmother told me that great clouds of smoke seemed to be rising from every part of the city and that a large number of injured people were walking along the road to Mount Hiji. Then, 'Does it hurt you very much?' she asked.

" 'No, not so much,' I replied.

" 'All right, don't worry,' she said. 'Just hold onto me.'

"Near Matoba, someone in a first aid party put some ointment on my wounds. He evidently thought that I, like so many others, had been burnt. My grandmother and I continued a little longer, but soon

I suddenly felt terribly tired and sleepy. 'Grandma,' I said, 'please let me rest here a while. I can't go on any more.'

" 'What are you talking about?' she cried. 'You can't stay here— you'd be trampled to death. Take courage, we must go on a little further.'

"Somewhat comforted, I plodded on, still holding tight to her, but when we reached the parade grounds, I felt as though I was finished. I simply dropped to the ground and told my grandmother I could not move any further, even though the heat from all the burning houses around us was overwhelming. My grandmother helped me up. 'We have to go on a bit more,' she said. 'Here embers may fall on us any second.'

"At last we got to a bomb shelter, where I dropped into a kind of coma. Later my grandmother told me that in my delirium, I kept crying for water. She left me for a while, and when she returned, she gave me a bottle of the precious liquid to drink, telling me she had had to go a long way to get it. I still remember how delicious that water tasted.

"Others in the shelter were also crying out for water, and so I asked my grandmother to give what remained in the bottle to them. 'How can you say such a thing?' she answered. 'I had to go a terribly long way to get it. Now go back to sleep.' But I was like a child—I simply could not realize how difficult it had been for her to obtain that precious drop of water.

"Then she said: 'Stay here quietly. I've heard they're giving out food—I'll see what I can get.' After about half an hour she came back with several rice balls. 'Try to eat one,' she said.

"But I knew I could not. 'All I want is water,' I replied. My lips, in which countless tiny fragments of glass were embedded, had swollen to twice their normal size. How, I wondered, could I put a rice ball through those swollen lips?"

CHAPTER 5 **ALL DAY: THE MILITARY**

Private first-class Haruo Masumoto, who had gone AWOL the day before and who was now about to be punished for it by having to spend the hot August day helping to dig a bomb shelter, was (at 8:16 A.M.) standing at attention in front of Eleventh Infantry Regiment headquarters (a little under three thousand feet from the hypocenter), awaiting orders. When he picked himself up a few minutes later, he discovered that he had been thrown some one hundred feet; he discovered also that his uniform had been reduced to tatters. As he began to recover from the shock, he realized that he had been burnt: the upper right side of his body was causing him considerable pain, and his left hand had been stripped of its skin.

Seeing that the regimental barracks were blazing, Masumoto decided that an enemy bomb had touched off a powder magazine. He decided further that this was probably not a very healthy place to be, so he began to run in the direction of Shiroshima-machi. When he had got as far as the Kyōbashi River, however, he discovered that the Tokiwa Bridge, which spanned it at that point, had been shattered in two, like a toy in the hands of an angry child. There was nothing to do, then, but to try to swim across the river.

Making his way down to the water's edge, he encountered a soldier whose arm had been badly injured. Masumoto unwound his own leggings and bound them around the wounded arm. He was still, after all, a member of the medical corps. In the water he saw several bodies being washed downstream as well as a man struggling ineptly against the current. Hurriedly Masumoto flung several wooden planks into the river, shouting to the struggling man: "If you can't swim, hold onto a board—that way you may get across." He took off his wrist-watch (which he thought was still running) and wrapped it in a hand-kerchief, which he tied around his head. Then, just as he was about to enter the swirling waters, an elderly woman, whose face was badly burnt, stopped him and asked him to take her with him. Sadly he shook his head: he knew there was nothing he could do for her; the most he could do, in his shocked and weakened condition, would be to get himself across.

In this he succeeded. Having reached the other bank, he started limping toward Mount Futaba, where he saw other soldiers who had escaped staring incredulously back at the huge clouds of black smoke that enveloped the city. Wondering what on earth could have happened to Hiroshima, Masumoto recalled the dire prediction of the young American prisoner of war who had foretold that the whole city would be destroyed by a single bomb. Was this it, then? And what had happened to the young American?

Masumoto could go no further. Having reached a grove of trees, where he saw other wounded soldiers, he lay down on the ground in the shade. His side and hand were aching badly, and he felt like vomiting; he would have liked to go looking for his wife, but he realized he lacked the strength. Just then a soldier who seemed to be less wounded than the others called on all who could still walk to assemble and march to the parade ground. Masumoto, along with a few others, ignored the call; they were too weak to move.

When, however, a noncommissioned officer set up a picture of the emperor, all the soldiers rose and stood shakily at attention before it. Seeing that some of them were about to drop, the noncommissioned officer quickly issued the order for them to stand at ease. Then he led all those who were still capable of movement in the direction of the parade ground.

Masumoto fell back under the shade of the tree, where he lay until evening, drifting occasionally off into sleep, then waking and staring with empty eyes at the yellowing leaves above him. At last, as the hot August sun began to sink behind the horizon, he got slowly to his feet and began to walk away from the city. When he reached a small suburban village, he saw many other refugees, both civilian and military. Passing a farmhouse, he went in and asked for a glass of water. The farmer offered him a place to sleep for the night, and Masumoto gratefully accepted.

He was but one of the estimated ninety thousand members of the armed forces who were in Hiroshima that day. The city's history as a military center had begun with the Sino-Japanese War of 1894-5, when imperial headquarters was established in Hiroshima Castle, and Ujina (3.7 miles from the city center) was the main port of embarkation for Japanese soldiers destined to fight on the Chinese mainland. Ujina filled the same function during the Russo-Japanese War (1904–05), during the Manchurian Incident of the mid-thirties, and during a large part of the Pacific war. On the nearby island of Etajima was an academy for naval officers, while the port of Kure, only a few miles distant, was a major naval base.

Towards the end of the Pacific war, when preparations were being made to fight the final battle, the supreme command divided the country in two, establishing the headquarters of the First General Army in Tokyo in the east and of the Second General Army in Hiroshima in the west. The commander in chief of the Second General Army was Field Marshal Shunroku Hata; his chief of staff was Lieutenant General Seizaburō Okazaki; and Hata's staff was composed of over four hundred officers. The defense of Hiroshima, as well as of the entire Chūgoku area, was in the hands of Chūgoku Military District headquarters, whose commander (on 6 August) was Lieutenant General Yōji Fujii. Fujii's chief of staff was Major General Shūitsu Matsumura. One American magazine said that Hiroshima had stronger air defense than Berlin itself; in fact, despite Hiroshima's bristling military importance, it was defended by only a dozen old-fashioned antiaircraft guns. The *Enola Gay* had had little to worry about so far as interception was concerned.

In the Operations Section of the Second General Army (situated on the second floor of a building almost exactly a mile from the hypocenter) were three high-ranking officers: the chief of the section and two staff officers. They were hurled to the floor by the blast, their bodies pierced by fragments of shattered glass. When, in a few moments, they regained their senses, they immediately began to discuss what kind of bomb it was that had struck the city. The information staff officer, who had been picking up overseas broadcasts, said it was probably a peculiar new weapon of which he had heard frecquent intimations.

Just then another staff officer, who had not been injured, arrived for work; and together the four men decided to send badly wounded soldiers to the garrison hospital in trucks and to transfer the rest to Mount Futaba, where they would establish new headquarters. But soon the trucks that had started off with the badly hurt returned; the trucks could not get through.

At this, the four officers made their way on foot to Mount Futaba, to get an overall view of the devastated city. What they saw was wholly unlike anything they had seen before. The chief of the operations section said he must obviously report to the supreme command in Tokyo as soon as possible. One of the staff officers drafted a communication to the effect that "a special and very powerful" bomb had been dropped on Hiroshima, "causing great damage to the city." Since all communications facilities had been destroyed, a messenger had to be sent to Ujina to cable the report to Tokyo.

The capital was soon to receive further confirmation from Satoshi Nakamura, a reporter with the Dōmei News Agency. At the moment the bomb exploded, Nakamura was just starting to eat breakfast in the house where he had been staying—that of a friend in Rakurakuen, about eight miles from the city. The glass windows facing east, toward Hiroshima, were all shattered, and Nakamura himself was thrown to the floor. He recovered almost at once and, supposing that a one-ton bomb had been dropped, ran outside. There he saw a great cloud of black smoke mushrooming up over the city to what appeared to be a height of perhaps fifteen thousand feet, where it abruptly turned into a tremendous ball of red flame. To Nakamura it looked like the sudden blossoming of some gigantic flower.

He jumped on a bicycle and began pedalling toward the city. After passing through the little town of Itsukaichi, he felt an unusually strong wind, which was followed by a heavy downpour of what appeared to be rain mixed with sand and dust. In any case, the drops were large and extremely dark, almost black. He saw that his fingers, gripping the handlebars of the bicycle, trying to keep it steady, had in a few seconds become stained with this black rain.

The wind was so fierce he could no longer control the bicycle. He got down and started walking. The rain lasted for less than half an hour, then it suddenly stopped, and the sky was once again a clear summer blue. Doubting the evidence of his own senses, the reporter continued on until he reached the outskirts of Koi, at the western edge of Hiroshima. From there it appeared that all the bridges had been burnt down, so Nakamura decided not to try to get into the city but to go instead to the nearby village of Hara, where the Japan Broadcasting Corporation maintained branch facilities.

The transmitting station was surrounded by paddy fields; it stood only a little over three miles north of the hypocenter. As he approached, Nakamura found it hard to believe his eyes. Two hordes of people were moving in opposite directions: those staggering north, out of the city, were all injured, bleeding or burnt, and all naked, or nearly so; those streaming south, out of the further suburbs toward the city, did not appear to be injured but were frantically calling out the names of those they were seeking.

Nakamura threaded his way through the two opposing lines until finally he reached the broadcasting station. The building seemed intact, but when he got inside he learned that its transmitting facilities were dead save for a single telephone line to the Okayama broadcasting station (some ninety miles from Kobe). Nakamura explained to the man in charge that, as a Dōmei reporter, it was his duty to get the news of the bombing of Hiroshima to Tokyo as soon as possible, and he asked permission to use the telephone for less than five minutes. Permission was immediately granted.

To the man at the Okayama end, Nakamura said, "Please relay the message I will now give you to Dōmei's Okayama office at once." The voice that replied was hardly audible: "All right, but please read slowly —I've got to take it down in longhand."

Nakamura then dictated probably the most important story any reporter had ever told: "At around 8:16 A.M., 6 August," he read, "one or two enemy planes flew over Hiroshima and dropped one or two special bombs (they may have been atomic), completely destroying the city. Casualties are estimated at one hundred seventy thousand dead."

The time was then 11:20 A.M. After Nakamura hung up he wondered if he had exaggerated the number of fatalities. He turned to the man at the station, who had been listening as he made his telephone call, and asked: "Does that figure sound right to you? A hundred and seventy thousand?"

"No, it sounds all wrong!" cried the other. "It should be nearer two hundred thousand! There was a flash and a boom, and then Hiroshima vanished from the face of the earth."

Nakamura went outside and sat wearily down under an acacia tree. He knew he should be starting to write a longer news story, but for the moment he felt unequal to the task. His notebook and his pencil were in his hands. "Devils!" he wrote. "Devils!" Then, after a time: "So this is the end of the war." Alas, poor Nakamura was a bit too optimistic.

Marshal Hata, commander in chief of the Second General Army, was in his quarters on Mount Futaba, praying for the repose of the souls of the war dead, when the blast struck him. He was thrown violently to the matted floor in front of the *kamidana*, the alcove shrine where he had been offering his prayers, but soon picked himself up to discover—happily for him—that he was uninjured.

At that same moment, Hata's chief of staff, Lieutenant General Okazaki, was reading a newspaper at his residence in Kamiyanagimachi (about four thousand feet from the hypocenter). Although he had received a serious back wound, he managed, with the help of his adjutant, to reach a small island in the Kyōbashi River. There he remained until around three in the afternoon, when he was picked up by a rescue team composed of navy personnel. Not until then did his injured back receive any treatment. He was brought back to headquarters, by which time he was running a high fever and was almost delirious.

Of the more than four hundred staff officers of the Second General Army, about a quarter died within moments of the explosion, and most of the others were injured, more or less seriously. Three thousand officers and men of the Fifty-ninth Army were also killed, including their commander, Lieutenant General Fujii. Those who survived sought places of refuge—some down on the river banks, others up in the mountains—but none of them knew what to do next. Their orders had not envisaged a calamity of the kind that had struck them.

Japan, at that time, was partitioned not only into prefectures but also into eight larger districts, called governments-general, which comprised local administrative bodies. The deputy superintendent general of the Chūgoku Regional Government-General was a man named Naoaki Hattori. Around two o'clock that afternoon he appeared in the office of Colonel Kumao Imoto, who was head of the Operations Section of Second General Army headquarters. His face discolored, his head swathed in bandages, Hattori reported to the colonel that the superintendent general had been killed and that—for all practical purposes—there no longer existed either a prefectural or a municipal government in Hiroshima. Rescue and first aid operations must therefore, he said, be delegated to the army, and he asked Colonel Imoto to make as quickly as possible what arrangements he could to provide food for the survivors. His own wife, Hattori added woodenly, had also been killed.

But the army was little better able to function than the civilian administrative bodies. Wondering how he was to feed the survivors, Colonel Imoto conferred with one of his staff officers, and the two men agreed to request Marshal Hata to place Hiroshima under limited martial law. Although imperial approval was theoretically necessary before martial law could be proclaimed, Hata agreed that in the present emergency the emperor's approval would have to be by-passed. Accordingly, he ordered Lieutenant General Fumio Saeki, commander of a transport corps in the port of Ujina, to assume responsibility for the imposition of limited martial law, making use of troops garrisoned in the vicinity of the city to enforce it.

This would leave headquarters of the Second General Army free to play its assigned role in defending the homeland. Both Colonel Imoto and his staff officer, Lieutenant Colonel Masakatsu Hashimoto, believed that the enemy would now attempt an invasion very soon as a follow-up to the unprecedented bombing of Hiroshima; and it would be the task of tke Second General Army to meet the enemy and to repel him. The two men, Imoto and Hashimoto, had both been badly

50. Shadows burnt onto the side of a tank about 2,300 yards from the hypocenter.

51. A streetcar which was 670 yards from the hypocenter at the time of the blast.

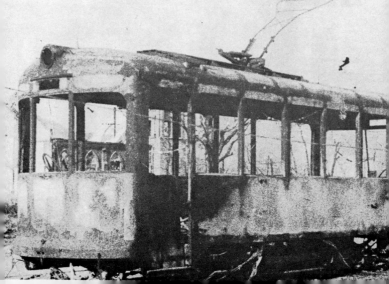

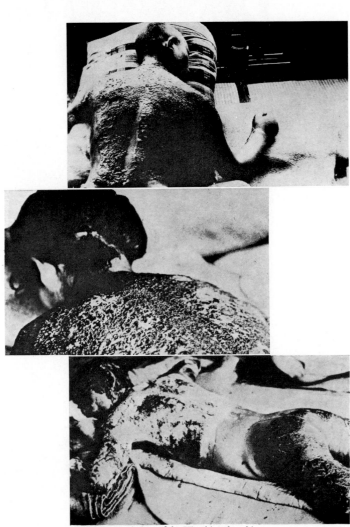

52–57. Burnt victims of the Hiroshima bombing.

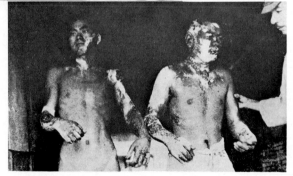

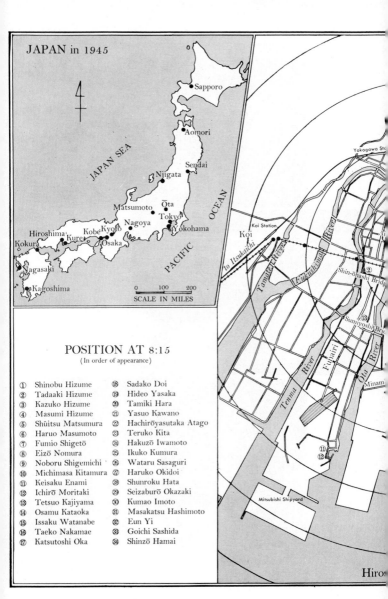

JAPAN in 1945

JAPAN SEA

Sapporo

Aomori

Sendai

Niigata

Matsumoto   Ōta

Nagoya   Tokyo

Kyoto   Yokohama

Kobe

Hiroshima

Kokura   Kure   Osaka

Nagasaki

Kagoshima

PACIFIC OCEAN

0   100   200
SCALE IN MILES

POSITION AT 8:15
(In order of appearance)

①	Shinobu Hizume	⑱	Sadako Doi
②	Tadaaki Hizume	⑲	Hideo Yasaka
③	Kazuko Hizume	⑳	Tamiki Hara
④	Masumi Hizume	㉑	Yasuo Kawano
⑤	Shūitsu Matsumura	㉒	Hachirōyasutaka Atago
⑥	Haruo Masumoto	㉓	Teruko Kita
⑦	Fumio Shigetō	㉔	Hakuzō Iwamoto
⑧	Eizō Nomura	㉕	Ikuko Kumura
⑨	Noboru Shigemichi	㉖	Wataru Sasaguri
⑩	Michimasa Kitamura	㉗	Haruko Okidoi
⑪	Keisaku Enami	㉘	Shunroku Hata
⑫	Ichirō Moritaki	㉙	Seizaburō Okazaki
⑬	Tetsuo Kajiyama	㉚	Kumao Imoto
⑭	Osamu Kataoka	㉛	Masakatsu Hashimoto
⑮	Issaku Watanabe	㉜	Eun Yi
⑯	Taeko Nakamae	㉝	Goichi Sashida
⑰	Katsutoshi Oka	㉞	Shinzō Hamai

Yokogawa Sta.

Koi Station

Koi

To Itsukaichi

Tamagawa River

Fukushima River

Shin-ōhashi Bridge

②

Sumiyoshi Brid.

Tenma River

Fukuiri

Ōta River

Minam

Mitsubishi Shipyard

⑪
⑫

Hiro

HIROSHIMA in 1945

Ōta River

Ushida

Shiroshima

Tokiwa Bridge

Sanjō Bridge

Mt. Futaba

Second General Army

Hiroshima East Parade Ground

ygoku Military District

Headquarters

Asano Park (Sen-tei)

Hiroshima Military District Headquarters

na West Parade Grounds

Hiroshima Station

NHK

Noborichō

Kamiyachō

Yasu Bridge

Doten

Enkō River

Mukainada Station

Fuchu

Mt. Hiji

Kyōbashigawa

Hiratsuka

Hijiyama

Hiroshima Higher Normal School

Senda

to Kure

suki Bridge

Minami

Toyo Industry

Kyōsai Hospital

Niho

Ujina

Ujina Port

Bay

0   0.5   1
SCALE IN MILES

4 miles

58. A typical Hiroshima clock after the blast still shows the time of the explosion.

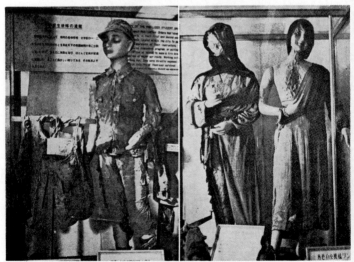

59, 60. Dummies, hung with articles of clothing from actual victims, demonstrate how the clothes were torn and people were burnt at the time of the explosion.

61. Flowerpots made of stone. Note the difference between the sides that were exposed to the blast and those that were not.

62. A deformed vessel, which at the time of the blast contained water and was inside a metal safe 1,200 yards from the hypocenter.

63. The shadow of a man who was sitting on the steps at the time of the blast.

64. Burns on bamboo trunks situated about 4,000 yards from the hypocenter.

65. This English translation of a Japanese poem is inscribed on the back of a memorial stone in a Hiroshima park.

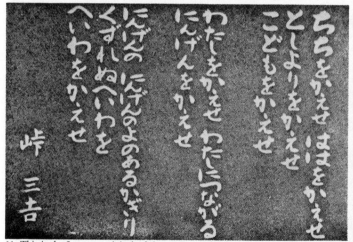

66. This is the Japanese original of the poem translated above. It is engraved in big letters on the front of the same stone.

burnt, and when, a little later, they were treated by a navy surgeon from Ujina, he told them, in all honesty, that he did not believe they could be saved. So far as he was aware, he said, no medicine existed that would heal what he called "burns caused by heat rays." Thanking him, the two officers continued with their preparations for the immediate defence of the homeland.

Major General Shūitsu Matsumura succeeded in extricating himself from his collapsed house. His uniform had been ripped away, leaving him only his *fundoshi* (a kind of loincloth), and his body was a mass of bleeding wounds. His only thought, once he was outside his house, was to get to Hiroshima Military District headquarters, of which he was chief of staff. But Matsumura was new to the city, and now he saw that the landmarks by which he was accustomed to guide himself no longer existed.

Then, just as he passed the building housing the Japan Broadcasting Corporation's Hiroshima station, which had begun to burn, he saw fleeing from it a man whom he knew. This was Masanobu Furuta, one of the announcers. Furuta had been broadcasting a communiqué from Chūgoku Military District headquarters, warning that three enemy aircraft had been sighted over Saijo, when he had been thrown to the floor by the force of the blast. He had not, however, been injured.

"Do you know Hiroshima well?" Matsumura asked.

"I should," replied Furuta. "I was born here."

"Then would you mind showing me the way to headquarters? I don't know where it is any more. Even the keep of the castle is gone."

When the two men entered the West Parade Ground, they found it hard to believe the evidence of their own eyes and ears. The field was littered with the bodies of dead and wounded soldiers, lying about like a vast school of fish stranded on the beach. Many, crying for help, rolled about on the ground, trying to assuage the pain of their burns and wounds. Out of the trenches rose a hellish cacophony of groans and moans, and all the while a seemingly endless stream of nearly naked soldiers, their bodies covered with burns, fled from the barracks. They held their arms high, so as to avoid any painful contact with the seared flesh.

Headquarters, Matsumura saw, was already a blazing inferno. Furuta had left, so Matsumura now asked one of the soldiers if he knew of any place where they might find refuge. "Sentei," the man replied promptly. The chief of staff, accordingly, guided by his ensign, a man named Abe, led the soldiers who could still walk toward Asano Park. During that frightful trek to the old gardens, Matsumura witnessed sights far more terrible than anything he had ever seen on any battlefield. Burnt, bleeding, and blackened spectres staggered along the road for a time, then suddenly fell by the wayside and could move no more. It did not seem possible that they might still be alive. From under great smoldering piles of rubble came faint cries for help; but what help could men barely able to walk themselves offer the trapped victims?

When they reached Sentei, Matsumura and his men lay down on the ground under the shade of some pine trees. A few of the most seriously injured soldiers apparently felt that death was not far off, for they now asked those who were not so badly hurt to take last messages and send them to their families. A master sergeant, who had miraculously found a notebook in his tattered uniform, began writing the messages down, along with the names and addresses of the recipients.

Matsumura himself felt his mind beginning to wander. Vaguely he wondered if he was destined to die of loss of blood, for his many wounds were still bleeding profusely. He recalled that he had been warned not to drink any water, but his thirst was overwhelming. He accepted a cup of water from one of his men and gulped it down, only to vomit it up a few moments later. The water, he noted dispassionately, was now a yellowish color. With that, he drifted into sleep, to be awakened shortly by Abe with the news that the garden had burst into flame and that they must seek refuge elsewhere immediately.

Wearily they made their way down to the river and crossed to a small island. It was already crowded with refugees. One young lad whose face was burnt and swollen pleaded with the soldiers to help him. But what could they do? The Little Boy, at eight seconds past 8:16 in the morning, had erased all distinction between soldier and civilian. The flesh that was burnt was the same flesh.

"Another bomb!" cried one of the soldiers suddenly, plunging into the river; but he was wrong—it was only the sun glowing lividly through the thick haze that hung above the city. For a time, there on the island, Matsumura and a medical officer named Inoue discussed what kind of bomb it could have been that had fallen on Hiroshima. Both had seen a crimson ball of fire, and now they knew that everyone who had been exposed to that fire had suffered terrible and mysterious burns. Neither man, however, divined the nature of the bomb.

Matsumura now decided he must do what he could to get help for the stricken folk of Hiroshima from troops that had been stationed outside the city. Since all lines of communication were obviously down, he decided to walk toward Ushida, where Lieutenant General Yamamoto, chief of ordnance, had his quarters. Matsumura was accompanied by Inoue, Abe, and a private first-class named Sugihara. The four men found that Yamamoto's house, midway up a mountain, had been partially destroyed but, being high up, had escaped the worst of the blast; and so had Yamamoto himself. In fact, when he greeted Matsumura, he even attempted a joke; he must have been one of the few men in Hiroshima that day to have done so.

"Is your son safe?" he asked.

But Matsumura's only children were girls. He thought Yamamoto knew it. Then, seeing a smile on the other's face, he understood. His loincloth was soaked in blood, and the word Yamamoto had used—*musuko*—does indeed mean "son," but it also, in popular jargon, means "penis." With a wry smile, Matsumura replied, "Thank you, my son is safe. The blood you see comes from wounds above my son."

Some neighbors brought in bowls of rice, but the men had no appetite, although to be polite they tried to eat it. The rice, however, tasted as though it had grains of sand mixed in it.

As far back as 1910, Japan had promulgated its so-called Treaty of Annexation with Korea; during the years that followed, Korea had become, for all practical purposes, a Japanese colony. The government encouraged members of the royal house of Yi to marry into the imperial family of Japan and also required several Korean princes of the blood to come to Japan, where they were given honorary posts in the army and navy. One was Prince Eun Yi, a Second General Army staff officer.

An ardent horseman, Prince Yi used to ride from his residence in Koi to Second General Army headquarters each morning. At 8:16 on the morning of 6 August he happened to be passing the Fukuya Department Store. He was hurled off his horse by the blast and severely injured; the two military policemen who were escorting him were never heard of again. The prince himself walked down to the river, where he took shelter beneath Aioi Bridge. Almost at once, search parties were sent out to look for him, since he was officially a member of Japan's imperial family. When, at length, he was found, he was taken immediately to the naval hospital on the island of Ninoshima.

Even less fortunate were the recruits about to be inducted into the Eleventh Infantry Regiment. The armed forces had already drafted all able-bodied men (and some who were not) under the age of forty; the new recruits who, at 8:16 A.M. on 6 August, had just bid farewell to their families outside the gate of the West Parade Ground were all past that age. It had been a tearful farewell, for most of the new soldiers were convinced that Japan was losing, or had already lost, the war and that they themselves stood little chance of ever returning to their wives and children. The epicenter of the bomb was almost directly over their heads: they, as well as those who had come to say goodby to them, were all destroyed in a moment of time. To this day, not one survivor has been found of those middle-aged, unbellicose family men who were the army's newest recruits in its implacable drive to win one last major battle.

CHAPTER 6   **NOON TO EVENING**

When the bomb struck, Lieutenant Colonel Shigeo Tamura was in his room at Jigozen, far from the hypocenter. Thus, although it was immediately obvious to him that something terrible had happened to Hiroshima, he had no idea of the extent of the devastation. He walked from Jigozen to the Iguchi Station of a private electric railway, whence he proceeded to the port of Ujina. There, and on the neighboring island of Etajima, he was in charge of training a detachment of the army's Akatsuki Corps ("the Dawn Corps"), the army's equivalent to the navy's kamikaze squadrons. The soldiers of the Akatsuki Corps were being trained to pilot flimsy plywood boats, each of which packed two torpedoes, and their mission, when the expected invasion finally came, was to attack enemy ships. In the course of the attack, they would lose, as they very well knew, both their boats and their lives.

Throughout the day, Tamura heard horrifying tales of what was going on in nearby Hiroshima, but it was not until four in the afternoon that he was ordered to take a squadron of his men into the city to help rescue still surviving victims. As soon as he reached Hiroshima, he was to place himself and his men under Commanding Officer Saitō, who was in charge of rescue operations at Senda-machi. Now, for the first time, Tamura saw with his own eyes the unbelievable devastation that had overtaken the once prosperous city.

The task assigned to this detachment of the Akatsuki Corps was to help extinguish the fires of still burning buildings, for which purpose they were given some elderly water pumps. Their task, they soon realized, was completely hopeless. In many of the buildings the fires had died a natural death—there was nothing left to burn; while those that were still blazing were beyond cure by such decrepit and feeble manually operated pumps. Because of snarled communications with command headquarters on Mount Futaba, it was not until nightfall that Tamura and his men received orders to cease their futile efforts at fire fighting and to start undertaking rescue operations.

Not everyone, however, had waited for instructions from Futaba. Emergency first aid stations had already been set up in various parts of the stricken city, and hospitals had already started treating the injured. On the north side of Mount Hiji, in the Hiroshima Girls' Commercial High School (some seventy-two hundred feet from the hypocenter), was stationed an army medical unit known as the Medical Education Squad, commanded by Captain Goichi Sashida. Immediately after the blast, Captain Sashida climbed up to headquarters, somewhat higher up on Mount Hiji, but found that it had been almost wholly destroyed. He decided that he would have to act on his own.

About fifteen of his men, including a sergeant major named Nakamura, were still capable of working, so Sashida ordered them, under Nakamura's direction, to gather together all the absorbent cotton, bandages, and white cloth they could find. They were also to get hold of containers of all sorts—pots, pans, basins, bowls. Once that was done, the men were told to fill all the containers with a kind of unguent made by mixing zinc powder with edible oil. Sashida dipped a bit of cotton in the ointment and applied it to the burns on the palm of his hand. He felt some relief at once. "Okay," he said, "we're ready for business."

A number of the injured had already found their way to the station, some of them so horribly burnt that the orderlies realized, as they applied the unguent, that all they could supply was a modicum of comfort, that only death, which was clearly imminent, could offer the final relief. Yet they worked on tirelessly, and were gratified to see that many of the injured, when they felt the soothing ointment cover their burns, closed their eyes, the better to savor the temporary easing of their pain. As the afternoon wore on, the word spread, and the injured began arriving in ever increasing numbers.

It was not only their burns that had to be treated: there was also the painstaking, difficult task of extricating the countless fragments of shattered glass that were embedded in arms and legs, in blasted faces, and in torn bodies. Sashida, wielding a pair of forceps, could hear the bits of glass crunch one against the other within the bruised and bleeding flesh. Although he worked as gently as he could, he knew that what he was doing was terribly painful, yet no one cried out, no one said anything except a word of thanks.

After a time, he climbed up to headquarters again, but there was still no one to give him orders. Both officers and men lay on the ground, many of them critically injured, incapable of taking any action. From the height at which headquarters stood, Sashida could see great clouds of smoke still billowing out of the city's burning buildings. Like so many others in Hiroshima that day, Sashida could only wonder what kind of bomb had inflicted such overwhelming catastrophe. Nor did he stop to wonder long; he knew that his duty lay elsewhere.

When he got back to the first aid station, he saw that Nakamura, his sergeant major, had begun preparing food for the victims. Nakamura and a couple of the men had dug holes in the hillside, had built fires, and were boiling up a mixture of rice and barley which, when it was cooked, they formed into balls. Those who were not too badly injured were able to eat; others merely shook their heads. The members of the unit who had been treating the burns and the cuts were hungry; quickly they gobbled a bit of food, then went back to work. Sashida, once he had eaten some of the rice and barley, felt better able to go on.

Still the injured continued to stream into the station; and as their numbers increased, so did the numbers of the dead. Many had made the long and painful journey to no purpose: within moments of their arrival, even as their burns were being coated with the makeshift ointment, they died. Bodies lay everywhere, the dead and the wounded jumbled together. So here was another task for the already overworked medics. In Japan bodies are ceremonially cremated; but now there was no time for ceremony—the growing mounds of bodies had to be disposed of as expeditiously as possible. With the help of some of the victims who were not seriously hurt, the members of the medical corps gathered heaps of wood, which they lighted; then onto the flaming pyres they laid the bodies of the dead. Now the smell of burning flesh mingled with the other acrid odors that permeated the Hiroshima Girls' Commercial High School. Around the pyres stood relatives and friends, murmuring prayers for their vanishing dead; tears coursed down their seared faces. Many knew that they would soon be joining those they were praying for.

Kōichi Toda was a dentist who lived in the town of Kabe, some ten miles from the hypocenter. After the blast, he went to Gion (about three miles from the hypocenter), where a first aid station had been set up in a school for young men. Toda brought with him what little medicine and equipment he had and there joined forces with other doctors who had come to render what assistance they could to the world's first victims of an atomic blast. Here too it was decided that the best, perhaps the only, thing that could be done for those whose flesh had been burnt away was to coat the burns with oil or saline solution. Once victims had been treated, they were given straw mats to lie on in a nearby shrine.

Among those who helped with this work was a Catholic priest, who made countless trips between the first aid station and the shrine, carrying those who were unable to walk. Most of them had lost all of their clothes, almost all were badly burnt, and some had large gaping wounds. Soon the priest's black robe was soaked in blood; where the rays of the sun struck it, it glistened darkly.

Toda, who was still working indefatigably in the station, came upon a scene which almost made him feel he could not go on any longer. Two little girls, around three and five years old, had come for help. Both were burnt. The skin had already dropped from the legs of both, but the younger of the two little girls was in far worse shape than the older. Her face was so badly burnt, it did not look like a face at all, and her whole body, especially her chest, was pierced with fragments of glass, from which welled streams of blood. She had been blinded. The older girl, although her face was much swollen, could still see. She held her younger sister by the hand.

"Mother!" cried the three-year-old. "Mother, I can't see!"

But there was no mother to hear her, only a five-year-old sister who stared with great frightened eyes. Perhaps mother and father were still alive; more likely they were both dead.

Toda, as he did what he could for the two little girls, found that he had to make a tremendous effort to prevent his fierce anger from interfering with his work.

Probably there are no unused words left in any language with which to describe what occurred in the larger hospitals of Hiroshima that day. The Red Cross Hospital, for example, which stood only about four thousand feet from the hypocenter, was more than half demolished by the blast and most of its doctors and nurses had sustained serious injuries. Yet vast throngs of wounded converged on the hospital begging for help; it was the first place that many of them thought of. To make matters worse, the Red Cross Hospital of Hiroshima—like most hospitals in Japan at that time—suffered from a critical shortage of supplies; the armed forces had commandeered so much. The handful of doctors and nurses able to function did what they could; but soon the hospital was more like a morgue than a place of succor.

Even more crowded was the army hospital in Ujina. Vast as it was—the floor space of the hospital buildings themselves was about ten thousand square feet, while the compound in which they stood occupied nearly twenty-five thousand square feet—the place was soon overflowing with the wounded, the dying, and the dead. The victims of the bombing lay everywhere—in corridors, in bomb shelters, outside in the yard. Nurses went about writing down the names and addresses of the wounded on little bits of cloth, which they pinned onto whatever fragment of clothing still remained on the maimed bodies. There was little else either the nurses or the doctors could do—daub the mysterious burns with ointment, paint the wounds with mercurochrome, hardly anything more. As the day wore on, it was difficult to tell the dead from the living—or the dying. It has been estimated that more than half of those who came to Ujina for treatment died before the day was done.

The fact that the victims who came to the various hospitals and to some of the first aid stations seeking help were at least given a little something to eat that afternoon was due to the efforts not only of the doctors and nurses but also of the city's municipal officials. To be sure, the victims were only given balls of rice and barley and some dried bread, but, for those who were destined to survive, it helped them to outlive the day.

Shinzō Hamai, chief of the municipal Distribution Section, was at his house in Niho-machi (two and a half miles from the hypocenter) when the bomb was dropped. Much of the house was destroyed, but Hamai and the other members of his family were not seriously injured. Accordingly, he left the work of salvage and repair to the others, while he himself started off almost at once for his office. Customarily he made the trip by bicycle but that morning he found the roads impassable. As he walked on, he encountered hundreds of injured people staggering along in the opposite direction; then he saw that the street leading to his office was a blazing inferno.

He thought perhaps he could still reach it by taking a roundabout route, so he began to edge around the fires. On the way, he happened to meet a colleague named Kurose, the municipal treasurer. Kurose told Hamai that City Hall was already wholly engulfed in flame. As the two men stood discussing the problem of what to do, they were joined, again coincidentally, by two other high municipal officials: Morishita (the deputy mayor) and Nakahara (the city auditor). It was Hamai's idea that they establish emergency headquarters in a room in the Employment Agency, a building which was still standing. He suggested that the other three make their way there immediately, while he himself would go out and try to locate supplies of food for the survivors.

Hamai went first to Ujina, where he managed to secure not only a truck but also the help of a couple of college students, who had been drafted to work at an armored car training center in the port. The three men now headed toward the Fuchū-machi food depot in the suburbs of Hiroshima. As they edged their way slowly through the crowds of dazed and wounded survivors, the students tried to instil some hope in them by assuring them that they would soon, at least, have some food.

At Fuchū-machi, Hamai and his two helpers found another truck that had come from Kure. They loaded both trucks with bags of dried bread and then headed for the Employment Agency, where Hamai thought the other officials had installed themselves. There, however, they learned that the City Hall fire had subsided somewhat and that municipal headquarters had now been temporarily set up in the square in front of City Hall. When they reached it, Hamai's first thought was to unload the sacks of dried bread there in the open plaza, but the truck driver from Kure pointed out that the heat was still so intense the two vehicles might well burst into flame.

They therefore moved on to the Red Cross Hospital, where they divided up the sacks of bread, sending some to first aid stations and hospitals and some to other safe areas where the injured had taken refuge. Then Hamai made his way back to the plaza in front of City Hall, where an ever increasing number of injured were gathering in the hope of finding medical care and food. A girl of about twelve, badly burnt on her face, hands, and legs, asked Hamai to help her. He found a chair for her, and told her to sit quietly there for a moment or tow until he came back, when he would take her to a hospital. Her disfigured face broke into the semblance of a smile, and with a sign of relief she sat down. Hamai returned to her, as he had promised, in a very few minutes. She was still sitting in the chair, but when he went to help her up he found that she was already dead.

The rest of the day Hamai devoted his efforts tirelessly to the distribution of food. In this he had the help of a fellow municipal employee named Takubo. Where streets were still passable, the two men used trucks; otherwise, they carried the sacks of food on foot. Wherever they went that afternoon, through the shuffling crowds of the burnt and the wounded, they saw unforgettable scenes of horror. People lay dead with their heads still immersed in the troughs of water from which they had hoped to drink. Small children and infants were charred to a crisp, like fowl that had been left too long in a blazing oven. To many of the wounded the meager bits of food came as a life saver; for many of the others, who had reached the point of no return, the rice balls and the dried bread served no purpose.

One such was Kenji Masuda, a first-grade pupil in Hiroshima Prefectural First Middle School. He had been out of doors, in Sakai-machi, when the bomb fell, and he had been badly hurt, yet with a couple of his friends he managed to get as far as a primary school in Koi. There, a little later, his mother, frantically following his trail, found him—but he was already dead. Beside him lay an untouched ball of rice mixed with soy beans. Somehow one of the beans had got embedded in a wound in the dead boy's distended face.

At Ōno, about twelve miles from Hiroshima, was an army hospital for the treatment of soldiers afflicted with tuberculosis. On the morning of 6 August, the hospital had about four hundred patients; by afternoon, it had several thousands—neither military men nor tubercular but ordinary people of Hiroshima who had fled all that way in the hope of finding medical treatment and relief from their pain. Unlike the hospitals nearer the hypocenter, this one was relatively undamaged; and unlike civilian hospitals, it was better stocked with medical supplies, being under the aegis of the army. Its ten doctors and eighty nurses labored throughout the day and far into the night, by which time even its comparatively large supplies of medicine had been exhausted. There was nothing left to put on the burnt bodies but saline solution.

Late in the evening, one of the exhausted nurses, Misa Moriya, was accosted by an army officer who was in the hospital being treated for tuberculosis. "What's all this about?" he demanded angrily. "The whole day we army men have been ignored, while you've been treating a gang of civilians. You go and tell the doctors that won't do. We're the men who have to get well in order to fight for the country— not a lot of burnt civilians. What happened to them anyway?" Nurse Moriya could not answer, since she did not know: all she knew was that the burns were not like any she had ever encountered before.

She left the complaining officer and returned to that growing group of burnt civilians. Altogether forgotten was the pleasure she and another nurse had taken the day before in going to Hiroshima to buy colored paper and streamers with which to celebrate the Tanabata Matsuri (the Star Festival). In Tokyo, as in many other parts of the country, the day when the two loving stars were permitted to meet was officially celebrated on 7 July; but many other places, including Hiroshima, preferred to celebrate the holiday a month later. Neither date was technically correct, for Tanabata was a lunar festival and should have been observed on the seventh day of the seventh month according to the lunar calendar. Carrying their packages of colored paper, the two nurses had walked back to the hospital along the banks of the Ōta River, singing the song of Tanabata. But that year, in Hiroshima, there were to be no gay decorations hanging from bamboo trees, no streamers inscribed with suitable wishes. That year the people of Hiroshima had other things on their minds.

In the transmitting station of the Japan Broadcasting Corporation in the suburb of Hara, Satoshi Nakamura, the Dōmei reporter, was once again in communication with Dōmei's Okayama office. Nakamura was now speaking to Susumu Uematsu, head of the office; listening in on the call was a Dōmei employee, who was taking the conversation down in shorthand. Uematsu told Nakamura that his previous report that one hundred seventy thousand people had been killed by a single bomb, which had virtually destroyed the entire city of Hiroshima, could not possibly be true. He instructed Nakamura to file a more reasonable story, correcting his earlier and obvious exaggerations. Why, the army itself—

Nakamura exploded. "You tell those bastards in the army," he shouted into the telephone, "that they are the world's biggest fools! I'll give you a second story, and I'll give it to you now. Just tell those bastards in the army to read it!"

He then proceeded to dictate a more detailed report of all that he had witnessed since his first brief announcement that a most unusual bomb had fallen on Hiroshima. He described the throngs of critically wounded—the naked, the burnt, the bleeding; he described the mountains of dead and the pervasive stench of burning flesh. In an effort to be as circumstantial as possible, Nakamura added: "People who were wearing white clothing sustained burns only on their hands and faces and other exposed parts of their bodies. They suffered no burns underneath their clothing, whereas those who were dressed in black, were severely burned over their entire bodies. There were women who were almost entirely naked clutching their breasts and walking to places of refuge. All were badly burned." Nakamura continued with his account, quite unaware that tears were streaming down his cheeks and splashing onto the notebook in front of him.

CHAPTER 7 **AFTERMATH**

Nightfall brought little or no relief. The cool night breezes served only to fan the flames of the still burning buildings, to carry smoldering embers from one wooden dwelling to another, and to harass the victims of the bombing who huddled out of doors beneath bridges, beside river banks, and in open squares. The waters of the Inland Sea were at high tide; the seven rivers of Hiroshima were swollen by the incoming water. People who had sought refuge by the river banks moved further away from the rising water if they could; those who could not were carried away. The fact that the city had no electric power rendered vastly more difficult the work of the rescue team as well as of those who were trying to administer first aid.

On Nakajima Island, where the Ōta River forks, Tetsuo Kajiyama, son of the chief priest of Jisenji Temple, sat with his critically injured mother, hearing her tell how fire had gradually encircled their dwelling and how at last she had leapt into the river. The boy, a fifth-grader in a primary school, listened in silence as he and his mother waited for the long night to end. Somewhere in the dark Tetsuo heard a woman asking her husband how he, so seriously injured, was planning to get a job in future. The man did not reply.

Many spent the night on Aioi Bridge, surrounded by the dead and the dying. At some point, a rescue team found them and to those who were still able to eat distributed balls of rice. After the rescuers left to look for other survivors who were in need of food, weak voices could be heard from beneath the bridge, crying for help. Soon they faded into silence. Were the owners of the voices asleep or dead? Probably by morning it would come to the same thing: there would be more bodies to burn, more smoke to add to the pall that shrouded the city.

Ten-year-old Noboru Shigemichi did not reach the suburban village where his mother and brothers were living until after dark. He had walked ten miles that day. His reward came when his mother took him into her arms and told him how brave he had been; but when she asked about her husband, the boy could tell her nothing, for he had not even attempted to go to their house in Hiroshima. The family reunion remained incomplete.

Despite the darkness, large numbers of injured were still being taken to first aid stations, such as that at the foot of Mount Hiji, as well as to the various hospitals. The doctors and nurses, hampered by a lack of proper medical supplies, were now hampered still further by a lack of electric power. When their flashlights gave out, they tried to make do with candles. The mercurochrome with which they had painted the wounds glowed with a strange phosphorescent light.

At the Kyōsai hospital, young Masumi sat beside her injured mother, Mrs. Hizume. The groans of the injured all about her kept her awake, and like all the others she felt devoured by thirst. Shin Utsu, chief of the hospital's general affairs section, walked the corridors, candle in hand; there was little he could do for the injured, wedged one against the other, but bring them the water that they craved. It was no good remembering how, only a few hours before, he had watched his son die; it was better to try to keep in mind the precepts of the Lord Buddha.

Ikuko Kumura, along with ten schoolmates and their teacher, had taken refuge in the hangar of an airport at Yoshijima. A woman with three small children joined the group, the burned bodies of all four of them smeared with ointment. The children cried out in pain; there was nothing their mother could do for them. During the night, some soldiers came with food. Unable to eat, Ikuko went outside and lay down on the ground. She felt sick in her stomach and sick at heart, watching the red sky over Hiroshima, wondering what had happened to her family in Ushida-machi. When a couple of her friends joined her, Ikuko told them about the matchbox bomb. For a time they talked about it, then fell into silence; but sleep came to none of them.

Haruko Okidoi, who had been blinded in both eyes by flying glass, also lay on the ground, with a stone beneath her head for a pillow. She listened to the voice of her elderly grandmother, who sat beside her. "Can anyone tell me," muttered the old woman, "why we got into this war? Our country has been destroyed, Hiroshima has vanished forever. All we can do is pray. And your husband, Haruko, is still at the front. He knows nothing about what has happened to Hiroshima. What can we do, what can any of us do but pray?" The old voice droned on; at last Haruko fell asleep.

Katsutoshi Oka, the teacher in a municipal middle school, having heard that a dozen or more of his pupils were lying injured near Doba-shi Bridge, brought them some balls of rice and a canteen of warm water. He got there about nine in the evening to find the boys, all of them naked, crying for water and complaining of feeling cold. After giving a little water to those who could drink, he built a fire and then talked quietly to the boys, each in turn, hoping somehow to keep them alive until morning, for they had all been seriously injured.

There were many others beside the river who were in need of help, and Oka distributed what little food and water he had left. One girl took the rice ball he offered but instead of eating it herself broke it into little pieces and tried to feed her more critically wounded sister. About three in the morning a rescue team came from the Akatsuki Corps. An army surgeon issued orders that those who were still alive were to be taken to a first aid station. Oka surrendered his stewardship, and about 4:30 in the morning arrived back at his demolished school, to snatch a couple of hours' sleep within the shadow of its ruins.

Lieutenant Colonel Shigeo Tamura, of the Akatsuki Corps, spent the entire night in rescue work. He went wherever he heard the sound of voices; if he no longer had food to give, he could at least bring water to the parched and the dying. At the foot of Minami-ōhashi Bridge, he heard a young girl crying out against the cold. He hurried to a nearby inn, where he was known, and borrowed a quilt for her, but when he tried to cover her, she thanked him and asked him to give the quilt instead to her teacher, who was lying nearby and who was far more seriously injured. The water that he offered she accepted gratefully. About an hour later Tamura returned to find that both the girl and her teacher were dead.

Prince Yi, lying in the naval hospital at Ninoshima, died at four in the morning. His adjutant, Lieutenant Colonel Hiroshi Yoshinari, who by chance had not been with him at the moment of the explosion but who had attended him through the night, went outside, sat down on the hospital lawn, and shot himself.

Issaku Watanabe, the first-year student at Hiroshima Prefectural Daiichi Middle School whose mother had tried to feed him mandarin oranges, had been severely wounded and by the time he got to the reception center was running a high temperature. His mother kept putting wet towels on his forehead, but they did no good. He was soon delirious, and at six in the morning he died. He was twelve years old. His mother looked wearily away from his wasted body to see that the sun had risen on a new day in Hiroshima.

It was not a happy sight. The city was no longer burning: in a great circle, five miles in diameter, there was nothing left to burn. Everywhere lay dead bodies and the bodies of those who were about to die;

everywhere wandered those who were less critically injured, seeking mothers and fathers, sons and daughters, brothers and sisters, husbands and wives. But there were so many bodies. Even people who were not much injured were appalled; and after a long and weary time, many of them abandoned the search as fruitless.

Some persisted. One man, whose dwelling in Tenjin-machi had been wholly destroyed, kept frantically searching for his son, who was thirteen years old. When he reached the shore of the Ōta River, he saw a pair of shoes at the river's edge that he thought must be the ones he had recently bought for the boy. The body itself was submerged; when the man lifted it out of the water, he discovered that he had not been mistaken.

About four in the morning, Lieutenant Colonel Tamura had rested for an hour; then, with some fifty men of the Akatsuki Corps, he resumed rescue operations. Those who had survived the night were laid gently in trucks and transported to hospitals and first aid stations. When the rescue corps got to Asano Park, they found the garden itself a charred wasteland, but some who had sought refuge there were still alive. Their bodies were almost as black as the burnt trees; but still they pulled themselves to their feet and begged for help. Where the skin had dropped away, the flesh had begun to rot; the smell was indescribably foul. Many of the children who had survived seemed to have gone mad; they kept up a constant stream of murmurs, but no one could understand what they were saying.

As soon as it was light, Major General Shūitsu Matsumura, accompanied by two soldiers, descended from Ushida to the site of Hiroshima Castle, where Chūgoku Military District headquarters had been installed. Matsumura could hardly recognize it: the keep was altogether gone, the barracks had been burnt down, even the lotus plants growing in the castle moat had been shaved off, as though by a gigantic razor. Only charred and blackened concrete superstructures were still standing.

Matsumura now discovered that Inoue, the commander of the medical unit, had already set up a first aid station on the site. The general's first thought, on seeing Inoue, was that the army must now, at all costs, be rehabilitated. Then the general's glance shifted to the high mounds of bodies, bodies of men who had been working at head-quarters when the bomb exploded. He realized that before the army could be rebuilt, the bodies of its dead would have to be cremated.

In the afternoon, command headquarters of the Second General Army, situated in a bomb shelter on Mount Futaba, was the scene of a meeting between officers of the army and prefectural and municipal officials. The main topic of discussion was how to prevent the Hiro-shima survivors from falling into a state of hopelessness and lethargy. But no one seemed to have any very clear idea how that was to be done. Finally the decision was reached that a proclamation be posted in various parts of the city, and a little later that day, in the name of the mayor, Genshin Takano, the following message was proclaimed:

"The present catastrophe is the result of a horrible and inhuman air raid. The enemy's intention is clearly to undermine the fighting spirit of the Japanese people. Citizens of Hiroshima, the damage is great! But that is only to be expected during a war. Keep up your spirits! Do not lose heart!"

Were the citizens of Hiroshima invigorated by this stirring message? More likely they were strengthened by the food that was distributed throughout the day by municipal employees and by the knowledge that more and more rescue teams from every part of the prefecture were coming to their aid. By the end of the day, these totaled thirty-three in all, including 190 policemen and 2,700 members of civilian vigilance corps.

At the badly damaged but crowded and still functioning Red Cross Hospital, its deputy director, Fumio Shigetō, having examined a large number of wounded, was already convinced that their burns were highly unusual. Then one of the hospital's X-ray technicians showed him some undeveloped film that, though it had been sealed in a lead box, was as black as though it had been exposed to light. Shigetō no longer had any doubt that the bomb which had fallen on Hiroshima was one that emitted radioactivity. It was at that moment he began his long struggle against what he called in Japanese "atomic disease" (in English, "radiation sickness")—a struggle tkat is still going on at the

Atomic Bomb Hospital and the Red Cross Hospital, both of which he serves as director.

Ikuko Kumura, who had spent the night in the airport at Yoshijima, got a ride into the city on a truck, then started walking toward her house. When she reached the Gokoku Shrine, she paused to pray for the safety of her family, then continued on. As she was crossing the bridge that led to her house, she encountered one of the boys in the neighborhood, a student at a military academy. To her intense relief, he told her that her family had all survived. She hurried on. Soon she saw a familiar row of cherry trees and behind them her house—still standing intact.

Haruko Okidoi had been carried on a stretcher from the East Parade Ground, where she had spent the night attended by her grandmother, to a first aid station in a temple near Mount Futaba. The first question she asked of the doctor who began to treat her was: "Will I ever see again?"

"We will do our best," he replied. "Your eyes have stopped bleeding, but there are still a great many fragments of glass embedded in them." All he could do, for the moment, was to wash them thoroughly with a solution of boric acid.

Then she lay down in a corner of the temple grounds to wait. Her grandmother told her to take off her dress, which was stiff with bloodstains. She said she would wash it for her. When the young woman hesitated, the old grandmother said, "Don't be ashamed. Everyone else is half-naked too." All around her, she could hear the voices of people looking for members of their families; and her thoughts, as she lay on the ground waiting for her grandmother to return, were not on her own plight but on the doubtful fate of her daughter, who had left for school that morning before the bomb fell and from whom she had heard nothing since. Although she could not see, she could still cry.

Mrs. Hizume, lying in the hospital, was also thinking not about herself but about the other members of her family. Her younger daughter, Masumi, had gone to the family house in Minami-machi to fetch some food and some utensils to cook it in. But what about her older daughter? What about her son Tadaaki? What about her husband? Mrs. Hizume had had, so far, no word of any of them.

Just then a young girl, wholly naked, appeared beside her bed, in her hands a blackened blouse. "Would you please help me put this on?" she asked. But it was impossible. The girl's entire body was a mass of burns, from which oozed a foul yellowish fluid. "I'm Fudeko, seventeen years old," she said. Mrs. Hizume made room for the girl in her bed and, after she had lain down, carefully put the blackened blouse over the distorted body. Then she gave the girl some water, and the girl fell into a feverish sleep, crying out now and then for her mother.

Soon Mrs. Hizume's younger daughter, Masumi, returned and prepared some food, which she gave to her mother as well as to others who were lying nearby. In the afternoon came the older daughter, Kazuko. She told her mother she had spent the night at the house of a friend in the village of Hesaka. When Mrs. Hizume asked her if she had been hurt, she said her hands had been cut by flying glass from the Fukuya Department Store windows. After returning to the city from Hesaka, she had gone home to change her clothes and there had learned from neighbors where her mother and younger sister were. But there was still no word of either father or brother.

Masumi opened a tin of oranges, and Mrs. Hizume pressed Kazuko to eat something, but Kazuko declined, saying she felt like vomiting. As the oranges were being distributed to other people nearby, Mrs. Hizume wondered whether Kazuko really felt sick or whether she had refused the oranges so that others might have them.

In a very few minutes the terribly burnt girl who was sharing Mrs. Hizume's bed died. While she waited for someone to come and carry the body away, she suddenly knew, with frightful certainty, that both her husband and older son were dead too. After the body was borne away, Mrs. Hizume saw that the bed was stained with the yellowish fluid that had seeped from the girl's wounds. It was all she could do to keep herself from crying out, "Everyone is going to die like that girl! Everyone of us will soon be dead!" But she remained silent.

Among those who did die were about twenty-three Americans. As *Time* magazine was to say twenty-six years later on 1 August 1971,

"Some months after the war ended, a former Japanese military police-man gave U.S. Occupation authorities twenty-three sets of dog tags (identification discs) that had been taken from U.S. prisoners of war who were in Hiroshima when the bomb was dropped.

"Most were captured airmen, and most doubtless died in the first shock wave."

At first, despite an unequivocal announcement from Washington, and despite the horrifying reports that reached Tokyo from Hiro-shima, the Japanese government refused to accept the fact that an atomic bomb had been dropped on Hiroshima. The morning news-papers of 8 August merely carried a brief announcement from imper-ial headquarters stating that "a few enemy planes" had severely dam-aged Hiroshima, using "a wholly new type of bomb."

In the afternoon of that day, an investigating team arrived from Tokyo. It was headed by Lieutenant General Seizō Arisue, chief of the second department of the general staff office, and it included Dr. Yoshio Nishina as well as Lieutenant Colonel Seiichi Niizuma, a techni-cal officer who had studied physics at Tokyo Imperial University. Two days later, the Arisue mission, as it was called, was joined by another survey team headed by Professor Bunsaku Arakatsu of Kyoto Imperial University.

The two groups met in both the morning and the afternoon of 10 August at the army's arsenal in Hijiyama-machi. The joint conclu-sions that they reached were presented to imperial headquarters that same day in a formal paper entitled "Report on the Survey of the Hiroshima Bombing." They said there could be no doubt that the bomb which fell on Hiroshima on 6 August had made use of atomic energy. Japanese scientists who had been working on similar projects were shocked to learn that the Americans had succeeded where they they had failed; but they were in no doubt either that Hiroshima had been the world's first victim of an atomic bombing.

Mrs. Hizume was released from the hospital on 12 August and re-turned to her home in Minami-machi. Within a short time she learned that her husband and son had indeed both died in the blast, and she now watched her two daughters die of radiation sickness. An inability to eat, diarrhea, a low blood count, a high temperature—these were the first symptoms; then all the hair of the head began to fall out, and the body was soon covered by a rash of purple spots. Kazuko died on 6 September; Masumi lingered on for six years, finally succumbing to the disease in 1951, at the age of twenty.

The most conspicuous feature of radiation sickness is the formation of the so-called keloid scars that follows the healing of the burns. Atomic radiation has also been ascertained to be the cause of abnormal births and of various forms of cancer that may not make their presence known for some time and that still—a quarter of a century later—account for a large percentage of deaths among atomic victims. The Hiroshima Atomic Bomb Hospital reported that in the first six months of 1971, thirty-three patients died there, twenty-three of them of cancer. Up to mid-1971 the leukemia death rate among survivors was running at over sixteen times the national average, and deaths from other forms of cancer at eight times the national average. The full genetic effect will not be known for three or four generations; as if to demonstrate this point, in the *Asahi Evening News* for 11 October 1971 there appeared the following report from Nagasaki:

"Funeral services are being held in Nagasaki City, Kyushu, today for 15-year-old Toshihiro Miyazaki who died at 11:35 p.m. Saturday of a malignant lymphatic tumor at Mitsubishi Hospital.

"He had apparently inherited the 'atom bomb disease' from his parents, who were both exposed to radiation from the atom bombing of Nagasaki in August, 1945.

"Toshihiro was the oldest son of Toshio, 40, and Sachiko, 39, Miyazaki. Mr. Miyazaki is an employee of the Nagasaki Shipyard of Mitsubishi Heavy Industries.

"He was living in Kumamoto Prefecture when Nagasaki was atom bombed 9 August 1945. He went that night to Nagasaki City to seek his parents, brothers, and sisters who were living in that city only 600 meters away from the blast center. He was exposed to radiation.

"Mrs. Miyazaki was living in Nagasaki City at the time and was only three kilometers from the blast center."

Fumio Shigetō, head of the Hiroshima Atomic Bomb Hospital, has noted that those who were exposed to the radiation age faster than other people.

One of them, old beyond his time, ill and in pain, told the authors: "All I can say is this, I hope an atomic bomb—no, I hope a lot of atomic bombs—will fall everywhere, and destroy the whole world."

EPILOGUE

EPILOGUE

On 6 August," President Truman wrote later, "the fourth day of the journey home from Potsdam, came the historic news that shook the world. I was eating lunch with members of the *Augusta*'s crew when Captain Frank Graham, White House Map Room watch officer, handed me the following message:

TO THE PRESIDENT:

FROM THE SECRETARY OF WAR:

> Big Bomb dropped on Hiroshima 5 August at 7:15 P.M. Washington time. First reports indicate complete success which was even more conspicuous than earlier test.

"I was greatly moved. I telephoned Byrnes aboard ship to give him the news and then said to the group of sailors around me, 'This is the greatest thing in history. It's time for us to get home.' "[1]

In Washington, Secretary Stimson released the presidential announcement that had been prepared before the bombing. It said, in part: "We have spent two billion dollars on the greatest scientific gamble in history—and won. . . . We are now prepared to obliterate more rapidly and completely every productive enterprise the Japanese have above ground in any city. We shall destroy their docks, their factories, and their communications. Let there be no mistake; we shall completely destroy Japan's power to make war.

"It was to spare the Japanese people from utter destruction that the ultimatum of 26 July was issued at Potsdam. Their leaders promptly rejected that ultimatum. If they do not now accept our terms, they may expect a rain of ruin from the air, the like of which has never been seen on this earth."

On 6 August, in Tokyo, the emperor was informed by his chief aide-de-camp that Hiroshima had been almost wholly destroyed—apparently by a single bomb (although that fact had not been absolutely ascertained) of a wholly new type. Early in the morning of the following day, the foreign ministry relayed to the emperor's grand chamberlain, Fujita, news of the announcement that had been broadcast from Washington. Fujita brought the news at once to the Obunko, where the emperor was then living; His Majesty ordered an immediate investigation.

But many officials of both the government and the military insisted that the bomb could not have been atomic. Even the United States, they said, was not capable of producing and delivering a bomb of so uncertain a nature. They were not prepared to accept the word of either the president of the United States or of eyewitnesses in Hiroshima. Furthermore, they said, there were many "countermeasures" that might be taken. The decision was reached that the words "atomic bomb" should not be used, at least for the time being, in reporting the catastrophe to the people of Japan.

Throughout the day of 7 August the emperor awaited further word—but none came. On 8 August Tōgō reported to His Majesty on what he knew of the situation in Hiroshima as well as on the Washington announcement. The emperor, speaking so softly he could hardly be heard, agreed that Japan now had no choice but to terminate the war on the basis of the Potsdam Proclamation; she could no longer hope to seek more favorable terms. Tōgō was instructed to make every effort to end hostilities at once.

Upon hearing from Tōgō of the emperor's desire, the prime minister attempted to convene a session of the Supreme Council for the Direction of War for that same day but was told that such a meeting would not be possible, since one of the Big Six was out of town that day.

On 8 August (Moscow time), the Japanese ambassador had his long awaited meeting with Molotov. The foreign minister curtly asked

Satō to be seated, then proceeded to read a short document that ended: "In view of the above, the Soviet Government declares that from tomorrow, that is from 9 August, the Soviet Union will consider herself in a state of war against Japan." This, then, was the end of the imperial government's protracted negotiations to secure Soviet good offices. Within two hours, Soviet troops had begun their invasion of Manchuria. The Soviet-Japanese Neutrality Pact, which was not due to expire for another eight months, had been tossed into the wastepaper basket.

On 9 August the plutonium bomb fell on Nagasaki. The emperor instructed Marquess Kido to relay to the prime minister the imperial desire to end the war at once. At 10:30 that morning the Big Six met in emergency session in an underground bomb shelter near the Obunko. Despite all that had happened, there was still a lack of unanimity. Three of the supreme councillors—Suzuki, Tōgō, and Yonai—favored immediate acceptance of the Potsdam Proclamation, with the sole proviso that the imperial house be retained; the other three—the war minister and the two chiefs of staff—proposed other conditions: a short occupation by a minimal force, the demobilization of Japanese troops by Japanese officers, and the trying of war criminals by Japanese courts. After two and a half hours of discussion, no decision had been reached, and the meeting was adjourned.

In further attempts to achieve a consensus, two cabinet meetings were held that afternoon and evening: from 2:30 to 5:30 P.M. and from 6:30 to 10:00 P.M. The deadlock continued: there was still no unanimity of opinion, and without it the cabinet was powerless to act. Suzuki and Tōgō now agreed that there was but one way to break the deadlock—a way unheard of in the annals of Japan. At eleven o'clock that night they petitioned the emperor to convene an imperial conference, *despite the lack of unanimity within the cabinet.* Hitherto the emperor had been present at such conferences only to give his sanction to what his ministers had already agreed upon. Now, in an unprecedented action, he was about to be called upon to make a decision.

At 2:30 in the morning of 10 August, accordingly, the emperor entered his underground bomb shelter to hear a restatement of the various arguments. One subject that seemed of particular importance was the wording of the Japanese insistence that the imperial house be maintained; but the chief point of difference remained the same: should Japan accept the proclamation with only the single proviso concerning the imperial structure or should she seek to gain concessions from the Allies on all four provisos? The talk went on and on. The familiar arguments were expressed again and again.

At last the prime minister, pointing out that opinion was still clearly and hopelessly divided, begged the emperor's pardon for asking him to decide which proposal should be adopted. Quietly, in a brief statement, His Majesty said that it was clear to him that the war could no longer be fought; that, although it was unbearable for him to see his loyal troops disarmed and his loyal ministers punished, "the time has come when we must bear the unbearable"; and that, therefore, he favored acceptance of the Potsdam Proclamation with the single proviso outlined by the foreign minister. With that, the emperor turned and left the conference room.

Almost immediately a cabinet meeting was held at the official residence of the prime minister. There the wording of Japan's acceptance was finally agreed upon, and in a communication dated 10 August the Allied powers were informed that "The Japanese Government are ready to accept the terms enumerated in the joint declaration which was issued at Potsdam on 26 July 1945 by the heads of the Governments of the United States, Great Britain, and China, and later subscribed to by the Soviet Government, with the understanding that the said declaration does not comprise any demand which prejudices the prerogatives of His Majesty as a Sovereign Ruler." That same day Tokyo was heavily bombed again; and while the government tried to prepare the people for imminent surrender, without actually saying that surrender was imminent, the army continued to issue communiqués exorting those same people to fight on to the end.

It was a complex and difficult situation, and it was not rendered either less complex or less difficult by the reply of the American secretary of state, James Byrnes. With regard to the Japanese proviso, Byrnes announced, "our position is as follows:

"From the moment of surrender the authority of the Emperor and the Japanese Government to rule the state shall be subject to the Supreme Commander of the Allied powers who will take such steps as he deems proper to effectuate the surrender terms."

Byrnes had not accepted the Japanese demand—but neither had he altogether rejected it. America had her wartime allies to consider; Japan, the intransigence of her military; both, the saving of face. The events of the next few days have been told before, notably in *Japan's Longest Day*,[2]—the complicated story of all the backstage maneuvering that finally resulted in the momentous imperial conference of 14 August, when the emperor did what only he could do: using the mysterious magic of his rank, he commanded an end to hostilities. "I desire," he said in closing his brief, historic address to his ministers, "that the cabinet prepare as soon as possible an imperial rescript announcing the termination of the war."

Although fanatical elements of the military tried to prevent the emperor's recording of the rescript from being broadcast to the nation and the world, they failed. The following day, at noon, most of the people of Japan heard, for the first time in their lives, the voice of their emperor; and from him they learned, tears streaming down many of their faces, that Japan had been defeated.

In Washington President Truman promptly issued a statement which began: "I have received this afternoon a message from the Japanese Government in reply to the message forwarded to that Government by the Secretary of State on 11 August. I deem this reply a full acceptance of the Potsdam Declaration which specifies the unconditional surrender of Japan. In the reply there is no qualification."

The Pacific war, which opened with the Japanese attack on Pearl Harbor in 1941, had indeed come to a close; Japan had suffered her first defeat; she would soon be occupied by enemy troops; the agony of war was ended at last—the uncertainties of peace were about to begin. But through all the high-sounding words, through all the machinations dictated by power politics on both sides of the ocean, through all the demands and counterdemands, through all the face-saving devices, we still hear no final, unequivocal answer to the question why the world's first atomic bomb had ever to be dropped upon Hiroshima; nor do we yet fully understand what effect that bomb has had, and may still have, upon the planet Earth and the people who dwell there—not upon the dead and the dying (we know that now) but upon the rest of us, the survivors.

NOTES

PREFACE

1. Elliott Roosevelt, *As He Saw It*, Duell, Floan and Pearce, New York, 1946, pp. 131–132.

ONE

1. David Irving, *The German Atomic Bomb*, Simon and Schuster, New York, 1967, p. 92.

2. Arthur Holly Compton, "Atomic Power: Its Birth and Meaning," *Commerce* (January 1953), copyright 1953 by the Chicago Association of Commerce and Industry; quoted in *The Cosmos of Arthur Holly Compton*, Alfred A. Knopf, New York, 1967, pp. 244–245.

3. David Irving, *op. cit.*, p. 121.

4. Lansing Lamont, *Day of Trinity*, Atheneum, New York, 1965, p. 31.

5. Arthur Holly Compton, *op. cit.*, pp. 246–7.

6. David Irving, *op. cit.*, pp. 164–165.

7. Lansing Lamont, *op. cit.*, p. 111.

8. William L. Laurence, *Dawn over Zero*, Simon & Schuster, New York, 1946, pp. 147–148.

9. Society for Assisting the Imperial Rule.

10. Lansing Lamont, *op. cit.*, pp. 83–84.

11. Leslie R. Groves, *Now It Can Be Told: The Story of the Manhattan Project*, Harper & Brothers, New York, 1961, p. 265.

12. David Irving, *op. cit.*, p. 259.

13. Leslie R. Groves, *op. cit.*, p. 266.

TWO

1. A complete English-language reconstruction of the text of the memorial is to be found in Robert J. C. Butow, *Japan's Decision to Surrender*, Stanford University Press, Stanford, Calif., 1954, pp. 47–50. Dr. Butow's reconstruction is based upon several documents, including "a draft translation of the Memorial prepared toward the latter part of 1945 by Mr. Tomohiko Ushiba, secretary and aide to Prince Konoye." Mr. Ushi-

ba's translation is the basis for that which appeared in *Japan's Struggle to End the War*, published by the Strategic Bombing Survey, Government Printing Office, Washington, D.C., 1946.

2. Robert J. C. Butow, *op. cit.*

3. Leo Szilard, "A Personal History of the Bomb," *The University of Chicago Round-table*, 25 September 1949, p. 14.

4. Henry L. Stimson and McGeorge Bundy, *On Active Service in Peace and War*, Harper & Brothers, New York, 1947, pp. 615–616.

5. Ellis M. Zacharias, *Secret Missions*, New York, G. P. Putnam's Sons, 1946, p. 335.

6. Harry S. Truman, *Years of Decision*, Doubleday and Co., Garden City, 1955, p. 79.

7. Ibid., p. 82.

8. Harrison, who was appointed secretary to the committee, was president of the New York Insurance Company—a fact that some citizens of Hiroshima might later have found to have an irony of its own.

9. Lansing Lamont, *op. cit.*, p. 70.

10. Harry S. Truman, *op. cit.*, p. 207.

11. Herbert Feis, *op. cit.*, p. 40.

12. *In the Matter of J. Robert Oppenheimer, Transcript of Hearing before Personnel Security Board, U.S. Atomic Energy Commission*, Washington, D.C., p. 31.

13. Arthur Holly Compton, *Atomic Quest*, Oxford University Press, New York, 1956, p. 219.

14. Henry L. Stimson and McGeorge Bundy, *op. cit.*, pp. 616–617.

15. Arthur Holly Compton, *op. cit.*, pp. 238–239.

16. Henry L. Stimson and McGeorge Bundy, *op. cit.*, p. 617.

17. James F. Byrnes, *Speaking Frankly*, Harper & Brothers, New York, 1947, p. 262.

18. Leo Szilard, *op. cit.*, pp. 14–15.

19. James F. Byrnes, *All in One Lifetime*, Harper & Brothers, New York, 1958, p. 284.

20. "A Report to the Secretary of War, June 1945," *Bulletin of Atomic Scientists*, 1 May 1964.

21. Henry L. Stimson, "The Decision to Use the Atomic Bomb," *Harper's Magazine*, February, 1947.

22. Arthur Holly Compton, *op. cit.*, pp. 239–241.

23. Sources used in compiling the three previous paragraphs: Ernest J. King and Walter M. Whitehill, *Fleet Admiral King*, W. W. Norton, New York, 1952, p. 606; see also p. 621. Henry L. Stimson and McGeorge Bundy, *op. cit.*

24. Harry S. Truman, *op. cit.*, p. 416.

25. Ibid., p. 417.

26. Ibid., p. 420.

27. Ibid., p. 419.

28. Henry L. Stimson and McGeorge Bundy, *op. cit.*, p. 627.

29. Joseph C. Grew, *Turbulent Era*, Houghton Mifflin Co. Boston, 1952, Vol. II, p. 1406.

30. Ibid., p. 1407.

31. This means much the same in Japanese as it does in English.

32. *The Forrestal Diaries*, edited by Walter Millis, Viking Press, New York, 1951, p. 74.

33. James F. Byrnes, *Speaking Frankly*, Harper & Brothers, New York, 1947, p. 211.

34. Harry S. Truman, *op. cit.*, p. 335.

35. Ibid., p. 337.

36. Ibid., p. 396.

37. Ibid., pp. 340–342.

38. Lansing Lamont, *op. cit.*, pp. 247–8.

39. Winston S. Churchill, *Triumph and Tragedy*, Houghton Mifflin Co., Boston, 1953, p. 638.

40. Ibid., p. 639.

41. Harry S. Truman, *op. cit.*, pp. 420–421.

42. Ibid., p. 416.

43. Leo Szilard, *op. cit.*, p. 15.

44. Arthur Holly Compton, *op. cit.*, pp. 243–244.

45. Len Giovannitti and Fred Freed, *The Decision to Drop the Bomb*, Coward-McCann, New York, 1965, pp. 167–170.

46. Ibid., p. 171.

47. Joseph C. Grew, *op. cit.*, p. 1433.

48. Harry S. Truman, *op. cit.*, pp. 402–404.

49. Lord Atlee, "The Hiroshima Choice," *The Observer*, London, 6 September 1959.

50. Harry S. Truman, *op. cit.*, p. 411.

51. Ibid., pp. 411–412.

52. Ibid., p. 411.

EPILOGUE

1. Ibid., p. 421.

2. Pacific War Research Society, The, *Japan's Longest Day*, Kodansha International, Tokyo and Palo Alto, Calif., 1968.

BIBLIOGRAPHY OF BOOKS IN JAPANESE

BOOKS ON THE ATOMIC BOMB AND BOMBING

Genbaku no ko ("Children of the Atomic Bombing"), Arata Osada, Iwanami Shoten

Genshi bakudan no hanashi ("The Story of the Atomic Bomb"), Shin Shida, Tokyo University Press

Genshiryoku to kokusai seiji ("Atomic Energy and International Politics"), Kakuzō Maeshiba, Tōyō Keizai Shimpōsha

Genshi sensō ("Nuclear War"), Mitsuo Taketani, Asahi Shinbun

Genshiryoku to kokusai seiji ("Atomic Energy and International Politics"), Hisashi Maeda, Iwanami Shoten

Kakusenryaku jidai no gaikō ("Foreign Diplomacy During the Age of Nuclear Strategy"), Atsuhiro Kobayashi, Bungei Shunjū

Genshi bakudan ("The Atomic Bomb"—a magazine essay), Yoshio Nishina, Iwanami Shoten

BOOKS ON VICTIMS OF THE A-BOMB

Genbaku taikenki ("Experiences of the A-Bombing"), compiled by the Hiroshima Atomic Bombing Experience Publication Association, Asahi Shinbun

Hiroshima no shōgen ("Hiroshima Testimonial"), compiled by the Hiroshima Peace and Cultural Books Publication Association, Nihon Hyōronsha

Hoshi wa miteiru ("The Stars Are Looking On"), compiled by Masayuki Akita, Masu Shobō

Genbaku bakushinchi ("Epicenter of the Atomic Explosion"), compiled by Kiyoshi Shimizu, Nippon Hōsō Shuppan Kyōkai

Genbaku shichō ("Mayor of the Atomic Bombed City"), Shinzō Hamai, Asahi Shinbun

Genbaku no ki ("Account of the Atomic Bombing"), Goichi Sashida, Shakai Shinpōsha

Sensen kara shūsen made ("From the Declaration to the Termination of the War"), Shūitsu Matsumura, Nihon Shūhōsha

Genbaku nijūgo nen ("Twenty-fifth Anniversary of the Atomic Bombing"), compiled by the Mainichi Shinbun, Mainichi Shinbunsha

Genshibakudan saigai chōsa hōkokusho ("Collection of Reports Concerning Damage by the Atomic Bomb"), compiled by the Japan Science Council, Nippon Gakujutsu Shinkō-kai

Shinshū Hiroshima-shi shi ("New History of Hiroshima City"), compiled by the Editorial Committee for Recording the History of Hiroshima City, Hiroshima City

Hiroshima nikki ("Hiroshima Diary"), Michihiko Hachiya, Asahishinbun

Gensuibaku higai hakusho ("White Paper on Damage Caused by the A- and H-bombs"), compiled by the Special Committee of the Japan Council for the Prohibition of Atomic and Hydrogen Bombs, Nihon Hyōronsha

Genbaku yurusumaji ("The Atomic Bomb Must Never be Used Again"), compiled by Editorial Committee for Accounts by Victims of the Atomic Bomb in Hiroshima Prefecture, Shin Nihon Shinsho

Hiroshima no kiroku ("Record of Hiroshima"), compiled by the Chūgoku Shinbun, Miraisha

Shōgen wa kienai ("Testimonies Do Not Disappear"), compiled by the Chūgoku Shinbun, Miraisha

Honoo no naka kara nijū nen ("Twenty Years from the Day of the A-bombing"), compiled by the Chūgoku Shinbun, Miraisha

Genbaku 500 nin no shōgen ("Testimonies by 500 Victims of the Atomic Bombing"), compiled by the Asahi Shinbun, Asahi Shinbun

Seiki no senkō ("Flash of the Century"), Eijirō Inatomi, Hiroshima Tosho

Kabane no machi ("City of Corpses"—novel), Yōko Ōta, Kawade Shobō

Ningen o kaese ("Give Back the Human"—collection of poems), Sankichi Tōge, Fūdo-sha

Genbaku ("Atomic Bomb"), Tatsutarō Hattori, Uno Shoten

Zetsugo no kiroku ("Final Record"), Toyohumi Ogura, Chūōsha

BOOKS ON THE TERMINATION OF THE WAR

Ushinawareshi seiji ("Lost Politics"), Fumimaro Konoye, Asahi Shinbun

Heiwa eno doryoku ("Efforts toward Peace"), Fumimaro Konoye, Nihon Denpō Tsūshin-sha

Haisen hishi ("Secret History of Japan's Defeat"), Bunren Chō, Jiyū Shobō

Kōfukuji no shinsō ("Truth about Japan's Surrender"), Hisatsune Sakomizu, Jikyoku-geppōsha

Shūsenki ("Account of Japan's Defeat"), Kainan Shimomura, Kamakura Shobō

Taiheiyō kaisen-shi ("History of Naval Battles in the Pacific"), Sōkichi Takagi, Iwanami Shoten

Shūsen hishi ("Secret History of Japan's Defeat"), Kainan Shimomura, Kōdansha

Mizūri e no dōtei ("Way to the Missouri"), Toshikazu Kase, Bungei Shunjū

Taiheiyō-sensō rikusen gaishi ("History of Ground Battles in the Pacific War"), Saburō Hayashi, Iwanami Shoten

Jidai no ichimen ("One Aspect of the Age"), Shigenori Tōgō, Kaizōsha

Shūsenshiroku ("History of Japan's Defeat"), compiled by the Foreign Ministry, Shinbun Geppōsha

Genbaku-ki Tokyo e ("A Plane Carrying an A-bomb Flies to Tokyo"), Noboru Kimura, Masu Shobō

Rikugun sōgiiinchō ("Chairman of the Funeral Committee for the Japanese Army"), Sumihisa Ikeda, Nihon Shuppan-kyōdō

Daitōasensō zenshi ("Complete History of the Greater East Asian War"), Takushirō Hattori, Hara Shobō

Dainiji-sekaitaisen gaikō-shi ("Diplomatic History of World War II"), Hitoshi Ashida, Jijitsūshinsha

Nihon shūsenshi ("History of Japan's Defeat"), compiled by Shigeru Hayashi, Yomiuri Shinbun

Haisen no kiroku ("Record of Japan's Defeat"), General Staff Office, Hara Shobō

Jijūchō no kaisō ("Reminiscences of a Grand Chamberlain"), Hisanori Fujita, Kōdansha

Teikoku rikugun no saigo ("Last Days of the Imperial Army"), Masanori Itō, Bungei Shunjū

Odorashita mono ("The Instigator"), Hiromichi Fujimoto, Hokushin Shobō

Shūsen no hyōjō ("Expression of Defeated Japan"), Kantarō Suzuki, Rōdō Bunka Sha

Konton no ki ("Chaos"), Hideo Mimasu, Bunchōsha

Taiheiyō-sensō shūketsu ron ("Discussions on Ways to Bring About an End to the Pacific War"), compiled by the Japan Foreign Diplomacy Council, Tokyo University Press

Kaiko 80 nen ("Eighty Years in Retrospect"), Naotake Satō, Jijitsūshinsha

Shōwa-shi no tennō ("The Emperor in Showa History"), compiled by the Yomiuri Shinbun, Yomiuri Shinbun

Tokyo hibaku ki ("Accounts of Airraids over Tokyo"), compiled by the Asahi Shinbun, Asahi Shinbun

Kaze wa sugiyuku ("The Wind Blows Past"), Teru Mori, Rinjinsha

Konoye Fumimaro ("Konoye Fumimaro"), compiled by the Biography Publication Association, Biography Publication Association

Nihon haisen ki ("Japan's Defeat"), Tetsurō Shiga, Shimbunsha

DIARIES

Daihonei kimitsu nikki ("Secret Diary of Imperial Headquarters"), Suketaka Tanemura, Diamond-sha

Higashikuni nikki ("Higashikuni Diary"), Norihiko Higashikuni, Tokuma Shoten

Sokai gakudō no nikki ("Diaries of Evacuated Children"), Mihoko Nakane, Chūō Kōron-sha

Jōhō tennō ni tassezu ("The Emperor Does Not Receive Information"), Morisada Hosokawa, Isobe Shobō

Ankoku nikki ("Black Diary"), Kiyoshi Kiyosawa, Tōyō Keizai Shinpōsha

Haisen nikki ("Diary of the Defeated"), Jūzō Unno, Kōdansha

Ōki nikki ("Oki Daiary"), Misao Ōki, Asahi Shinbun

Nagatacho ichibanchi ("Official Residence of the Prime Minister"), Shōgo Nakamura, News-sha

Bansō ("Late Frost"), Kuromitsu Sōma, Tōzai Bunmeisha

Tokyo shōjin ("Tokyo Burns Down"), Hyakken Uchida, Kōdan Sha

Rasai nikki ("Record of Disaster"), Kafū Nagai, Fusō Shobō

Kaisen karano nikki ("Diary from the Start of the War"), Aiko Takahashi

Shi no kage ni ikite ("Living in the Shadow of Death"), Munekatsu Oguma, Taihei Shuppansha

Senchūha fusen nikki ("Diary of a Man Who Did Not Go to the War"), Fūtarō Yamada, Banchō Shobō

Tokyo Kūshū ("Tokyo Airraids"), Norikazu Ōya, Kawade Shobō

Owarazaru toki no akashi ni ("Testimony to Endless Time"), Shūhei Hayama, Tōjusha

Jūgo nikki ("Homefront Diary"), Kakuji Kakizaki, Kinki Shoten

Sumiyaki nikki ("Charcoal Making Diary"), Kunio Yanagita, Shūdōsha

Kano nengetsu ("Those Years and Months"), Rintarō Fukuhara, Azumashobō

Jūrokusai no taiheiyō-sensō ("I Was Sixteen Years Old During the Pacific War"), Kenji Nagai, Shūdan Keisei

Takami Jun nikki ("Takami Jun Diary"), Jun Takami, Keisō Shobō

Musei sensō nikki ("Musei War Diary"), Musei Tokugawa, Chūō Kōronsha

Senchū nikki ("War Diary"), Yoshishige Kozai, Keisō Shobō

Kido nikki ("Kido Diary"), Kōichi Kido, Tokyo University Press

* Articles which appeared in magazines have been omitted, unless of special importance.

DISCOVER JAPAN   Words, Customs, and Concepts
Volumes 1 & 2
The Japanese Culture Institute

Essays and photographs illuminate 200 ideas and customs of contemporary Japan. "The one book you must have if you're heading for Japan ..."   — *Essex Journal*

PB, Vol. 1: ISBN 0-87011-835-8, 216 pages
PB, Vol. 2: ISBN 0-87011-836-6, 224 pages

GEISHA, GANGSTER, NEIGHBOR, NUN
Scenes from Japanese Lives
Donald Richie

A collection of 48 highly personal portraits of Japanese—both famous and obscure. "His portraits are unforgettable."   — Tom Wolfe

PB, ISBN 4-7700-1526-7, 212 pages
Previously published in hardcover as Different People.

HAGAKURE
The Book of the Samurai
Tsunetomo Yamamoto
Translated by William Scott Wilson

"A guidebook and inspiration for ... anyone interested in achieving a courageous and transcendent understanding of life."   — *East West Journal*

PB, ISBN 0-87011-606-1, 180 pages

THE HIDDEN ORDER
Tokyo Through the Twentieth Century
Yoshinobu Ashihara
Translated by Lynne E. Riggs

Looking at architecture as a metaphor for culture, a renowned Japanese architect considers the apparent chaos of Tokyo.

PB, ISBN 4-7700-1664-6, 160 pages

THE JAPANESE EDUCATIONAL CHALLENGE
A Commitment to Children
Merry White

Examines educational values in Japan, and differences between the Japanese and American school systems. "The best account I know of Japan as a learning society."   — Ronald P. Dore

PB, ISBN 4-7700-1373-6, 224 pages
Available only in Japan.

THE JAPANESE NEGOTIATOR
Subtlety and Strategy Beyond Western Logic

Robert M. March

Shows how Japanese negotiate among themselves and examines case studies, providing practical advice for the Western executive.

PB, ISBN 0-87011-962-1, 200 pages

THE JAPANESE THROUGH AMERICAN EYES

Sheila K. Johnson

A revealing look at the images and stereotypes of Japanese produced by American popular culture and media.

PB, ISBN 4-7700-1450-3, 208 pages   Available only in Japan.

JAPAN'S LONGEST DAY

Pacific War Research Society

A detailed account of the day before Japan surrendered, based on eyewitness testimony of the men involved in the decision to surrender.

PB: ISBN 0-87011-422-0, 340 pages

MANGA! MANGA!
The World of Japanese Comics

Frederick L. Schodt
Introduction by Osamu Tezuka

A profusely illustrated and detailed exploration of the world of Japanese comics.

PB, ISBN 0-87011-752-1, 260 pages

NEIGHBORHOOD TOKYO

Theodore C. Bestor

A highly readable glimpse into the everyday lives, commerce, and relationships of some 2,000 neighborhood residents of Tokyo.

PB, ISBN 4-7700-1496-1, 368 pages   Available only in Japan.

THE INLAND SEA

Donald Richie

An award-winning documentary—part travelogue, part intimate diary and meditation—of a journey into the heart of traditional Japan.

PB, ISBN 4-7700-1751, 292 pages

Social Sciences and History

THE THIRD CENTURY
America's Resurgence in the Asian Era

Joel Kotkin and Yoriko Kishimoto

Argues that the U.S. must adopt a realistic and resilient attitude as it faces serious competition from Asia. "Truly powerful public ideas."
— *Boston Globe*

PB, ISBN 4-7700-1452-X, 304 pages
Available only in Japan.

THE UNFETTERED MIND
Writings of the Zen Master to the Sword Master

Takuan soho
Translated by William Scott Wilson

Philosophy as useful to today's corporate warriors as it was to seventeenth-century samurai.

PB, ISBN 0-87011-851-X, 104 pages

THE UNSPOKEN WAY
**Haragei, or The Role of Silent Communication
in Japanese Business and Society**

Michihiro Matsumoto

Haragei, a uniquely Japanese concept of communication, affects language, social interaction, and especially business dealings.

PB, ISBN 0-87011-889-7, 152 pages

WOMANSWORD
What Japanese Words Say About Women

Kittredge Cherry

From "cockroach husband" to "daughter-in-a-box," a mix of provocative and entertaining words that collectively tell the story of Japanese women.

PB, ISBN 4-7700-1655-7, 160 pages

WORDS IN CONTEXT
Takao Suzuki
Translation by Akira Miura

One of Japan's foremost linguists explores the complex relationship between language and culture, psychology and lifestyle.

PB, ISBN 0-87011-642-8, 180 pages

Japan's Modern Writers

BEYOND THE CURVE
Kobo Abe
Translated by Juliet Winters Carpenter

"Abe is Japan's most gifted, important, and original writer of serious fiction." —Alan Levy, *The New York Times Magazine*

PB, ISBN 4-7700-1690-5, 248 pages

GHOSTS
A Tale of Childhood and Youth
Morio Kita
Translated by Dennis Keene

The award-winning story of a man obsessed with memories of the past who struggles to interpret various dreams of his mother and sister, lost during the war.

PB, ISBN 4-7700-1743-X, 200 pages

SELF PORTRAITS Stories
Osamu Dazai
Translated by Ralph McCarthy

The women, suicide attempts, and life-or-death struggle against a staid literary establishment of Japan's most engaging *enfant terrible.*

PB, ISBN 4-7700-1689-1, 232 pages

SILENCE
Shusaku Endo
Translation by William Johnston

"A remarkable work, a somber, delicate, and startlingly empathetic study." —John Updike

PB, ISBN 0-87011-536-7, 312 pages

THE SHOWA ANTHOLOGY
Modern Japanese Short Stories
Edited by Van C. Gessel and Tomone Matsumoto

Twenty-five superbly translated stories from the Showa era (1926 - 1989) "All the stories shine." — *Publishers Weekly*

PB, ISBN 4-7700-1708-1, 464 pages